Junior Praise

Compiled by

Phil Burt, Peter Horrobin and Greg Leavers

COMBINED MUSIC EDITION

Collins

Collins
A division of HarperCollins*Publishers*
77-85 Fulham Palace Road
Hammersmith
London W6 8JB

First published in Great Britain in 1997 by Marshall Pickering
Reissued 2004

10 9 8 7 6 5 4 3 2 1

A catalogue record for this book is available from the British Library

ISBN 0 00 718467 0

Combined Words Edition ISBN 0 00 718468 9

Music and text set by Barnes Music Engraving Ltd, East Sussex, England
Printed and bound in Great Britain by The Bath Press, Bath

Preface

Since its publication in 1986, *Junior Praise* has set a standard which few other books have been able to follow. The secret of the book's success, like its sister volume for adults, *Mission Praise,* has been the mixing of traditional and modern hymns and songs, and the sensitive alteration of those items not readily understood by children.

Junior Praise 2 appeared in 1992, adding a new collection of more than 200 songs to the original songbook. This new combined music edition brings together both compilations in one volume, retaining the numbering from the original volumes to match the existing combined words edition.

As we hoped, the provision of a separate melody line has made it easy for children to accompany items on recorders, flutes, xylophones, violins etc., and we have retained this for the combined edition. We have also included guitar chords, together with the 'Notes to guitarists' and a chord chart. This edition also includes first line and subject indexes.

I would stress again our over-riding purpose in offering this book for use in schools throughout the world: we want children, through music, to understand that God wants them to enjoy the experience of knowing, loving, serving and worshipping Him. The discipline of Christian commitment will help children to grow up as men and women of integrity. We pray anew that all those who use this book will do so with this ideal at heart.

Greg Leavers

1 A boy gave to Jesus

Words and music: Peter Horrobin
Music arranged Phil Burt

1 A boy gave to Jesus five loaves and two fish,
not much, you might say, for a crowd;
but Jesus, He took them and smiled at the lad,
gave thanks to His Father and blessed them out loud.

2 The boy then saw Jesus take loaves and the fish,
not much for the folk on that day;
but Jesus, He broke them and smiled at the lad,
gave bits to disciples to then give away.

3 Then all worshipped Jesus as enough loaves and fish
were given to everyone there.
But Jesus just watched them, and smiled at the lad
who'd given his lunch-box for Jesus to share.

2

Abba Father

Words and music: Dave Bilbrough
Music arranged Roland Fudge

Thoughtfully

Ab - ba Fa - ther, let me be Yours and

Yours a - lone. May my

will for ev - er be ev - er -

- more Your own. Ne - ver let my

* This item appears in the key of B♭ in the first edition of *Junior Praise*.

Abba Father, let me be
Yours and Yours alone.
May my will for ever be
evermore Your own.
Never let my heart grow cold,
never let me go,
Abba Father, let me be
Yours and Yours alone.

3 Alleluia, alleluia, give thanks

ALLELUIA NO. 1

Words and music: Donald Fishel
Music arranged Betty Pulkingham

He is the King of cre - a - tion. Al - le -

Alleluia, alleluia,
give thanks to the risen Lord;
alleluia, alleluia,
give praise to His name.

1 Jesus is Lord of all the earth,
He is the King of creation.
Alleluia, alleluia . . .

2 Spread the good news through all the earth,
Jesus has died and has risen.
Alleluia, alleluia . . .

3 We have been crucified with Christ;
now we shall live for ever.
Alleluia, alleluia . . .

4 God has proclaimed the just reward,
life for all men, alleluia.
Alleluia, alleluia . . .

5 Come let us praise the living God,
joyfully sing to our Saviour:
Alleluia, alleluia . . .

4(i)   All people that on earth do dwell

Words: William Kethe (1520–94)
in this version Jubilate Hymns
Music: Roger Jones
arranged Phil Burt

All peo-ple that on earth do dwell, sing to the Lord with cheer-ful voice: serve Him with joy, His prais - es tell, come now be - fore Him and re - joice! Know that the Lord is God in - deed, He formed us all with - out our aid; __

we are the flock He loves to feed, the sheep who by His hand are

made. - dore!

1 All people that on earth do dwell,
   sing to the Lord with cheerful voice:
   serve Him with joy, His praises tell,
   come now before Him and rejoice!
   Know that the Lord is God indeed,
   He formed us all without our aid;
   we are the flock He loves to feed,
   the sheep who by His hand are made.

2 O enter then His gates with praise,
   and in His courts His love proclaim;
   give thanks and bless Him all your days:
   let every tongue confess His name.
   The Lord our mighty God is good,
   His mercy is for ever sure;
   His truth at all times firmly stood,
   and shall from age to age endure.

3 All people that on earth do dwell
   sing to the Lord with cheerful voice:
   serve Him with joy, His praises tell,
   come now before Him and rejoice!
   Praise God the Father, God the Son,
   and God the Spirit evermore;
   all praise to God, the Three-in-One,
   let heaven rejoice and earth adore!

4(ii) All people that on earth do dwell
(alternative arrangement)

ALL PEOPLE LM

Words: William Kethe (1520–94)
in this version Jubilate Hymns
Music: Roger Jones
arranged Roger Mayor

Latin feel ♩ = 116

All peo-ple that on earth do dwell, sing to the Lord with cheer-ful voice: serve Him with joy, His prais - es tell, come now be - fore Him and re - joice! Know that the Lord is

1 All people that on earth do dwell,
 sing to the Lord with cheerful voice:
 serve Him with joy, His praises tell,
 come now before Him and rejoice!
 Know that the Lord is God indeed,
 He formed us all without our aid;
 we are the flock He loves to feed,
 the sheep who by His hand are made.

2 O enter then His gates with praise,
 and in His courts His love proclaim;
 give thanks and bless Him all your days:
 let every tongue confess His name.
 The Lord our mighty God is good,
 His mercy is for ever sure;
 His truth at all times firmly stood,
 and shall from age to age endure.

3 All people that on earth do dwell
 sing to the Lord with cheerful voice:
 serve Him with joy, His praises tell,
 come now before Him and rejoice!
 Praise God the Father, God the Son,
 and God the Spirit evermore;
 all praise to God, the Three-in-One,
 let heaven rejoice and earth adore!

5

All over the world

Words and music: Roy Turner
Music arranged Roland Fudge

All over the world the Spirit is moving, all over the world as the prophet said it would be; all over the world there's a mighty revelation of the glory of the Lord, as the waters cover the sea.

1 All over the world the Spirit is moving,
   all over the world as the prophet said it would be;
   all over the world there's a mighty revelation
   of the glory of the Lord, as the waters cover the sea.

2 All over His Church God's Spirit is moving,
   all over His Church as the prophet said it would be;
   all over His Church there's a mighty revelation
   of the glory of the Lord, as the waters cover the sea.

3 Right here in this place the Spirit is moving,
   right here in this place as the prophet said it would be;
   right here in this place there's a mighty revelation
   of the glory of the Lord, as the waters cover the sea.

6(i) All things bright and beautiful

Royal Oak   76 76 with refrain

Words: Cecil Frances Alexander (1818–95)
Music: English traditional melody
arranged Martin Shaw (1875–1958)

All things bright and beau-ti-ful, all crea-tures great and_ small,

all things wise and won-der-ful, the Lord God made them all.

Each lit-tle flower that o-pens, each lit-tle bird that sings, He_

Music arrangement: © J Curwen & Sons Ltd / William Elkin Music Services,
Station Road Industrial Estate, Salhouse, Norwich, Norfolk NR13 6NY

made their glow-ing_ col - ours, He_ made their ti - ny_ wings.

All things bright and beautiful,
all creatures great and small,
all things wise and wonderful,
the Lord God made them all.

1 Each little flower that opens,
   each little bird that sings,
   He made their glowing colours,
   He made their tiny wings.
   All things bright . . .

2 The purple-headed mountain,
   the river running by,
   the sunset, and the morning
   that brightens up the sky;
   All things bright . . .

3 The cold wind in the winter,
   the pleasant summer sun,
   the ripe fruits in the garden,
   He made them every one.
   All things bright . . .

4 He gave us eyes to see them,
   and lips that we might tell
   how great is God almighty,
   who has made all things well.
   All things bright . . .

6(ii) All things bright and beautiful

ALL THINGS BRIGHT AND BEAUTIFUL
76 76 with refrain

Words: Cecil Frances Alexander (1818–95)
Music: William Henry Monk (1823–89)

All things bright and beau - ti-ful, all crea - tures great and small,

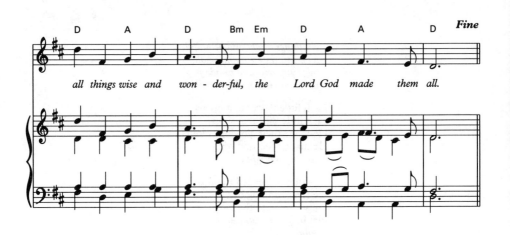

all things wise and won - der-ful, the Lord God made them all.

Fine

Each lit - tle flower that o - pens, each lit - tle bird that sings, He

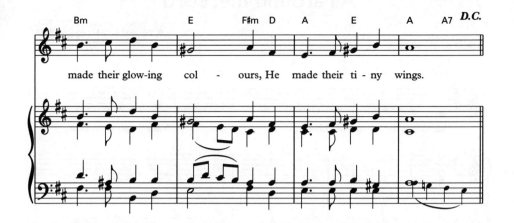

made their glow-ing col - ours, He made their ti - ny wings.

All things bright and beautiful,
all creatures great and small,
all things wise and wonderful,
the Lord God made them all.

1 Each little flower that opens,
   each little bird that sings,
   He made their glowing colours,
   He made their tiny wings.
   All things bright ...

2 The purple-headed mountain,
   the river running by,
   the sunset, and the morning
   that brightens up the sky;
   All things bright ...

3 The cold wind in the winter,
   the pleasant summer sun,
   the ripe fruits in the garden,
   He made them every one.
   All things bright ...

4 He gave us eyes to see them,
   and lips that we might tell
   how great is God almighty,
   who has made all things well.
   All things bright ...

7

All around me, Lord

Words and music: Greg Leavers
Music arranged Phil Burt

All around me, Lord, I see Your goodness,
all creation sings Your praises,
all the world cries, 'God is love!'

8 Amazing grace

AMAZING GRACE   CM

Words: John Newton (1725–1807)
Music: traditional
arranged Roland Fudge

1 Amazing grace – how sweet the sound –
  that saved a wretch like me!
  I once was lost, but now am found,
  was blind, but now I see.

2 'Twas grace that taught my heart to fear,
  and grace my fears relieved;
  how precious did that grace appear
  the hour I first believed.

3 Through many dangers, toils and snares,
  I have already come;
  'tis grace has brought me safe thus far,
  and grace will lead me home.

4 When we've been there ten thousand years
  bright shining as the sun,
  we've no less days to sing God's praise
  than when we've first begun.

9 As with gladness

Dix   77 77 77

Words: William Chatterton Dix (1837–98)
altered Horrobin/Leavers
Music: from a chorale by Conrad Kocher (1786–1872)

As with glad-ness men of old   did the guid-ing   star be-hold;

as   with joy they hailed its light,   lead-ing on-ward, beam-ing bright,

so, most gra-cious God,   may we   led by You for   ev - er be.

1 As with gladness men of old
did the guiding star behold;
as with joy they hailed its light,
leading onward, beaming bright,
so, most gracious God, may we
led by You for ever be.

2 As with joyful steps they sped,
Saviour, to Your lowly bed,
there to bend the knee before
You whom heaven and earth adore,
so may we with one accord,
seek forgiveness from our Lord.

3 As they offered gifts most rare,
gold and frankincense and myrrh,
so may we, cleansed from our sin,
lives of service now begin,
and in love our treasures bring,
Christ, to You our heavenly King.

4 Holy Jesus, every day
keep us in the narrow way;
and when earthly things are past,
bring our ransomed souls at last
where they need no star to guide,
where no clouds Your glory hide.

5 In the heavenly country bright
need they no created light;
You its light, its joy, its crown,
You its sun which goes not down.
There for ever may we sing
hallelujahs to our King.

10 Angels from the realms of glory

IRIS 87 87 with refrain

Words: James Montgomery (1771–1854)
in this version Jubilate Hymns
Music: French carol melody

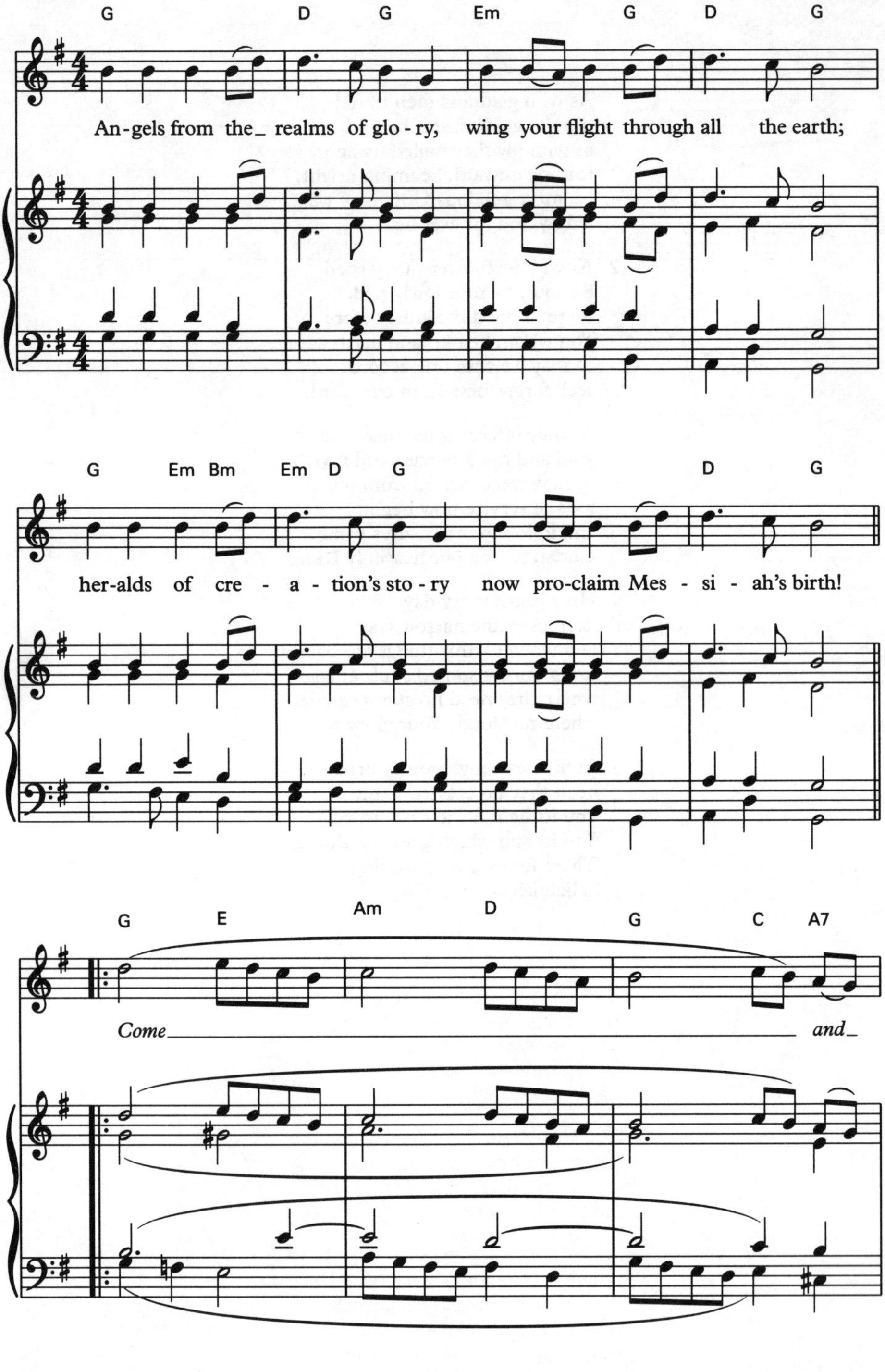

G D G Em G D G
An-gels from the_ realms of glo-ry, wing your flight through all the earth;
G Em Bm Em D G D G
her-alds of cre - a - tion's sto - ry now pro-claim Mes - si - ah's birth!
G E Am D G C A7
*Come_ and_*

1.   wor - ship Christ, the new - born King;

2.   wor - ship Christ the new - born King.

1 Angels from the realms of glory,
   wing your flight through all the earth;
   heralds of creation's story
   now proclaim Messiah's birth!
     Come and worship
     Christ, the new-born King;
     come and worship,
     worship Christ the new-born King.

2 Shepherds in the fields abiding,
   watching by your flocks at night,
   God with man is now residing:
   see, there shines the infant light!
     Come and worship . . .

3 Wise men, leave your contemplations!
   brighter visions shine afar;
   seek in Him the hope of nations,
   you have seen His rising star:
     Come and worship . . .

4 Though an infant now we view Him,
   He will share His Father's throne,
   gather all the nations to Him;
   every knee shall then bow down:
     Come and worship . . .

Ask! Ask! Ask!

Words and music: Anon
Music arranged Phil Burt

Ask! Ask! Ask! and it shall be giv-en you; Seek! Seek! Seek! and you shall

find; Knock! Knock! Knock! it shall be o-pened un-to you, your

heaven-ly Fa-ther is so kind. He knows what is best for His

chil-dren in bo - dy, soul and mind; So ask! Ask! Ask!

Knock! Knock! Knock! Seek and you shall find.

Ask! Ask! Ask! and it shall be given you;
Seek! Seek! Seek! and you shall find;
Knock! Knock! Knock! it shall be opened unto you,
your heavenly Father is so kind.
He knows what is best for His children
in body, soul and mind;
So ask! Ask! Ask! Knock! Knock! Knock!
Seek and you shall find.

12 Away in a manger

CRADLE SONG 11 11 11 11

Words: verses 1, 2 Anon
verse 3 J T McFarland (c1906)
Music: William James Kirkpatrick (1838–1921)

A - way in a___ man - ger, no___ crib for a bed, the___ lit - tle Lord Je - sus laid___ down His sweet head; the stars in the___ bright sky looked down where He lay; the___ lit - tle Lord Je - sus a - sleep in the hay.

1 Away in a manger, no crib for a bed,
the little Lord Jesus laid down His sweet head;
the stars in the bright sky looked down where He lay;
the little Lord Jesus asleep in the hay.

2 The cattle are lowing, the baby awakes,
but little Lord Jesus, no crying He makes:
I love You, Lord Jesus! look down from the sky
and stay by my side until morning is nigh.

3 Be near me, Lord Jesus; I ask You to stay
close by me for ever and love me, I pray;
bless all the dear children in Your tender care,
and fit us for heaven to live with You there.

13(i)   At the name of Jesus

EVELYNS   65 65 D

Words: Caroline Maria Noel (1817–77)
altered Horrobin/Leavers
Music: William Henry Monk (1823–89)

At the name of Je - sus ev - ery knee shall bow,

ev - ery tongue con - fess__ Him King of glo - ry now.__

'Tis the Fa-ther's plea - sure we should call Him Lord,

who from the be - gin - ning was the migh - ty Word.

1   At the name of Jesus
    every knee shall bow,
    every tongue confess Him
    King of glory now.
    'Tis the Father's pleasure
    we should call Him Lord,
    who from the beginning
    was the mighty Word.

2   Humbled for a season,
    to receive a name
    from the lips of sinners
    unto whom He came,
    faithfully He lived here
    spotless to the last,
    raised was He victorious,
    when from death He passed.

3   Lifted high, triumphant,
    far above the world,
    into heaven's glory,
    our ascended Lord;
    to the throne of Godhead,
    at the Father's side,
    there He reigns resplendent
    who for man had died.

4   In your hearts enthrone Him;
    there let Him subdue
    all that is not holy,
    all that is not true;
    crown Him as your captain
    in temptation's hour,
    let His will enfold you
    in its light and power.

5   Brothers, this Lord Jesus
    shall return again,
    with His Father's glory,
    with His angel-train;
    for all wreaths of empire
    meet upon His brow,
    and our hearts confess Him
    King of glory now.

13(ii) At the name of Jesus

CAMBERWELL   65 65 D

Words: Caroline Maria Noel (1817–77)
altered Horrobin / Leavers
Music: Michael Brierley

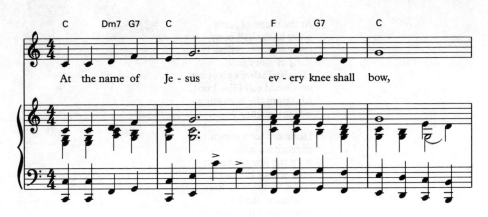

At the name of Je-sus ev-ery knee shall bow,

ev-ery tongue con-fess Him King of glo-ry__ now.

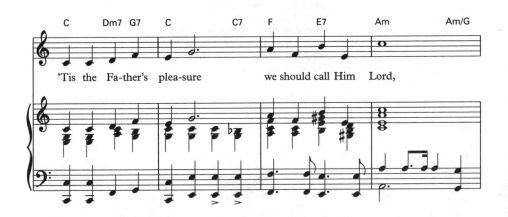

'Tis the Fa-ther's plea-sure we should call Him Lord,

who from the be - gin - ning was the migh - ty

Word.

now.

1 At the name of Jesus
   every knee shall bow,
   every tongue confess Him
   King of glory now.
   'Tis the Father's pleasure
   we should call Him Lord,
   who from the beginning
   was the mighty Word.

2 Humbled for a season,
   to receive a name
   from the lips of sinners
   unto whom He came,
   faithfully He lived here
   spotless to the last,
   raised was He victorious,
   when from death He passed.

3 Lifted high, triumphant,
   far above the world,
   into heaven's glory,
   our ascended Lord;
   to the throne of Godhead,
   at the Father's side,
   there He reigns resplendent
   who for man had died.

4 In your hearts enthrone Him;
   there let Him subdue
   all that is not holy,
   all that is not true;
   crown Him as your captain
   in temptation's hour,
   let His will enfold you
   in its light and power.

5 Brothers, this Lord Jesus
   shall return again,
   with His Father's glory,
   with His angel-train;
   for all wreaths of empire
   meet upon His brow,
   and our hearts confess Him
   King of glory now.

14 Be bold, be strong

Words and music: Morris Chapman
Music arranged Andy Silver

Be bold, be strong,
for the Lord your God is with you;
be bold, be strong,
for the Lord your God is with you!
 I am not afraid, (No! No! No!)
 I am not dismayed, (Not me!)
for I'm walking in faith and victory:
come on and walk in faith and victory,
for the Lord your God is with you.

15 Behold, what manner of love

Words and music: Patricia van Tine

A two-part round

Moderato

Be - hold, what man - ner of love the Fa - ther has giv - en un - to us,____ Be - hold, what man - ner of

love the Fa - ther has giv - en un - to us,

Behold, what manner of love the Father has given unto us,
Behold, what manner of love the Father has given unto us,
that we should be called the sons of God,
that we should be called the sons of God.

16   Big man

Words and music: Graham Kendrick
Music arranged Phil Burt

Big man stand-ing by the blue wa-ter-side, mend-ing nets by the blue sea. A-long came Je-sus, He said, 'Si-mon Pe-ter, won't you leave your nets and come, fol-low me.' *You don't need a-ny-thing, I've got ev-ery-thing, but, Pe-ter, it's going to be a*

1 Big man standing by the blue waterside,
   mending nets by the blue sea.
   Along came Jesus, He said,
   'Simon Peter, won't you leave your nets and come, follow me.'
       You don't need anything, I've got everything,
       but, Peter, it's going to be a hard way.
       You don't have to worry now, come on and hurry now,
       I'll walk beside you every day.

2 Life wasn't easy for the big fisherman,
   but still he followed till his dying day.
   Along came Jesus, He said,
   'Simon Peter, there's a place in heaven where you can stay.'
       You don't need anything . . .

17 Bind us together, Lord

Words and music: Bob Gillman
Music arranged Norman Warren

Bind us to-geth-er, Lord, bind us to-geth-er with cords that can-not be bro - ken;

bind us to-geth-er, Lord, bind us to-geth-er, O bind us to-geth-er with love.

There is on - ly one God, there is on - ly one King,

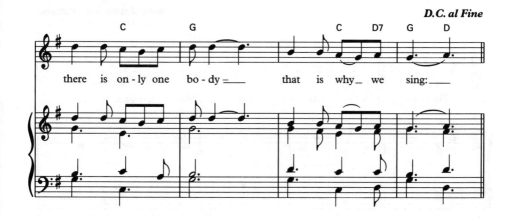

there is on-ly one bo-dy —— that is why— we sing:___

Bind us together, Lord,
bind us together
with cords that cannot be broken;
bind us together, Lord,
bind us together,
O bind us together with love.

1 There is only one God,
   there is only one King,
   there is only one body –
   that is why we sing:
      Bind us together . . .

2 Made for the glory of God,
   purchased by His precious Son.
   Born with the right to be clean,
   for Jesus the victory has won.
      Bind us together . . .

3 You are the family of God,
   You are the promise divine,
   You are God's chosen desire,
   You are the glorious new wine.
      Bind us together . . .

18 Barabbas was a bad man

Words and music: Peter Horrobin

1 Barabbas was a bad man,
   condemned to die was he,
   he'd done so many awful things,
   was bad as bad could be.

2 But Jesus was a good man,
   God's only Son was He.
   He did so many lovely things –
   the blind He made to see.

3 But Jesus some folk hated,
   they called, 'Put Him away!'
   when Pilate made them choose the one
   to free, that fatal day.

4 So Jesus, though a good man,
   was killed on Calvary,
   but three days on, He rose again
   to live eternally.

19   Bless the Lord, O my soul

Words: from Psalm 103
Music: Anon
arranged Roland Fudge

With breadth

Bless the Lord, O my soul, bless the Lord, O my soul, and all that is with - in me bless His ho - ly name. Bless the Lord, O my soul, bless the

Words: Copyright control

Lord, O my soul, and all that is with -

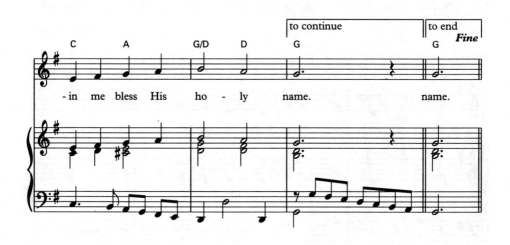

-in me bless His ho - ly name. name.

to continue | to end *Fine*

King of kings_____ (for ev - er and ev-er), Lord of lords_____ (for

Bless the Lord, O my soul,
bless the Lord, O my soul,
and all that is within me
bless His holy name.
Bless the Lord, O my soul,
bless the Lord, O my soul,
and all that is within me
bless His holy name.

King of kings (for ever and ever),
Lord of lords (for ever and ever),
King of kings (for ever and ever),
King of kings and Lord of lords!

Bless the Lord, O my soul . . .

20 Blessèd assurance

BLESSED ASSURANCE   Irregular

Words: Frances van Alstyne (1820–1915)
(Fanny J Crosby)
Music: Phoebe Palmer Knapp (1839–1908)

Bless-èd as - sur - ance, Je - sus is mine:___ O what a
fore - taste of glo-ry di - vine!___ Heir of sal - va - tion, pur-chase of
God;___ born of His Spi - rit, washed in His blood.___
This is my sto - ry, this is my song,___ prais-ing my

Sav - iour all the day long.___ This is my sto - ry, this is my

song,___ prais-ing my Sav - iour all the day long.___

1 Blessèd assurance, Jesus is mine:
O what a foretaste of glory divine!
Heir of salvation, purchase of God;
born of His Spirit, washed in His blood.
  This is my story, this is my song,
  praising my Saviour all the day long;
  this is my story, this is my song,
  praising my Saviour all the day long.

2 Perfect submission, perfect delight,
visions of rapture burst on my sight;
angels descending, bring from above
echoes of mercy, whispers of love.
  This is my story . . .

3 Perfect submission, all is at rest,
I in my Saviour am happy and blest;
watching and waiting, looking above,
filled with His goodness, lost in His love.
  This is my story . . .

21 Brothers and sisters

Words and music: Roger Jones

Bro - thers and sis - ters (Bro - thers and sis - ters) in

Je - sus our Lord, (in Je - sus our Lord,) bro - thers and sis - ters,

(bro - thers and sis - ters,) be - liev-ing His word! (be - liev-ing His word!)

Now we're un - i - ted, (Now we're un - i - ted,) made

1 Brothers and sisters
  in Jesus our Lord,
  brothers and sisters,
  believing His word!
  Now we're united,
  made one in His love,
  we're brothers and sisters
  in Jesus our Lord!

2 Jesus has saved us,
  from sin set us free.
  Always His people
  together we'll be!
  This is the story
  we're telling the world,
  we're brothers and sisters
  in Jesus our Lord!

3 Jesus has told us
  to be of good cheer,
  for He is with us,
  His Spirit is here!
  He gives us power
  His message to share.
  We're brothers and sisters
  in Jesus our Lord!

22 Be still and know

Words and music: Anon
Music arranged Roland Fudge

1 Be still and know that I am God.
Be still and know that I am God.
Be still and know that I am God.

2 I am the Lord that healeth thee.
I am the Lord that healeth thee.
I am the Lord that healeth thee.

3 In Thee, O Lord, I put my trust.
In Thee, O Lord, I put my trust.
In Thee, O Lord, I put my trust.

23 By blue Galilee

Words and music: E H Swinstead (d1976)

By blue Galilee Jesus walked of old,
by blue Galilee wondrous things He told.
Saviour, still my teacher be,
showing wondrous things to me
as of old by Galilee, blue Galilee.

24 Children of Jerusalem

CHILDREN'S PRAISE   77 77 with refrain

Words: John Henley (1800–42)
altered Horrobin/Leavers
Music: from Curwen's *Tune Book*, 1842

Child-ren of Je - ru - sa - lem sang the praise of Je - sus' name;
child - ren, too, of mo - dern days, join to sing the Sav - iour's praise: *Hark! hark! hark! while child-ren's voi - ces sing,*

1 Children of Jerusalem
   sang the praise of Jesus' name;
   children, too, of modern days,
   join to sing the Saviour's praise:
      Hark, hark, hark! while children's voices sing,
      hark, hark, hark! while children's voices sing
      loud hosannas, loud hosannas,
      loud hosannas to our King.

2 We are taught to love the Lord,
   we are taught to read His word,
   we are taught the way to heaven;
   praise for all to God be given:
      Hark, hark, hark . . .

3 Parents, teachers, old and young,
   all unite to swell the song;
   higher let God's praises rise,
   as hosannas fill the skies:
      Hark, hark, hark . . .

25 Christ triumphant

CHRIST TRIUMPHANT   85 85 79

Words: Michael Saward
Music: Michael Baughen

With triumphant vigour

Christ tri-um-phant, ev-er reign-ing, Sav-iour, Mas-ter, King,___ Lord of heaven, our lives sus--tain-ing, hear us as we sing:___ Yours the glo-ry and the crown,___ the high re-

- nown, _____ the e - ter - nal name. _____

1 Christ triumphant, ever reigning,
Saviour, Master, King,
Lord of heaven, our lives sustaining,
hear us as we sing:
  Yours the glory and the crown,
  the high renown, the eternal name.

2 Word incarnate, truth revealing,
Son of Man on earth!
power and majesty concealing
by your humble birth:
  Yours the glory . . .

3 Suffering servant, scorned, ill-treated,
victim crucified!
death is through the cross defeated,
sinners justified:
  Yours the glory . . .

4 Priestly King, enthroned for ever
high in heaven above!
sin and death and hell shall never
stifle hymns of love:
  Yours the glory . . .

5 So, our hearts and voices raising
through the ages long,
ceaselessly upon You gazing,
this shall be our song:
  Yours the glory . . .

26 Clap your hands, all you people

A four-part round

Words and music: Jimmy Owens
Music arranged David Peacock

Clap your hands, all you peo-ple, shout un-to God with a voice of tri-umph,

clap your hands, all you peo-ple, shout un-to God with a voice of praise! Ho -

-san - na, ho - san - na, shout un - to God with a voice of tri - umph,

praise Him, praise Him, shout un - to God with a voice of praise!

27 Cleanse me from my sin

Words and music: R Hudson Pope (1879–196.

Cleanse me from my sin, Lord, put Your power with - in, Lord,

take me as I am, Lord, and make me all Your own.

Keep me day by day, Lord, in Your per - fect way, Lord,

make my heart Your pal - ace, and Your roy - al throne.

Colours of day
(Light up the fire)

Words and music: Sue McClellan,
John Paculabo, Keith Ryecroft
Music arranged Douglas Coombes

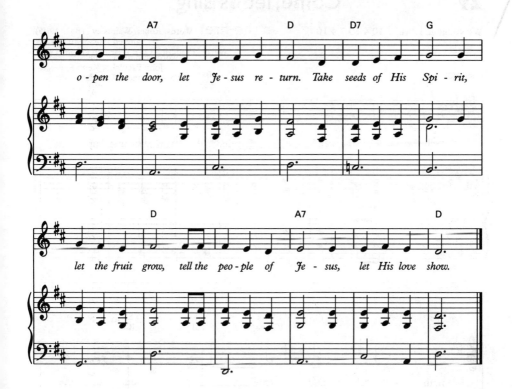

1 Colours of day dawn into the mind,
   the sun has come up, the night is behind.
   Go down in the city, into the street,
   and let's give the message to the people we meet.
      So light up the fire and let the flame burn,
      open the door, let Jesus return.
      Take seeds of His Spirit, let the fruit grow,
      tell the people of Jesus, let His love show.

2 Go through the park, on into the town;
   the sun still shines on, it never goes down.
   The Light of the world is risen again,
   the people of darkness are needing our friend.
      So light up the fire . . .

3 Open your eyes, look into the sky,
   the darkness has come, the sun came to die,
   the evening draws on, the sun disappears,
   but Jesus is living, His Spirit is near.
      So light up the fire . . .

29 Come, let us sing

WONDERFUL LOVE 10 4 10 7 4 10

Words: Robert Walmsley (1831–1905)
altered Horrobin/Leavers
Music: Frederick Luke Wiseman (1858–1944)

Come, let us sing of a won-der-ful love,

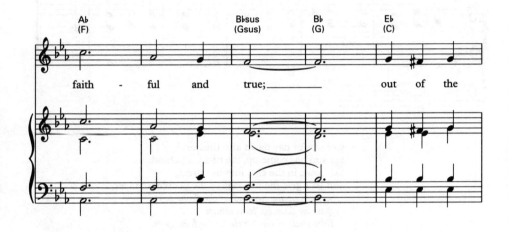

faith - ful and true;_____ out of the

heart of the Fa - ther a - bove,_____ stream-ing to

me and to you:_____ won - der - ful

love_____ dwells in the heart of the Fa - ther a - bove.

1 Come, let us sing of a wonderful love,
   faithful and true;
   out of the heart of the Father above,
   streaming to me and to you:
   wonderful love
   dwells in the heart of the Father above.

2 Jesus, the Saviour, this gospel to tell,
   joyfully came;
   came with the helpless and hopeless to dwell,
   sharing their sorrow and shame;
   seeking the lost,
   saving, redeeming at measureless cost.

3 Jesus is seeking all lost people yet;
   why can't they see?
   Turning to Him, He forgives and forgets,
   longing to set their hearts free.
   Wonderful love
   dwells in the heart of the Father above.

4 Come fill my heart with Your wonderful love,
   come and abide,
   lifting my life till it rises above
   envy and falsehood and pride;
   seeking to live
   life that is humble, with strength that You give.

30   Come, listen to my tale

Words and music: Anon
Music arranged Phil Burt

Ni - ne-veh, you see – to dis - o-bey's a ve - ry fool-ish no - tion. ___ But

God for-gave his sin, sal - va-tion en-tered in, way down in the mid-dle of the

way down in the mid-dle of the way down in the mid-dle of the o - cean. ___

Come, listen to my tale
of Jonah and the whale,
way down in the middle of the ocean.
Well, how did he get there?
Whatever did he wear?
Way down in the middle of the ocean.
A-preaching he should be
at Nineveh, you see –
to disobey's a very foolish notion.
But God forgave his sin,
salvation entered in,
way down in the middle of the
way down in the middle of the
way down in the middle of the ocean.

31 Come on, let's get up and go

Words and music: Graham Kendrick
Music arranged Phil Burt

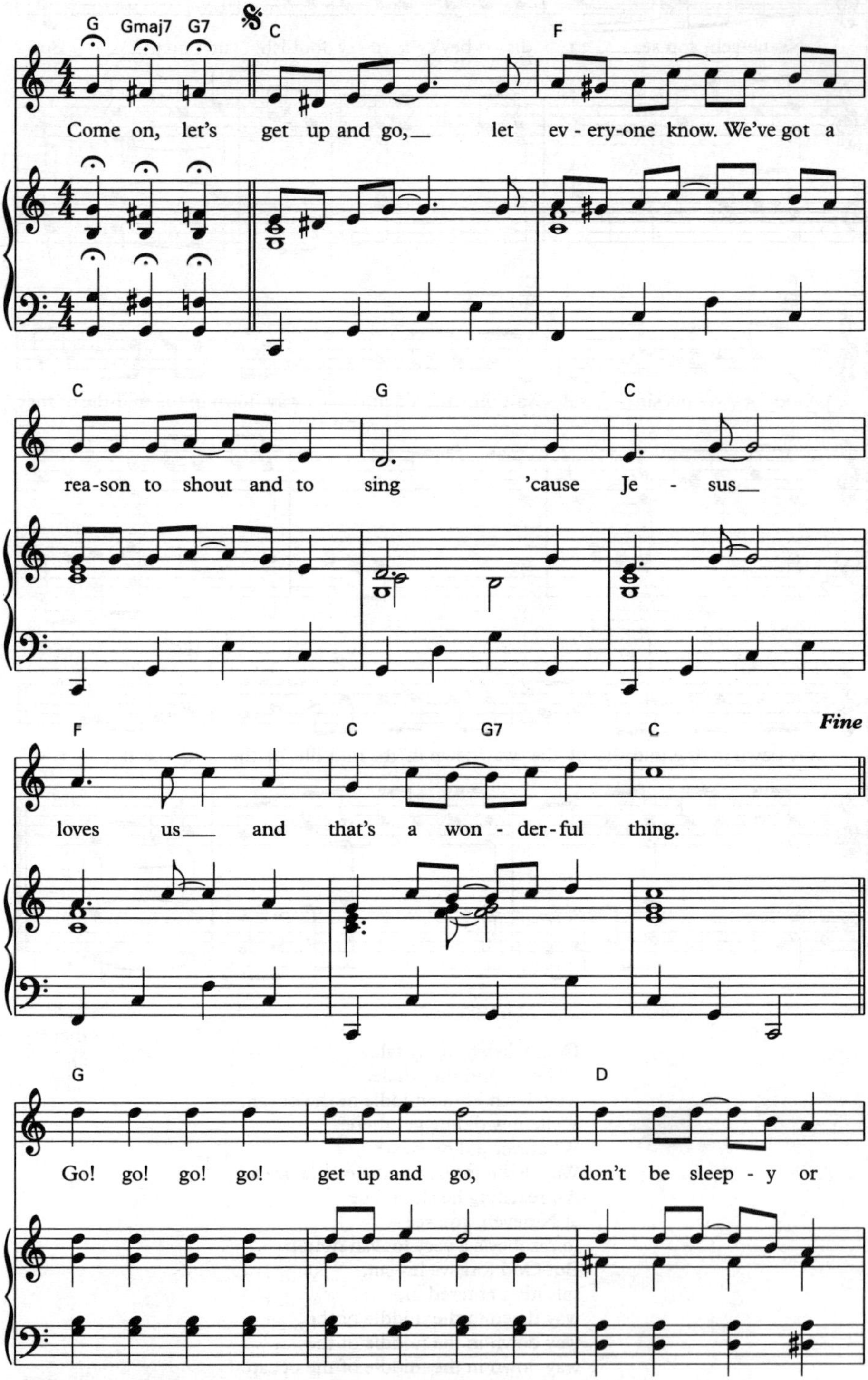

G Gmaj7 G7 C F
Come on, let's get up and go, let ev - ery-one know. We've got a
C G C
rea-son to shout and to sing 'cause Je - sus
F C G7 C
Fine
loves us and that's a won - der - ful thing.
G D
Go! go! go! go! get up and go, don't be sleep - y or

Come on, let's get up and go,
let everyone know.
We've got a reason to shout and to sing
'cause Jesus loves us
and that's a wonderful thing.

Go! go! go! go! get up and go,
don't be sleepy or slow!
You, you, you, you know what to do,
give your life to Him.

Come on, let's get up and go . . .

32   Come, you thankful people, come

St George's, Windsor   77 77 D

Words: Henry Alford (1810–71)
in this version Jubilate Hymns
Music: George Job Elvey (1816–93)

Come, you thank-ful peo - ple, come, raise the song of har - vest home!

Fruit and crops are gath - ered in safe be - fore the storms be - gin:

God our ma - ker will pro - vide for our needs to be sup - plied;

come, with all His peo - ple, come, raise the song of har - vest home!

1 Come, you thankful people, come,
raise the song of harvest home!
Fruit and crops are gathered in
safe before the storms begin:
God our maker will provide
for our needs to be supplied;
come, with all His people, come,
raise the song of harvest home!

2 All the world is God's own field,
harvests for His praise to yield;
wheat and weeds together sown
here for joy or sorrow grown:
first the blade and then the ear,
then the full corn shall appear –
Lord of harvest, grant that we
wholesome grain and pure may be.

3 For the Lord our God shall come
and shall bring His harvest home;
He Himself on that great day,
worthless things shall take away,
give His angels charge at last
in the fire the weeds to cast,
but the fruitful ears to store
in His care for evermore.

4 Even so, Lord, quickly come –
bring Your final harvest home!
Gather all Your people in
free from sorrow, free from sin,
there together purified,
ever thankful at Your side –
come, with all Your angels, come,
bring that glorious harvest home!

33 Come to Jesus, He's amazing

Words: Peter Horrobin
Music: Phil Burt

'Come to Je-sus, He's a-ma-zing!' peo - ple cried out when they saw

peo-ple walk-ing who were crip-pled, blind eyes see - ing, healed once more.

'Come to Jesus, He's amazing!'
people cried out when they saw
people walking who were crippled,
blind eyes seeing, healed once more.

34 Come and praise the Lord our King

Words: Traditional
adapted Geoffrey Marshall-Taylor
Music: Traditional
arranged Douglas Coombes

Come and praise the Lord our King, hal - le - lu - - jah, come and praise the Lord our King, hal - le - lu - jah.

1. Christ was born in Beth - le - hem, hal - le - lu - - jah, Son of God and Son of Man, hal - le - lu - jah

*Come and praise the Lord our King, hallelujah,
come and praise the Lord our King, hallelujah.*

1 Christ was born in Bethlehem, hallelujah,
Son of God and Son of Man, hallelujah.
Come and praise . . .

2 From Him love and wisdom came, hallelujah,
all His life was free from blame, hallelujah.
Come and praise . . .

3 Jesus died at Calvary, hallelujah,
rose again triumphantly, hallelujah.
Come and praise . . .

4 He will cleanse us from our sin, hallelujah,
if we live by faith in Him, hallelujah.
Come and praise . . .

5 He will be with us today, hallelujah,
and for ever with us stay, hallelujah.
Come and praise . . .

6 We will live with Him one day, hallelujah,
and for ever with Him stay, hallelujah.
Come and praise . . .

35

Deep and wide

Words and music: Sidney E Cox
Music arranged Andy Silver

Deep and wide, deep and wide,
there's a fountain flowing deep and wide;
deep and wide, deep and wide,
there's a fountain flowing deep and wide.

36   Daniel was a man of prayer

Words and music: Anon
Music arranged Phil Burt

Dan - iel was a man of prayer, dai - ly he prayed three times. Till one day they had him cast into a den of li - ons. In the den,

Daniel was a man of prayer,
daily he prayed three times.
Till one day they had him cast
into a den of lions.
In the den, in the den,
fear could not alarm him.
God just shut the lions' mouths
so they could not harm him.

37 Dear Lord and Father of mankind

REPTON   86 88 6 extended

Words: John Greenleaf Whittier (1807–82)
in this version Jubilate Hymns
Music: Charles Hubert Hastings Parry (1848–1918)

Dear Lord and Fa - ther__ of man-kind, for -

- give our fool - ish ways; re - clothe us in our

right - ful mind; in pur - er lives Your ser - vice_ find, in__

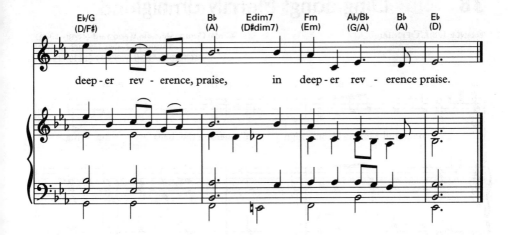

deep - er rev - erence, praise, in deep - er rev - erence praise.

1 Dear Lord and Father of mankind,
   forgive our foolish ways;
   re-clothe us in our rightful mind;
   in purer lives Your service find,
   in deeper reverence, praise.

2 In simple trust like theirs who heard,
   beside the Syrian sea,
   the gracious calling of the Lord,
   let us, like them, obey His word:
   'Rise up and follow Me!'

3 O Sabbath rest by Galilee!
   O calm of hills above,
   where Jesus shared on bended knee
   the silence of eternity,
   interpreted by love!

4 With that deep hush subduing all
   our words and works that drown
   the tender whisper of Your call,
   as noiseless let Your blessing fall,
   as fell Your manna down.

5 Drop Your still dews of quietness,
   till all our strivings cease;
   take from our souls the strain and stress,
   and let our ordered lives confess
   the beauty of Your peace.

6 Breathe through the heats of our desire
   Your coolness and Your balm;
   let sense be dumb, let flesh retire;
   speak through the earthquake, wind, and fire,
   O still small voice of calm!

Ding dong! Merrily on high

BRANLE DE L'OFFICIAL

Words: George Ratcliffe Woodward (1848–1934)
Music: 16th-cent. French melody
arranged Charles Wood and B V Burnett

Ding dong! Mer-ri - ly on high in heaven the bells are ring - ing.

Ding dong! Ve - ri - ly the sky is riven with an - gels sing - ing:

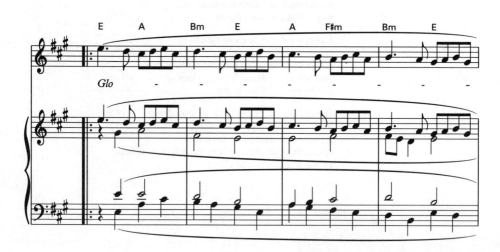

Glo - - - - - - - -

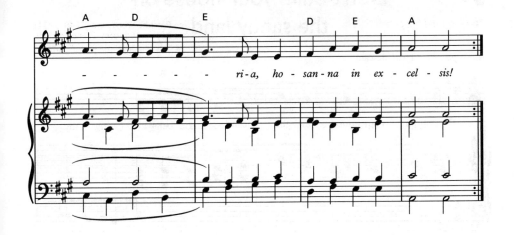

- - - - - ri-a, ho - san - na in ex - cel - sis!

1 Ding dong! Merrily on high
   in heaven the bells are ringing.
   Ding dong! Verily the sky
   is riven with angels singing:
   Gloria, hosanna in excelsis;
   gloria, hosanna in excelsis!

2 E'en so, here below, below,
   let steeple bells be swungen,
   and i-o, i-o, i-o,
   by priest and people sungen!
   Gloria . . .

3 Pray you, dutifully prime
   your matin chime, ye ringers;
   may you beautifully rime
   your eve-time song, ye singers:
   Gloria . . .

39 Don't build your house on the sandy land

Words and music: Karen Lafferty

A two-part round with descant

Don't build your house on the sand - y land,— don't build it too near the shore.___ Well, it might look kind of nice, but you'll have to build it twice, oh, you'll have to build your house once more. You'd bet - ter

* For round, when group 1 reaches this point, group 2 starts at the beginning. Also, add Descant for a third group.

Don't build your house on the sandy land,
don't build it too near the shore.
Well, it might look kind of nice,
but you'll have to build it twice,
oh, you'll have to build your house
    once more.

You'd better build your house upon a rock,
make a good foundation on a solid spot.
Oh, the storms may come and go,
but the peace of God you will know.

Rock of ages, cleft for me,
let me hide myself in Thee.

Do you want a pilot?

Words and music: E H Swinstead (d1976)

Do you want a pilot?
Signal then to Jesus;
do you want a pilot?
Bid Him come on board.
For He will safely guide
across the ocean wide,
until you reach at last
the heavenly harbour.

41   Father, hear the prayer we offer

GOTT WILL'S MACHEN

Words: Love Maria Willis (1824–1908)
Music: J L Steiner (1688–1761)

1   Father, hear the prayer we offer:
    not for ease that prayer shall be,
    but for strength, that we may ever
    live our lives courageously.

2   Not for ever in green pastures
    do we ask our way to be;
    but the steep and rugged pathway
    may we tread rejoicingly.

3   Not for ever by still waters
    would we idly rest and stay;
    but would smite the living fountains
    from the rocks along our way.

4   Be our strength in hours of weakness,
    in our wanderings be our guide;
    through endeavour, failure, danger,
    Father, always at our side.

42 Father, I place into Your hands

Words and music: Jenny Hewer

1 Father, I place into Your hands
   the things that I can't do.
   Father, I place into Your hands
   the times that I've been through.
   Father, I place into Your hands
   the way that I should go,
   for I know I always can trust You.

2 Father, I place into Your hands
   my friends and family.
   Father, I place into Your hands
   the things that trouble me.
   Father, I place into Your hands
   the person I would be,
   for I know I always can trust You.

3 Father, we love to seek Your face,
   we love to hear Your voice.
   Father, we love to sing Your praise,
   and in Your name rejoice.
   Father, we love to walk with You
   and in Your presence rest,
   for we know we always can trust You.

4 Father, I want to be with You
   and do the things You do.
   Father, I want to speak the words
   that You are speaking too.
   Father, I want to love the ones
   that You will draw to You,
   for I know that I am one with You.

43 Father, lead me day by day

ST MARTIN   77 77

Words: J P Hopps (1834–1912)
altered Horrobin/Leavers
Music: French traditional melody

Fa - ther, lead me day by day ev - er in your own good way;

teach me to be pure and true – show me what I ought to do.

1 Father, lead me day by day
   ever in your own good way;
   teach me to be pure and true –
   show me what I ought to do.

2 When in danger, make me brave;
   make me know that You can save.
   Keep me safe by Your dear side;
   let me in Your love abide.

3 When I'm tempted to do wrong,
   make me steadfast, wise and strong;
   and when all alone I stand,
   shield me with Your mighty hand.

4 When my work seems hard and dry,
   may I never cease to try;
   help me patiently to bear
   pain and hardship, toil and care.

5 May I do the good I know,
   be Your loving child below,
   then at last in heaven share
   life with You that's free from care.

44 Father, we adore You

Words and music: Terrye Coelho

A three-part round

Slowly, sustained

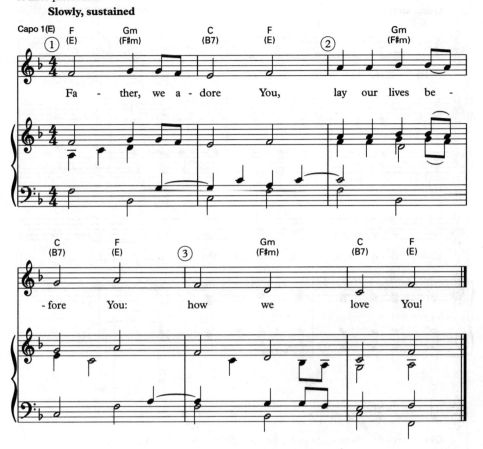

Father, we adore You, lay our lives be- -fore You: how we love You!

1 Father, we adore You,
  lay our lives before You:
  how we love You!

2 Jesus, we adore You,
  lay our lives before You:
  how we love You!

3 Spirit, we adore You,
  lay our lives before You:
  how we love You!

45 Father, we love You

Words and music: Donna Adkins

Fa - ther, we love You, we wor - ship and a - dore You: glo - ri - fy Your name in all the earth.

Glo - ri - fy Your name, glo - ri - fy Your name, glo - ri - fy Your name in all the earth.

1 Father, we love You,
  we worship and adore You:
  glorify Your name
  in all the earth.
  Glorify Your name,
  glorify Your name,
  glorify Your name
  in all the earth.

2 Jesus, we love You,
  we worship and adore You:
  glorify Your name
  in all the earth.
  Glorify Your name,
  glorify Your name,
  glorify Your name
  in all the earth.

3 Spirit, we love You,
  we worship and adore You:
  glorify Your name
  in all the earth.
  Glorify Your name,
  glorify Your name,
  glorify Your name
  in all the earth.

'Follow Me,' says Jesus

Words and music: Greg Leavers
Music arranged Phil Burt

'Fol - low Me,' says Je - sus, 'I can keep you safe.

I am the good shep - herd, so

why not be My sheep?_ If you're lost and

lone - ly I can keep you safe.____ I

gave My life to save you, so come, just fol-low Me.'

'Follow Me,' says Jesus,
'I can keep you safe.
I am the good shepherd,
so why not be My sheep?
If you're lost and lonely
I can keep you safe.
I gave My life to save you,
so come, just follow Me.'

47   For I'm building a people of power

Words and music: Dave Richards
Music arranged Roger Mayor

For I'm build-ing a peo-ple of pow-er___ and I'm mak-ing a peo-ple of praise, that will move through this land by My Spi-rit,___ and will glo-ri-fy My pre-cious name. Build Your Church, Lord, make us strong, Lord, join our hearts, Lord, through Your Son; make us

For I'm building a people of power
and I'm making a people of praise,
that will move through this land
   by My Spirit,
and will glorify My precious name.

Build Your Church, Lord,
make us strong, Lord,
join our hearts, Lord, through Your Son;
make us one, Lord, in Your body,
in the kingdom of Your Son.

48 For the beauty of the earth

ENGLAND'S LANE 77 77 77

Words: Folliott Pierpoint (1835–1917)
altered Horrobin/Leavers
Music: from an English melody
adapted and arranged by Geoffrey Shaw (1879–1943)

For the beau-ty of the earth, for the beau-ty of the skies, for the love which from our birth o-ver and a-round us lies; Fa-ther,

* This item appears in the key of C in the first edition of *Junior Praise*.

Music: by permission of Oxford University Press

un - to You we raise this our sac - ri - fice of praise.

1 For the beauty of the earth,
   for the beauty of the skies,
   for the love which from our birth
   over and around us lies;
   Father, unto You we raise
   this our sacrifice of praise.

2 For the beauty of each hour
   of the day and of the night,
   hill and vale, and tree and flower,
   sun and moon, and stars of light;
   Father, unto You we raise
   this our sacrifice of praise.

3 For the joy of love from God,
   that we share on earth below;
   for our friends and family,
   and the love that they can show;
   Father, unto You we raise
   this our sacrifice of praise.

4 For each perfect gift divine
   to our race so freely given,
   thank You, Lord, that they are mine,
   here on earth as gifts from heaven;
   Father, unto You we raise
   this our sacrifice of praise.

49 From the rising of the sun

From Psalm 113
Words and music: Paul Deeming

From the ris - ing of the sun to the go - ing down of the same,_ the Lord's name is to be praised. From the ris - ing of the

Praise ye the Lord,

praise Him, O ye ser-vants of the Lord, praise the name of the Lord; bless-èd be the name of the Lord from this time forth, and for ev - er - more.

From the rising of the sun
to the going down of the same,
the Lord's name is to be praised.
From the rising of the sun
to the going down of the same,
the Lord's name is to be praised.

Praise ye the Lord,
praise Him, O ye servants of the Lord,
praise the name of the Lord;
blessèd be the name of the Lord
from this time forth,
and for evermore.

Give me oil in my lamp

Words: A Sevison
Music: Anon
arranged Betty Pulkingham

Give me oil in my lamp, keep me burn-ing,_____ give me oil in my lamp, I pray; give me oil in my lamp, keep me burn-ing,_____ keep me burn-ing till the break of day.

1 Give me oil in my lamp, keep me burning,
   give me oil in my lamp, I pray;
   give me oil in my lamp, keep me burning,
   keep me burning till the break of day.
       Sing hosanna, sing hosanna,
       sing hosanna to the King of kings!
       Sing hosanna, sing hosanna,
       sing hosanna to the King!

2 Give me joy in my heart, keep me singing,
   give me joy in my heart, I pray;
   give me joy in my heart, keep me singing,
   keep me singing till the break of day.
       Sing hosanna . . .

3 Give me love in my heart, keep me serving,
   give me love in my heart, I pray;
   give me love in my heart, keep me serving,
   keep me serving till the break of day.
       Sing hosanna . . .

4 Give me peace in my heart, keep me resting,
   give me peace in my heart, I pray;
   give me peace in my heart, keep me resting,
   keep me resting till the break of day.
       Sing hosanna . . .

51 Glory to God in the highest

Words and music: Greg Leavers
Music arranged Phil Burt

Glo - ry to God in the high - est, peace_____ up-on earth, Je - sus Christ has come_____ to earth; that's why we sing, 'Je - sus the King, Je - sus has come for you.'_____

3rd time **to Coda**

Glory to God in the highest,
peace upon earth,
Jesus Christ has come to earth;
that's why we sing,
'Jesus the King,
Jesus has come for you.'

1 The shepherds who were sitting there
   were suddenly filled with fear;
   the dark night was filled with light,
   angels singing everywhere.
   Glory to God . . .

2 The next time we hear a song
   of worship from a heavenly throng,
   will be when Jesus comes again,
   then with triumph we'll all sing:
   Glory to God . . .

52 Glory to You, my God

TALLIS' CANON   LM

Words: Thomas Ken (1637–1711)
in this version Jubilate Hymns
Music: Thomas Tallis (1505–1585)

Glo - ry to You, my God, this night for all the bless-ings of the light;

keep me, O keep me, King of kings, be - neath Your own al - migh-ty wings.

1 Glory to You, my God, this night
for all the blessings of the light;
keep me, O keep me, King of kings,
beneath Your own almighty wings.

2 Forgive me, Lord, through Your dear Son,
the wrong that I this day have done,
that peace with God and man may be,
before I sleep, restored to me.

3 Teach me to live, that I may dread
the grave as little as my bed;
teach me to die, that so I may
rise glorious at the awesome day.

4 O may my soul on you repose
and restful sleep my eyelids close;
sleep that shall me more vigorous make
to serve my God when I awake.

5 If in the night I sleepless lie,
my mind with peaceful thoughts supply;
let no dark dreams disturb my rest,
no powers of evil me molest.

6 Praise God from whom all blessings flow
in heaven above and earth below;
one God, three persons, we adore –
to Him be praise for evermore!

53 God is so good

Words and music: Anon
Music arranged David Peacock

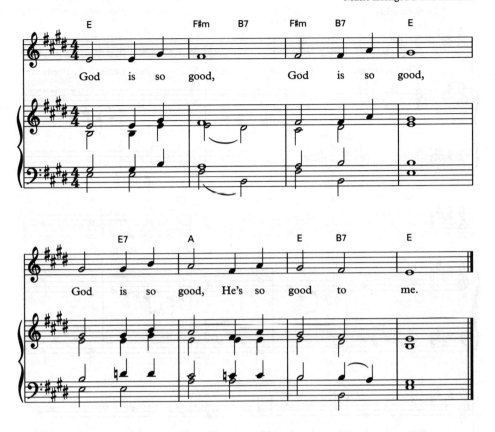

God is so good, God is so good, God is so good, He's so good to me.

1 God is so good,
God is so good,
God is so good,
He's so good to me.

2 He took my sin,
He took my sin,
He took my sin,
He's so good to me.

3 Now I am free,
now I am free,
now I am free,
He's so good to me.

4 God is so good,
He took my sin,
now I am free,
He's so good to me.

54 God forgave my sin

Words and music: Carol Owens

Smoothly

God for-gave my sin in Je - sus' name; I've been
born a - gain in Je - sus' name, and in Je - sus'
name I come to you to share His love as He
told me to. *He said: 'Free - ly, free - ly*

slowly   a tempo

1 God forgave my sin in Jesus' name;
   I've been born again in Jesus' name,
   and in Jesus' name I come to you
   to share His love as He told me to.
     He said:
     'Freely, freely you have received,
     freely, freely give;
     go in My name and because you believe,
     others will know that I live.'

2 All power is given in Jesus' name
   in earth and heaven in Jesus' name;
   and in Jesus' name I come to you
   to share His power as He told me to.
     He said . . .

55 God is good

Words and music: Graham Kendrick
Music arranged David Peacock

God is good – we sing and shout it, God is good –
we ce-le-brate; God is good – no more we doubt it,
God is good – we know it's true!
And when I think of His love for me, my heart fills with praise and I

* This item appears in the key of G minor in the first edition of *Junior Praise*.

God is good – we sing and shout it,
God is good – we celebrate;
God is good – no more we doubt it,
God is good – we know it's true!

And when I think of His love for me,
my heart fills with praise
and I feel like dancing;
for in His heart there is room for me,
and I run with arms opened wide.

God is good – we sing and shout it,
God is good – we celebrate;
God is good – no more we doubt it,
God is good – we know it's true! *Hey!*

56 God is our guide

FINLANDIA   11 10 11 10 11 10

Words: Christopher Porteous
Music: Jean Sibelius (1865–1957)

God is our guide, our light and our de-liv-erer,

He holds our hand, He walks be-side the way.

Lord, may our feet tread in the steps You taught us

to fol-low firm-ly as by faith each day,

Your word a light, a lamp to lead our foot-steps — we love the hours when You be-side us stay.

1 God is our guide, our light and our deliverer,
He holds our hand, He walks beside the way.
Lord, may our feet tread in the steps You taught us
to follow firmly as by faith each day,
Your word a light, a lamp to lead our footsteps –
we love the hours when You beside us stay.

2 God is our peace, our help and our protector,
we find His presence in the hour of need.
Lord, though the storms of life may leave us trembling,
Your words of comfort bring us peace within.
When we are weak and fear to face the future
we find such comfort in Your loving arms.

3 God is our hope, our joy and our salvation,
His love alone transforms the sinful heart.
Lord, how we sought Your Spirit's sweet renewing:
Your healing touch has filled our hearts with praise.
We come and worship Jesus, Lord and Saviour,
His love alone must fill our earthly days.

4 God is our strength, our rock and our redeemer
in times of trouble and in times of joy.
Lord, may our lives be full of sure thanksgiving,
our lips be full of symphonies of praise.
You gave us love, a risen, living Saviour,
we bring ourselves, a sacrifice of praise.

57 God is working His purpose out

BENSON Irregular

Words: Arthur Campbell Ainger (1841–1919)
in this version Jubilate Hymns
Music: Millicent Douglas Kingham (1866–1927)

God is work-ing His pur-pose out, as year suc-ceeds to year: God is work-ing His pur-pose out, and the time is draw-ing near: near-er and near-er draws the time, the

time that shall sure - ly be, when the earth shall be filled with the glo - ry of God, as the wa - ters co - ver the sea.

1 God is working His purpose out,
   as year succeeds to year:
   God is working His purpose out,
   and the time is drawing near:
   nearer and nearer draws the time,
   the time that shall surely be,
   when the earth shall be filled
   with the glory of God,
   as the waters cover the sea.

2 From utmost east to utmost west
   wherever man has trod,
   by the mouth of many messengers
   rings out the voice of God:
   listen to me, you continents,
   you islands, look to me,
   that the earth may be filled
   with the glory of God,
   as the waters cover the sea.

3 We shall march in the strength of God,
   with the banner of Christ unfurled,
   that the light of the glorious gospel of truth
   may shine throughout the world;
   we shall fight with sorrow and sin
   to set their captives free,
   that the earth may be filled
   with the glory of God,
   as the waters cover the sea.

4 All we can do is nothing worth
   unless God blesses the deed;
   vainly we hope for the harvest-tide
   till God gives life to the seed:
   nearer and nearer draws the time,
   the time that shall surely be,
   when the earth shall be filled
   with the glory of God,
   as the waters cover the sea.

God sent His Son

Words: Gloria and William J Gaither
Music: William J Gaither

1 God sent His Son, they call Him Jesus;
He came to love, heal, and forgive;
He lived and died to buy my pardon,
an empty grave is there to prove my Saviour lives.
  Because He lives I can face tomorrow;
  because He lives all fear is gone;
  because I know, I know He holds the future,
  and life is worth the living just because He lives.

2 How sweet to hold a new-born baby,
and feel the pride and joy he gives;
but greater still the calm assurance,
this child can face uncertain days because He lives.
  Because He lives . . .

3 And then one day I'll cross the river;
I'll fight life's final war with pain;
and then as death gives way to victory,
I'll see the lights of glory and I'll know He lives.
  Because He lives . . .

59   God so loved the world

Words and music: Peter Horrobin
Music arranged Phil Burt

1 God so loved the world
    He sent to us Jesus,
  God so loved the world He sent His Son.
  Alleluia, Jesus, Lord Jesus, Jesus,
  alleluia, Jesus, God sent His Son.

2 Jesus showed the world the love
    of the Father,
  Jesus showed the world how we must love.
  Alleluia, Jesus, Lord Jesus, Jesus,
  alleluia, Jesus, God sent His Son.

60 God's not dead

Words and music: Anon
altered Horrobin/Leavers
Music arranged Phil Burt

61 God, whose farm is all creation

SHIPSTON 87 87

Words: John Arlott (1914–91)
Music: English traditional melody
collected Lucy Broadwood (1858–1929)
arranged and harmonised Ralph Vaughan Williams (1872–1958)

1 God, whose farm is all creation,
  take the gratitude we give;
  take the finest of our harvest,
  crops we grow that men may live.

2 Take our ploughing, seeding, reaping,
  hopes and fears of sun and rain,
  all our thinking, planning, waiting,
  ripened in this fruit and grain.

3 All our labour, all our watching,
  all our calendar of care,
  in these crops of Your creation,
  take, O God; they are our prayer.

Music: from the *English Hymnal*
by permission of Oxford University Press

62 God whose Son was once a man

Words: Peter Horrobin
Music: Greg Leavers

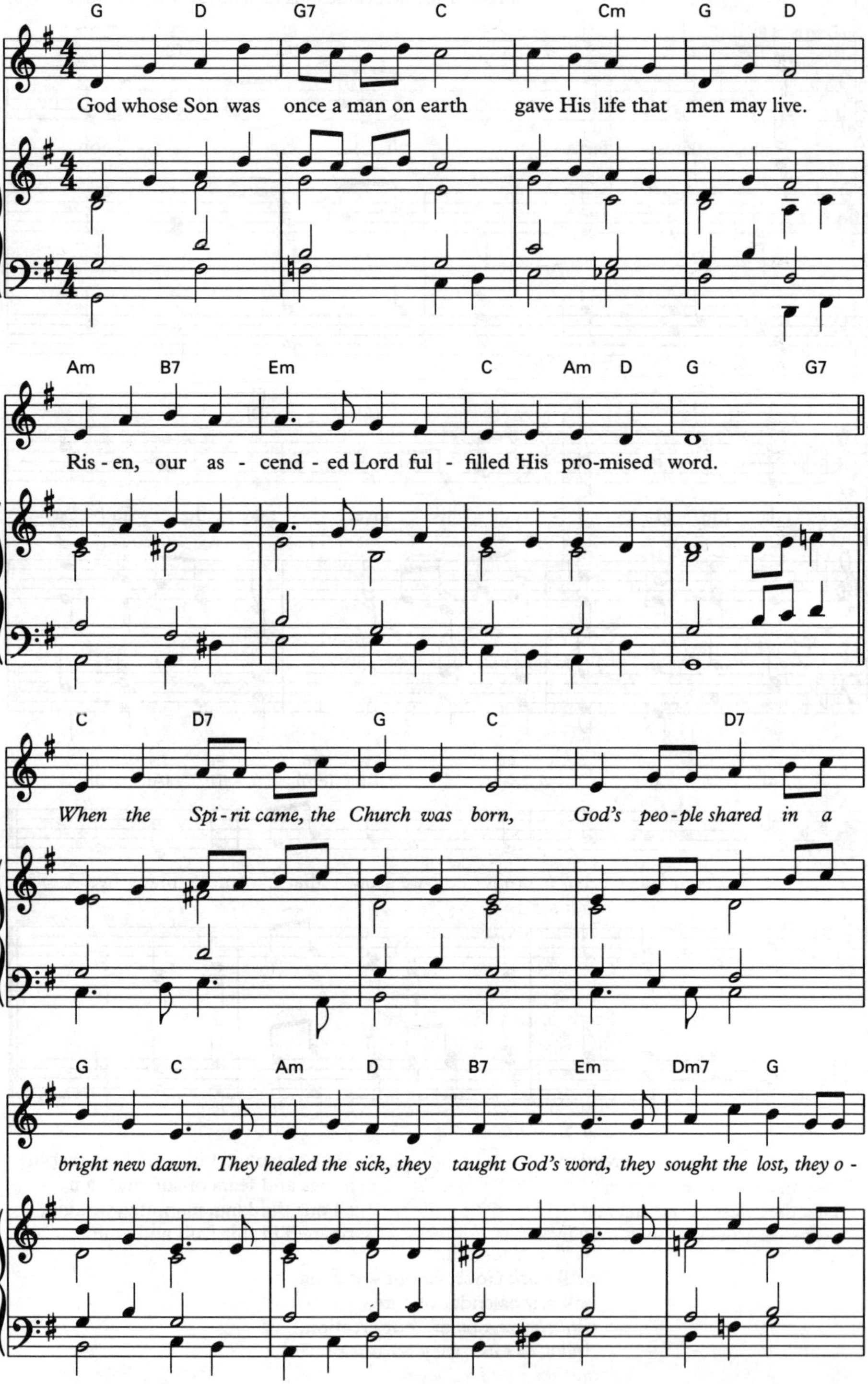

G D G7 C Cm G D
God whose Son was once a man on earth gave His life that men may live.
Am B7 Em C Am D G G7
Ris - en, our as - cend - ed Lord ful - filled His pro-mised word.
C D7 G C D7
When the Spi - rit came, the Church was born, God's peo - ple shared in a
G C Am D B7 Em Dm7 G
bright new dawn. They healed the sick, they taught God's word, they sought the lost, they o -

1 God whose Son was once a man on earth
   gave His life that men may live.
   Risen, our ascended Lord
   fulfilled His promised word.
       When the Spirit came, the Church was born,
       God's people shared in a bright new dawn.
       They healed the sick,
       they taught God's word,
       they sought the lost,
       they obeyed the Lord.
       And it's all because the Spirit came
       that the world will never be the same,
       because the Spirit came.

2 God whose power fell on the early church,
   sent to earth from heaven above;
   Spirit-led, by Him ordained,
   they showed the world God's love.
       When the Spirit came ...

3 Pour Your Spirit on the church today,
   that Your life through me may flow;
   Spirit-filled, I'll serve Your name
   and live the truth I know.
       When the Spirit comes, new life is born,
       God's people share in a bright new dawn.
       We'll heal the sick,
       we'll teach God's word,
       we'll seek the lost,
       we'll obey the Lord.
       And it's all because the Spirit came
       that the world will never be the same,
       because the Spirit came.

63 God, who made the earth

SOMMERLIED 5 6 6 4

Words: Sarah Betts Rhodes (1829–1904)
altered Horrobin/Leavers
Music: Herman von Muller (1859–1938)

God, who made the earth, the air, the sky, the sea, who gave the light its birth,___ will care for me.

1 God, who made the earth,
  the air, the sky, the sea,
  who gave the light its birth,
  will care for me.

2 God, who made the grass,
  the flower, the fruit, the tree,
  the day and night to pass,
  will care for me.

3 God, who made the sun,
  the moon, the stars, is He
  who, when life's clouds come on,
  will care for me.

4 God, who sent His son
  to die on Calvary,
  He, if I lean on Him,
  will care for me.

5 God, who gave me life
  His servant here to be,
  has promised in His word
  to care for me.

64 Great is Your faithfulness

GREAT IS YOUR FAITHFULNESS
11 10 11 10 with refrain

Words: Thomas O Chisholm (1866–1960)
in this version Jubilate Hymns
Music: William Marion Runyan (1870–1957)

Great is Your faith-ful-ness, O God my Fa-ther,
You have ful-filled all Your pro-mise to me;
You ne-ver fail and Your love is un-chang-ing;
all You have been You for-ev-er will be.

1 Great is Your faithfulness, O God my Father,
You have fulfilled all Your promise to me;
You never fail and Your love is unchanging;
all You have been You for ever will be.
    Great is Your faithfulness,
    great is Your faithfulness;
    morning by morning
    new mercies I see;
    all I have needed
    Your hand has provided –
    great is Your faithfulness,
    Father, to me!

2 Summer and winter, and spring-time and harvest,
sun, moon and stars in their courses above,
join with all nature in eloquent witness
to Your great faithfulness, mercy and love.
    Great is Your faithfulness . . .

3 Pardon for sin, and a peace everlasting,
Your living presence to cheer and to guide;
strength for today and bright hope for tomorrow,
these are the blessings Your love will provide.
    Great is Your faithfulness . . .

65 Go, tell it on the mountain

Words: Geoffrey Marshall-Taylor
Music: Anon
arranged Douglas Coombes

Go, tell it on the moun - tain, o - ver the hills and ev - ery-where;

go, tell it on the moun - tain that Je - sus is His name.

He pos-sessed no rich - es, no home to lay His head; He

saw the needs of oth - ers and cared for them in - stead.___

Go, tell it on the mountain,
over the hills and everywhere;
go, tell it on the mountain
that Jesus is His name.

1 He possessed no riches, no home to lay His head;
   He saw the needs of others and cared for them instead.
   Go, tell it on the mountain . . .

2 He reached out and touched them, the blind, the deaf, the lame;
   He spoke and listened gladly to anyone who came.
   Go, tell it on the mountain . . .

3 Some turned away in anger, with hatred in the eye;
   they tried Him and condemned Him, then led Him out to die.
   Go, tell it on the mountain . . .

4 'Father, now forgive them' – those were the words He said;
   in three more days He was alive and risen from the dead.
   Go, tell it on the mountain . . .

5 He still comes to people, His life moves through the lands;
   He uses us for speaking, He touches with our hands.
   Go, tell it on the mountain . . .

66 Hallelujah! for the Lord our God

Words and music: Dale Garratt

Triumphantly

Hal-le-lu-jah!_____ for the Lord our God the al-migh - ty_____ reigns._____ _ Hal-le-lu-jah!_____ for the Lord our God the al-migh - ty_____ reigns.

Hallelujah! for the Lord our God the almighty reigns.
Hallelujah! for the Lord our God the almighty reigns.
Let us rejoice and be glad and give the glory unto Him.
Hallelujah! for the Lord our God the almighty reigns.

67

Hallelu, hallelu

Words and music: Anon
Music arranged E J Hume

68 Hark, the glad sound

St Saviour   CM

Words: Philip Dodderidge (1702–51)
in this version Horrobin/Leavers
Music: Frederick George Baker (1840–1908)

1 Hark, the glad sound! the Saviour comes,
the Saviour promised long;
let every heart prepare a throne,
and every voice a song.

2 He comes, the prisoners to release
in Satan's bondage held;
the chains of sin before Him break,
the iron fetters yield.

3 He comes the broken heart to bind,
the wounded soul to cure;
and with the treasures of His grace
to enrich the humble poor.

4 Our glad hosannas, Prince of peace,
Your welcome shall proclaim;
and heaven's eternal arches ring
with Your belovèd name.

69 Hark! the herald-angels sing

MENDELSSOHN 77 77 D with refrain

Words: Charles Wesley (1707–88) and others
Music: Felix Mendelssohn-Bartholdy (1809–47)
arranged William H Cummings (1831–1915)

Hark! the her - ald - an - gels sing, _ 'Glo - ry to the new-born King!

Peace on earth, and mer - cy mild, _ God and sin - ners re - con - ciled.'

Joy - ful, all you na - tions rise, _ join the tri - umph of the skies; _

with th'an-gel - ic host pro-claim, 'Christ is __ born in Beth - le -hem!'

Hark! the her - ald - an - gels sing, 'Glo - ry __ to the new-born King!'

1 Hark! the herald-angels sing,
  'Glory to the new-born King!
  Peace on earth, and mercy mild,
  God and sinners reconciled.'
  Joyful, all you nations rise,
  join the triumph of the skies;
  with the angelic host proclaim,
  'Christ is born in Bethlehem!'
    Hark! the herald-angels sing,
    'Glory to the new-born King!'

2 Christ by highest heaven adored,
  Christ, the everlasting Lord,
  late in time behold Him come,
  offspring of a virgin's womb!
  Veiled in flesh the Godhead see!
  Hail, the incarnate Deity!
  Pleased as man with man to dwell,
  Jesus, our Immanuel.
    Hark! the herald-angels sing,
    'Glory to the new-born King!'

3 Hail, the heaven-born Prince of peace!
  Hail, the Sun of righteousness!
  Light and life to all He brings,
  risen with healing in His wings.
  Mild He lays His glory by,
  born that man no more may die;
  born to raise the sons of earth,
  born to give them second birth.
    Hark! the herald-angels sing,
    'Glory to the new-born King!'

70 Happiness is to know the Saviour

Words and music: Ira F Stanphill

Hap-pi-ness is to know the Sav-iour, liv-ing a life with-in His fav-our, hav-ing a change in my be-hav-iour, *1.* hap-pi-ness is the Lord. *2.* Lord. Real joy is mine, no mat-ter if tear-drops start; I've found the

sec - ret – it's Je - sus in my heart! Lord,

hap - pi-ness is the Lord, hap - pi-ness is the Lord!

1 Happiness is to know the Saviour,
   living a life within His favour,
   having a change in my behaviour,
   happiness is the Lord.

2 Happiness is a new creation,
   Jesus and me in close relation,
   having a part in His salvation,
   happiness is the Lord.
      Real joy is mine,
      no matter if teardrops start;
      I've found the secret –
      it's Jesus in my heart!

3 Happiness is to be forgiven,
   living a life that's worth the living,
   taking a trip that leads to heaven,
   happiness is the Lord,
   happiness is the Lord,
   happiness is the Lord!

71 Have you heard the raindrops

Words and music: Christian Strover

1 Have you heard the raindrops drumming on the rooftops?
Have you heard the raindrops dripping on the ground?
Have you heard the raindrops splashing in the streams
and running to the rivers all around?
There's water, water of life,
Jesus gives us the water of life,
there's water, water of life,
Jesus gives us the water of life.

2 There's a busy workman digging in the desert,
digging with a spade that flashes in the sun;
soon there will be water rising in the wellshaft,
spilling from the bucket as it comes.
There's water ...

3 Nobody can live who hasn't any water,
when the land is dry then nothing much grows;
Jesus gives us life if we drink the living water,
sing it so that everybody knows.
There's water ...

72 Have you seen the pussy cat

Words and music: P A Taylor
arranged Andy Silver

Have you seen the pus - sy cat sit - ting on the wall? Have you heard his beau-ti-ful purr? (*purr*) Have you seen the li - on stalk - ing round his prey? Have you heard his ter - ri - ble roar? (*roar*) One so big, one so small,

1 Have you seen the pussy cat sitting on the wall?
   Have you heard his beautiful purr? (*purr*)
   Have you seen the lion stalking round his prey?
   Have you heard his terrible roar? (*roar*)
       One so big, one so small,
       our heavenly Father cares for them all,
       one so big, one so small,
       our heavenly Father cares.

2 Have you seen the children coming home from school?
   Have you heard them shout, 'Hurray!' (*Hurray!*)
   Have you seen the grown-ups coming home from work,
   saying, 'What a horrible day!' (*What a horrible day!*)
       Some so big, some so small,
       our heavenly Father cares for them all,
       some so big, some so small,
       our heavenly Father cares.

73 He brought me to His banqueting house

Words and music: Anon
Music arranged Phil Burt

He brought me to His ban-quet-ing house and His
ban-ner o-ver me is love, He brought me to His
ban-quet-ing house and His ban-ner o-ver me is love, He
brought me to His ban-quet-ing house and His ban-ner o-ver me is

love, His ban-ner o-ver me__ is love.__

God loves you and I love you and that's the way it should be.

God loves you and I love you and that's the way it should be.__

1 He brought me to His banqueting house
  and His banner over me is love,
  He brought me to His banqueting house
  and His banner over me is love,
  He brought me to His banqueting house
  and His banner over me is love,
  His banner over me is love.
      God loves you and I love you
      and that's the way it should be.
      God loves you and I love you
      and that's the way it should be.

2 He feeds me at His banqueting table . . .
      God loves you . . .

3 He lifts me up to the heavenly places . . .
      God loves you . . .

4 There's one way to peace through the power of the cross . . .
      God loves you . . .

5 Jesus is the rock of my salvation . . .
      God loves you . . .

74 He gave me eyes so I could see

Words and music: Alan Pinnock

He gave me eyes so I could see the won-ders of the
world. With-out my eyes I could not see the
oth-er boys and girls. He gave me ears so
I could hear the wind and rain and sea. I've

got   to tell   it   to   the   world,   He   made   me!

1 He gave me eyes so I could see
  the wonders of the world.
  Without my eyes I could not see
  the other boys and girls.
  He gave me ears so I could hear
  the wind and rain and sea.
  I've got to tell it to the world,
  He made me!

2 He gave me lips so I could speak,
  and say what's in my mind.
  Without my lips I could not speak
  a single word or line.
  He made my mind so I could think
  and choose what I should be.
  I've got to tell it to the world,
  He made me!

3 He gave me hands so I could touch,
  and hold a thousand things.
  I need my hands to help me write,
  to help me fetch and bring.
  These feet He made so I could run,
  He meant me to be free.
  I've got to tell it to the world,
  He made me!

75 He is Lord, He is Lord

Words and music: Marvin Frey
Music arranged Roland Fudge

1 He is Lord, He is Lord,
He is risen from the dead
and He is Lord!
Every knee shall bow,
every tongue confess
that Jesus Christ is Lord.

2 He's my Lord, He's my Lord,
He is risen from the dead
and He's my Lord!
And my knee shall bow
and my tongue confess
that Jesus is my Lord.

76   He made the stars to shine

Words and music: Archie Hall

He made the stars to shine, He made the roll-ing sea, He made the moun-tains high, and He made me. But this is why I love Him – for me He bled and died, the Lord of all cre - a - tion__ be-came the cru - ci - fied.

77

He paid a debt

Words and music: Anon
Music arranged Phil Burt

He paid a debt He did not owe,___ I owed a
debt I could not pay.___ I need - ed some - one to
wash my sins a - way,_____ and now I sing a brand new song,

He paid a debt He did not owe,
I owed a debt I could not pay.
I needed someone to wash my sins away,
and now I sing a brand new song,
'Amazing grace!' the whole day long,
for Jesus paid a debt that I could never pay.

78 He's got the whole wide world

Words and music: Anon
Music arranged Phil Burt

1 He's got the whole wide world in His hands,
He's got the whole wide world in His hands,
He's got the whole wide world in His hands,
He's got the whole world in His hands.

2 He's got everybody here in His hands . . .

3 He's got the tiny little baby in His hands . . .

4 He's got you and me, brother, in His hands . . .

79

He's great! He's God

Words: Peter Horrobin and Greg Leavers
Music: Phil Burt and Greg Leavers

1 He's great! He's God!
   Jesus Christ is Lord.
   He's great! He's God!
   Trust His word.

2 His word is truth,
   for He cannot lie.
   His word is truth,
   to live by.

3 His love is strong,
   and will never end.
   His love is strong,
   praise His name.

4 He lives evermore
   as the King of kings.
   He lives evermore!
   Worship Him.

80 He who would valiant be

MONK'S GATE   11 11 12 11

Words: Percy Dearmer (1867–1936)
after John Bunyan (1628–88)
Music: English traditional melody
collected and arranged Ralph Vaughan Williams (1872–1958)

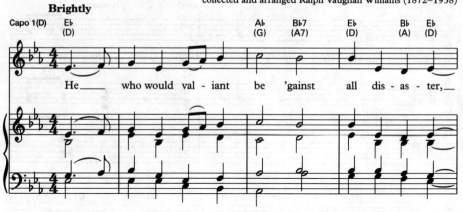

He___ who would val - iant be 'gainst all dis - as - ter,___

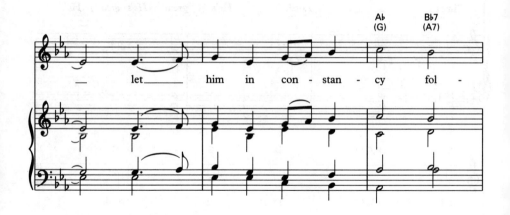

___ let___ him in con - stan - cy fol -

- low the Mas - ter.___ There's no dis - cour - age -

1 He who would valiant be
'gainst all disaster,
let him in constancy
follow the Master.
There's no discouragement
shall make him once relent
his first avowed intent
to be a pilgrim.

2 Who so beset him round
with dismal stories,
do but themselves confound –
his strength the more is.
No foes shall stay his might,
though he with giants fight:
he will make good his right
to be a pilgrim.

3 Since, Lord, Thou dost defend
us with Thy Spirit,
we know we at the end
shall life inherit.
Then fancies flee away!
I'll fear not what men say,
I'll labour night and day
to be a pilgrim.

81 Hévénu shalom

Words: Israeli traditional song
Music: Israeli traditional melody

He-vé-nu sha - lom a - lé-chem, Hé-vé-nu sha - lom a -

- lé-chem, Hé-vé-nu sha - lom a - lé-chem, Hé-vé-nu

sha - lom, sha - lom, sha - lom a - lé-chem. Hé - vé - nu sha - lom a - lé-chem.

Hévénu shalom aléchem,
Hévénu shalom aléchem,
Hévénu shalom aléchem,
Hévénu shalom,
shalom, shalom aléchem.

82 How great is our God

Words and music: Anon
Music arranged Phil Burt

With life

How great is our God, how great is His name, how great is His love for-ev-er the same. He rolled back the wa-ters of the migh-ty Red Sea, and He said, 'I'll ne-ver leave you, put your trust in Me.'

* This item appears in the key of E in the first edition of *Junior Praise*.

83 How did Moses cross the Red Sea?

Words and music: Hugh Mitchell
Music arranged Phil Burt

How did Mo-ses cross the Red Sea? How did Mo-ses cross the Red Sea?

How did Mo-ses cross the Red Sea? How did he get a - cross? Did he

swim? No! No! Did he row? No! No! Did he jump? No! No! No!

No! Did he drive? No! No! Did he fly? No! No! How

How did Moses cross the Red Sea?
How did Moses cross the Red Sea?
How did Moses cross the Red Sea?
How did he get across?
Did he swim? No! No!
Did he row? No! No!
Did he jump? No! No! No! No!
Did he drive? No! No!
Did he fly? No! No!
How did he get across?
God blew with His wind, puff, puff, puff, puff.
He blew just enough, 'nough, 'nough, 'nough, 'nough,
and through the sea He made a path –
that's how he got across.

84   How lovely on the mountains

Words and music: Leonard E Smith Jnr
Music arranged David Peacock

Triumphantly, with pace

How love-ly on the moun-tains are the feet of Him who brings good news, good news, pro-claim-ing peace, an-nounc-ing news of hap-pi-ness: our God reigns, our God reigns!

1 How lovely on the mountains are the feet of him
   who brings good news, good news,
   proclaiming peace, announcing news of happiness:
   our God reigns, our God reigns!
     Our God reigns, our God reigns,
     our God reigns, our God reigns!

2 You watchmen, lift your voices joyfully as one,
   shout for your King, your King.
   See eye to eye the Lord restoring Zion:
   your God reigns, your God reigns!
     Your God reigns, your God reigns,
     your God reigns, your God reigns!

3 Waste places of Jerusalem break forth with joy,
   we are redeemed, redeemed.
   The Lord has saved and comforted His people:
   your God reigns, your God reigns!
     Your God reigns, your God reigns,
     your God reigns, your God reigns!

4 Ends of the earth, see the salvation of your God,
   Jesus is Lord, is Lord.
   Before the nations He has bared His holy arm:
   your God reigns, your God reigns!
     Your God reigns, your God reigns,
     your God reigns, your God reigns!

85 Hushed was the evening hymn

SAMUEL   66 66 88

Words: John Drummond Burns (1823–64)
altered Horrobin/Leavers
Music: Arthur Seymour Sullivan (1842–1900)

Hushed was the eve - ning hymn, the tem - ple courts were dark;___ the lamp was burn - ing dim be - fore the sa - cred ark, when sud - den - ly a voice di - vine rang through the sil - ence of the shrine.

1 Hushed was the evening hymn,
   the temple courts were dark;
   the lamp was burning dim
   before the sacred ark,
   when suddenly a voice divine
   rang through the silence of the shrine.

2 The old man, meek and mild,
   the priest of Israel, slept;
   his watch the temple child,
   the little Samuel, kept:
   and what from Eli's sense was sealed
   the Lord to Hannah's son revealed.

3 O give me Samuel's ear,
   the open ear, O Lord,
   alive and quick to hear
   each whisper of Your word –
   like him to answer at Your call,
   and to obey You first of all.

4 O give me Samuel's heart,
   a lowly heart, that waits
   to serve and play the part
   You show us at Your gates,
   by day and night, a heart that still
   moves at the breathing of Your will.

5 O give me Samuel's mind,
   a sweet, unmurmuring faith,
   obedient and resigned
   to You in life and death,
   that I may read with childlike eyes
   truths that are hidden from the wise.

86 I am trusting You

BULLINGER 85 83

Words: Frances Ridley Havergal (1836–79)
Music: Ethelbert William Bullinger (1837–1913)

1 I am trusting You, Lord Jesus,
   You have died for me;
   trusting You for full salvation,
   great and free.

2 I am trusting You for pardon,
   at Your feet I bow;
   for Your grace and tender mercy,
   trusting now.

3 I am trusting You for cleansing,
   Jesus, Son of God;
   trusting You to make me holy
   by Your blood.

4 I am trusting You to guide me;
   You alone shall lead,
   every day and hour supplying
   all my need.

5 I am trusting You for power,
   Yours can never fail;
   words which You Yourself shall give me
   must prevail.

6 I am trusting You, Lord Jesus;
   never let me fall;
   I am trusting You for ever,
   and for all.

87 I am a lighthouse

Words and music: Graham Kendrick
Music arranged Phil Burt

I am a light-house, a shin-ing and bright house, out in the waves of a storm-y sea. The oil of the Spi-rit keeps my lamp burn - ing: Je - sus my Lord_ is the light in me. And when peo-ple see_ the good

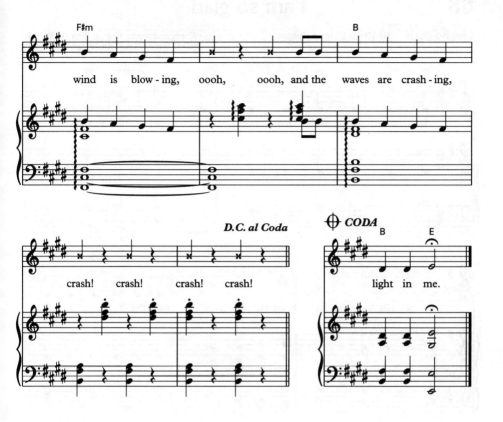

wind is blow-ing, oooh, oooh, and the waves are crash-ing,

D.C. al Coda

crash! crash! crash! crash!

⊕ *CODA*

light in me.

I am a lighthouse, a shining and bright house,
out in the waves of a stormy sea.
The oil of the Spirit keeps my lamp burning:
Jesus my Lord is the light in me.
And when people see the good things that I do,
they'll give praise to God who has sent us Jesus.
We'll send out a lifeboat of love and forgiveness
and give them a hand to get in.
I am a lighthouse . . .

While the storm is raging, whoosh, whoosh,
and the wind is blowing, oooh, oooh,
and the waves are crashing, crash! crash! crash! crash!

I am a lighthouse, a shining and bright house,
out in the waves of a stormy sea.
The oil of the Spirit keeps my lamp burning:
Jesus my Lord is the light in me.

88   I am so glad

I Am So Glad   10 10 10 10 with chorus

Words and music: Philipp Bliss (1838–76)
Music arranged A E Rusbridge (1917–69)

Je - sus loves me, Je - sus loves me, I am so glad that

Je - sus loves me, Je - sus loves e - ven me.

1 I am so glad that our Father in heaven
tells of His love in the book He has given:
wonderful things in the Bible I see;
this is the dearest, that Jesus loves me.
  I am so glad that Jesus loves me,
  Jesus loves me, Jesus loves me,
  I am so glad that Jesus loves me,
  Jesus loves even me.

2 Though I forget Him, and wander away,
He'll always love me wherever I stray;
back to His dear loving arms do I flee,
when I remember that Jesus loves me.
  I am so glad . . .

3 Oh, if there's only one song I can sing,
when in His beauty I see the great King,
this shall my song in eternity be:
'O what a wonder that Jesus loves me!'
  I am so glad . . .

4 If one should ask of me, 'How can I tell?'
Glory to Jesus, I know very well;
God's Holy Spirit with mine does agree,
constantly witnessing: Jesus loves me.
  I am so glad . . .

89   I am the way, the truth and the life

Words: Anon
Music: Traditional
arranged D J Crawshaw

'I am the way, the truth and the life,' that's what Je-sus said. 'I am the way, the truth and the life,' that's what Je-sus said. With-out the way there is no go-ing, with-out the truth there is no know-ing, with-out the

'I am the way, the truth and the life,'
that's what Jesus said.
'I am the way, the truth and the life,'
that's what Jesus said.
Without the way there is no going,
without the truth there is no knowing,
without the life there is no living.
'I am the way, the truth and the life,'
that's what Jesus said.

90   I can run through a troop

Words and music: Anon
Music arranged Phil Burt

I can run through a troop
and leap over a wall.
Hallelujah (glory, glory), hallelujah.
He's my Prince of peace,
He gives power to all.
Hallelujah (glory, glory), hallelujah.
Now there is no condemnation,
Jesus is the rock of my salvation.
I can run through a troop
and leap over a wall.
Hallelujah (glory, glory), hallelujah.

91 I danced in the morning
(Lord of the dance)

Words and music: Sydney Carter

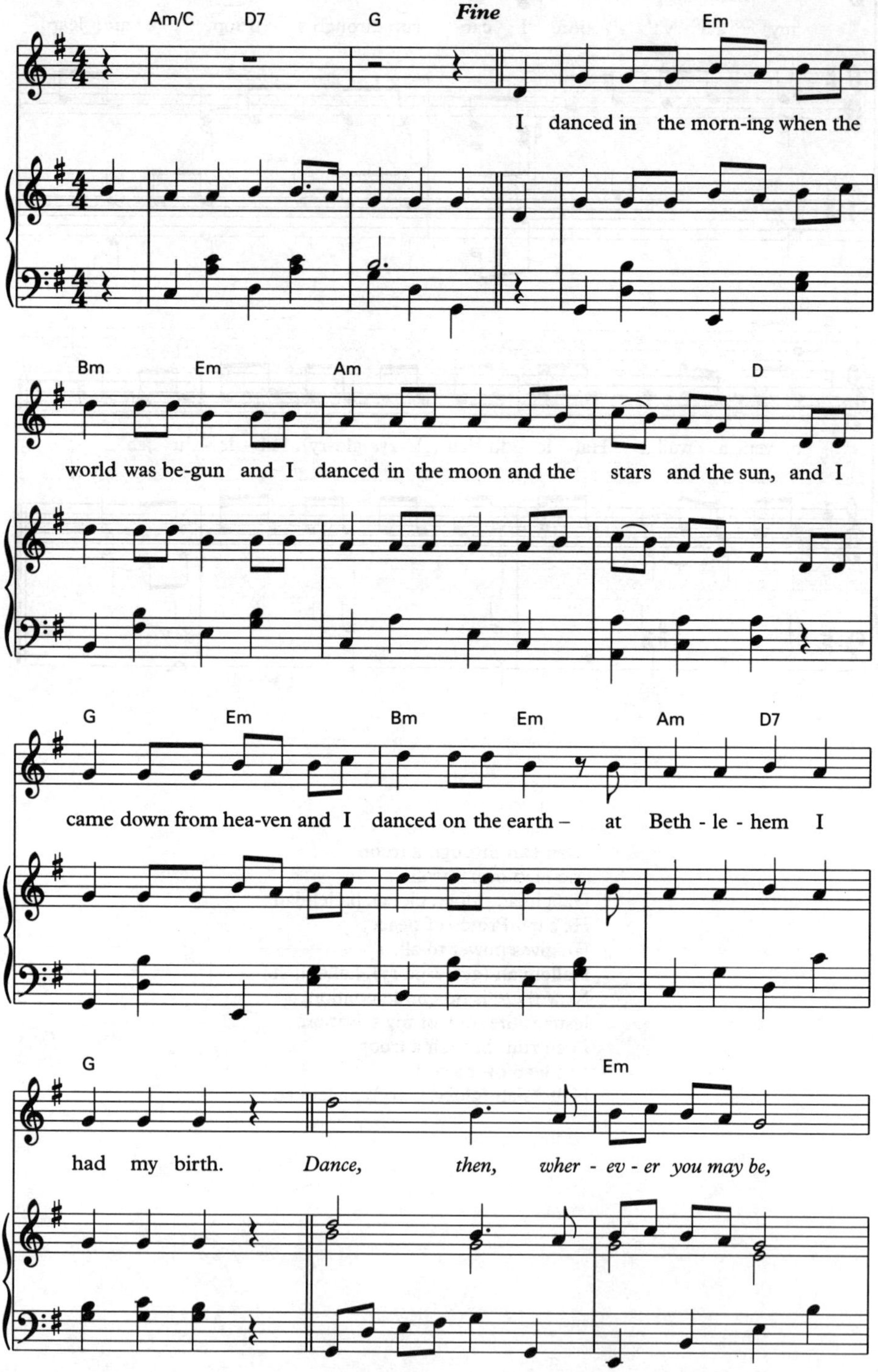

Am/C D7 G Fine Em
I danced in the morn-ing when the
Bm Em Am D
world was be-gun and I danced in the moon and the stars and the sun, and I
G Em Bm Em Am D7
came down from hea-ven and I danced on the earth – at Beth - le - hem I
G Em
had my birth. Dance, then, wher - ev - er you may be,

I am the Lord of the dance, said He, and I'll lead you all, wher-ev-er you may be, and I'll lead you all in the dance, said He.

1 I danced in the morning
   when the world was begun
   and I danced in the moon
   and the stars and the sun,
   and I came down from heaven
   and I danced on the earth –
   at Bethlehem I had my birth.
       Dance, then, wherever you may be,
       I am the Lord of the dance, said He,
       and I'll lead you all, wherever you may be,
       and I'll lead you all in the dance, said He.

2 I danced for the scribe and the pharisee,
   but they would not dance
   and they wouldn't follow me.
   I danced for the fishermen,
   for James and John –
   they came with me and the dance went on.
       Dance, then . . .

92   I do not know what lies ahead

Words and music: Alfred B Smith
and Eugene Clarke

I do not know what lies a - head, the way I can - not see; yet one stands near to be my guide, He'll show the way to me:

I know who holds the fu - ture, and He'll guide me with His hand; with God things don't just hap - pen, ev - ery - thing by Him is planned. So

as I face to-mor-row, with its prob-lems large and small, I'll trust the God of mir-a-cles, give to Him my all.

1 I do not know what lies ahead,
    the way I cannot see;
    yet one stands near to be my guide,
    He'll show the way to me:
      I know who holds the future,
      and He'll guide me with His hand;
      with God things don't just happen,
      everything by Him is planned.
      So as I face tomorrow,
      with its problems large and small,
      I'll trust the God of miracles,
      give to Him my all.

2 I do not know how many days
    of life are mine to spend;
    but one who knows and cares for me
    will keep me to the end:
      I know who holds . . .

3 I do not know the course ahead,
    what joys and griefs are there;
    but one is near who fully knows,
    I'll trust His loving care:
      I know who holds . . .

93 I'll be still

Words and music: Rick Founds and Todd Collins
Music arranged Phil Burt

I'll be still and know that You are God;
I'll be still and know You are the Lord;
I'll be still to worship and adore You,
blessèd One, Emmanuel, Jesus.

If I were a butterfly

Words and music: Brian Howard

If I were a but-ter-fly,— I'd thank You, Lord, for giv-ing me wings. And if I were a ro-bin in a tree, I'd thank You, Lord, that I could sing. And if I were a fish in the sea,— I'd wig-gle my tail— and I'd gig-gle with glee, but

1 If I were a butterfly,
   I'd thank You, Lord, for giving me wings.
   And if I were a robin in a tree,
   I'd thank You, Lord, that I could sing.
   And if I were a fish in the sea,
   I'd wiggle my tail and I'd giggle with glee,
   but I just thank you, Father, for making me 'me'.
   For You gave me a heart
   and You gave me a smile,
   You gave me Jesus
   and You made me Your child,
   and I just thank you, Father, for making me 'me'.

2 If I were an elephant,
   I'd thank You, Lord, by raising my trunk.
   And if I were a kangaroo
   You know I'd hop right up to You.
   And if I were an octopus,
   I'd thank You, Lord, for my fine looks,
   but I just thank You, Father, for making me 'me'.
   For You gave me a heart . . .

3 If I were a wiggly worm,
   I'd thank You, Lord, that I could squirm,
   and if I were a billy goat,
   I'd thank You, Lord, for my strong throat,
   and if I were a fuzzy wuzzy bear,
   I'd thank You, Lord, for my fuzzy wuzzy hair,
   but I just thank You, Father, for making me 'me'.
   For You gave me a heart . . .

95 If you see someone

Words and music: Annie and Neil Simpson
Music arranged Andy Silver

If you see some-one ly-ing in the road, don't leave him there, give him a hand.___ If you see some-one cry-ing in the road, don't leave him there, give him a hand.___ Does-n't mat-ter___ who you are;___ you might be a tramp or a

mo - vie star._____ Just re-mem-ber, who - ev - er you are,_ that it's

Je - sus ly - ing there, that it's Je - sus cry - ing there.

1 If you see someone lying in the road,
  don't leave him there, give him a hand.
  If you see someone crying in the road,
  don't leave him there, give him a hand.
  Doesn't matter who you are;
  you might be a tramp or a movie star.
  Just remember, whoever you are,
  that it's Jesus lying there,
  that it's Jesus crying there.

2 If Jesus sees you lying in the road,
  He won't leave you there, he'll give you a hand.
  If Jesus sees you crying in the road,
  He won't leave you there, he'll give you a hand.
  Doesn't matter who you are;
  you might be a tramp or a movie star.
  Just remember, whoever you are,
  that He sees you lying there,
  and He sees you crying there.

96 If you want joy, real joy

Words and music: Joseph Carlson
arranged W G Hathaway

If you want joy, real joy, won-der-ful joy, let Je - sus come in - to your heart. If you want joy, real joy, won-der-ful joy, let Je - sus come in - to your heart.___ Your sins He'll take a - way,___ your night He'll turn to

If you want joy, real joy, wonderful joy,
let Jesus come into your heart.
If you want joy, real joy, wonderful joy,
let Jesus come into your heart.
Your sins He'll take away,
your night He'll turn to day,
your heart He'll make over anew,
and then come in to stay.
If you want joy, real joy, wonderful joy,
let Jesus come into your heart.

97 I gotta home in gloryland

Words and music: Anon
Music arranged Phil Burt

1 I gotta home in gloryland that outshines the sun,
  I gotta home in gloryland that outshines the sun,
  I gotta home in gloryland that outshines the sun,
  way beyond the blue.
    Do, Lord, O do, Lord, O do remember me;
    do, Lord, O do, Lord, O do remember me;
    do, Lord, O do, Lord, O do remember me,
    way beyond the blue.

2 I took Jesus as my Saviour, you take Him too . . .
    Do, Lord, O do, Lord . . .

3 If you will not bear a cross, you can't wear a crown . . . .
    Do, Lord, O do, Lord . . .

98   I have decided to follow Jesus

Words: an Indian prince
Music: folk melody from India
arranged Cliff Barrows and Don Hustad

1 I have de-cid-ed to fo-llow Je-sus, I have de-cid-ed to fo-llow Je-sus, I have de-cid-ed to fo-llow Je-sus, no turn-ing back, no turn-ing back.

2 The world be-hind me, the cross be-fore me, the world be-

2 The world be-hind me, the cross be-fore me,

1 I have decided to follow Jesus, (*3 times*)
no turning back, no turning back.

2 The world behind me, the cross before me, (*3 times*)
no turning back, no turning back.

3 Though none go with me, I still will follow, (*3 times*)
no turning back, no turning back.

4 Will you decide now to follow Jesus? (*3 times*)
no turning back, no turning back.

99   I have seen the golden sunshine

FRIEND OF JESUS, FRIEND OF MINE

Words and music: Charlie Chester
and Benny Litchfield

mine. I've seen the light, I've seen the light, and that's why my heart

sings. I've known the joy, I've known the joy that lov-ing Je-sus brings.

1 I have seen the golden sunshine,
   I have watched the flowers grow,
   I have listened to the song birds
   and there's one thing now I know:
   they were all put there for us to share
   by someone so divine,
   and if you're a friend of Jesus
   (*clap, clap, clap, clap*)
   you're a friend of mine.

   I've seen the light, I've seen the light,
   and that's why my heart sings.
   I've known the joy, I've known the joy
   that loving Jesus brings.

2 I have seen the morning sunshine,
   I have heard the oceans roar,
   I have seen the flowers of springtime
   and there's one thing I am sure:
   they were all put there for us to share
   by someone so divine,
   and if you're a friend of Jesus
   (*clap, clap, clap, clap*)
   you're a friend of mine.

   I've seen the light . . .

100   I hear the sound

Words and music: Dave Moody
Music arranged Roland Fudge

I hear the sound of the army of the Lord;
I hear the sound of the army of the Lord;
it's the sound of praise,
it's the sound of war;
the army of the Lord,
the army of the Lord,
the army of the Lord is marching on.

101   I may never march in the infantry

Words and music: Anon
Music arranged Andy Silver

I may never march in the infantry,
ride with the cavalry, shoot with the artillery,
I may never zoom o'er the enemy,
for I'm in the Lord's army.
I'm in the Lord's army (Yes, sir!),
I'm in the Lord's army (Yes, sir!).
I may never march in the infantry,
ride with the cavalry, shoot with the artillery,
I may never zoom o'er the enemy,
for I'm in the Lord's army.

I met Jesus at the crossroads

Words and music: Anon
Music arranged Phil Burt

I met Je-sus at the cross-roads, where the two ways meet. Sa-tan too was stand-ing there, and he said, 'Come this way! Lots and lots of plea-sures I can give to you to-day.' But I said, 'No, there's Je-sus here, just

see what He of-fers me.____ Down here, my sins for-giv-en, up there, a home in hea-ven. Praise God! That's the way for me.'

I met Jesus at the crossroads,
where the two ways meet.
Satan too was standing there,
and he said, 'Come this way!
Lots and lots of pleasures
I can give to you today.'
But I said, 'No, there's Jesus here,
just see what He offers me.
Down here, my sins forgiven,
up there, a home in heaven.
Praise God! That's the way for me.'

103   I met You at the cross

Words: Eric A Thorn
Music: Roger Jones

I met You at the cross, Je-sus, my Lord; I heard You from that cross: my name You called – asked me to fol-low You all of my days,

1 I met You at the cross,
Jesus, my Lord;
I heard You from that cross:
my name You called –
asked me to follow You all of my days,
asked me for evermore Your name to praise.

2 I saw You on the cross
dying for me;
I put You on that cross:
but Your one plea –
would I now follow You all of my days,
and would I evermore Your great name praise?

3 Jesus, my Lord and King,
Saviour of all,
Jesus the King of kings,
You heard my call –
that I would follow You all of my days,
and that for evermore Your name I'd praise.

104   I'm feeding on the living bread

Words: Anon
altered Horrobin/Leavers
Music: Anon

I'm feeding on the living bread,
I'm drinking at the fountain head;
for all who drink, so Jesus said,
will never, never thirst again.
What, never thirst again?
No! never thirst again.
What, never thirst again?
No! never thirst again.
For all who drink, so Jesus said,
will never, never thirst again.

105 I'm singing for my Lord

Words: Oswald J Smith
Music: Redd Harper

Lyrics:

I'm singing for my Lord____ everywhere I go, singing of His wondrous love, that the world may know how He saved a wretch like me by His death on Calvary: I'm singing for my

Lord_____ ev - ery-where I go. go.

1 I'm singing for my Lord everywhere I go,
  singing of His wondrous love, that the world may know
  how He saved a wretch like me by His death on Calvary:
  I'm singing for my Lord everywhere I go.

2 I'm singing, but sometimes heavy is the rod,
  for this world is not a friend to the grace of God.
  Yet I sing the whole day long, for He fills my heart with song,
  I'm singing for my Lord everywhere I go.

3 I'm singing for the lost just because I know
  Jesus Christ, whose precious blood washes white as snow.
  If my songs to Him can bring some lost soul I'll gladly sing:
  I'm singing for my Lord everywhere I go.

4 I'm singing for the saints as they journey home;
  soon they'll reach that happy land where they'll never roam.
  And with me they'll join and sing praises to our Lord and King:
  I'm singing for my Lord everywhere I go.

I'm special

Words and music: Graham Kendrick
Music arranged Christopher Norton

With intensity

I'm spe-cial be-cause God has loved me, for He gave the best thing that He had to save me: His own Son Je-sus, cru - ci - fied to take the blame, for all the bad things I have done.

107   I'm very glad of God

Words and music: Alice M Pullen

I'm ve-ry glad of God: His love takes care of me. In ev-ery love-ly thing I see God smiles at me.

1 I'm very glad of God:
His love takes care of me.
In every lovely thing I see
God smiles at me.

2 I'm very glad of God:
His love takes care of me.
In every lovely sound I hear
God speaks to me.

108   In our work and in our play

HARTS

Words: W G Wills (1841–91)
altered Horrobin/Leavers
Music: Benjamin Milgrove (1731–1810)

1 In our work and in our play,
   Jesus, ever with us stay;
   may we serve You all our days,
   true and faithful in our ways.

2 May we in Your strength subdue
   evil tempers, words untrue,
   thoughts impure and deeds unkind,
   all things hateful to Your mind.

3 Jesus, from Your throne above,
   fill anew our hearts with love;
   so that what we say and do
   shows that we belong to You.

4 Children of the King are we,
   may we loyal to Him be:
   try to please Him every day,
   in our work and in our play.

109

In my need Jesus found me

Words and music: Gordon Brattle (1917–91)

In my need Je - sus found me, put His
strong arm a - round me, brought me safe home,
in - to the shel - ter of the fold.____
Gra - cious shep - herd that sought me, pre - cious

In my need Jesus found me,
put His strong arm around me,
brought me safe home,
into the shelter of the fold.

Gracious shepherd that sought me,
precious life-blood that bought me;
out of the night,
into the light and near to God.

110 Infant holy

INFANT HOLY 447 447 44447

From a Polish Carol
Words: tr. E M G Reed (1885–1933)
Music arranged A E Rusbridge (1917–69)

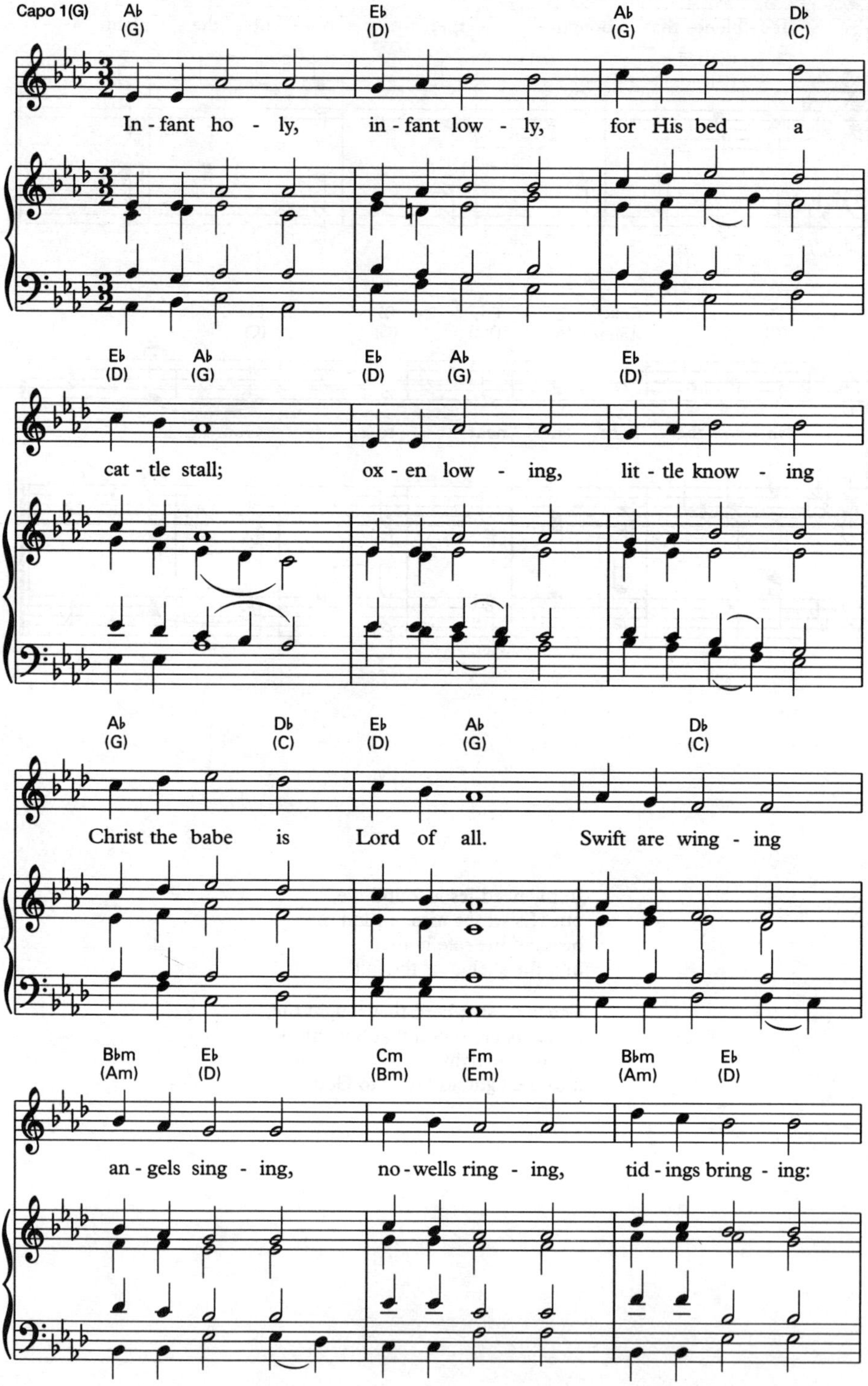

Capo 1(G)
Ab (G) Eb (D) Ab (G) Db (C)
In - fant ho - ly, in - fant low - ly, for His bed a
Eb (D) Ab (G) Eb (D) Ab (G) Eb (D)
cat - tle stall; ox - en low - ing, lit - tle know - ing
Ab (G) Db (C) Eb (D) Ab (G) Db (C)
Christ the babe is Lord of all. Swift are wing - ing
Bbm (Am) Eb (D) Cm (Bm) Fm (Em) Bbm (Am) Eb (D)
an - gels sing - ing, no - wells ring - ing, tid - ings bring - ing:

1 Infant holy, infant lowly,
   for His bed a cattle stall;
   oxen lowing, little knowing
   Christ the babe is Lord of all.
   Swift are winging angels singing,
   nowells ringing, tidings bringing:
   Christ the babe is Lord of all;
   Christ the babe is Lord of all!

2 Flocks were sleeping, shepherds keeping
   vigil till the morning new,
   saw the glory, heard the story –
   tidings of a gospel true.
   Thus rejoicing, free from sorrow,
   praises voicing, greet the morrow:
   Christ the babe was born for you;
   Christ the babe was born for you!

111   In the name of Jesus

Words and music: Anon
Music arranged Roland Fudge

In the name of Je - sus, in the name of Je - sus, we have the vic - to -

-ry. In the name of Je - sus, in the name of Je - sus,

de-mons will have to flee. Who can tell what

God can do? Who can tell of His love for you?

In the name of Jesus,
in the name of Jesus,
we have the victory.
In the name of Jesus,
in the name of Jesus,
demons will have to flee.
Who can tell what God can do?
Who can tell of His love for you?
In the name of Jesus, Jesus,
we have the victory.

112 In the stars His handiwork I see

Words and music: Ralph Carmichael
Music arranged Phil Burt

In the stars His han-di-work I see, on the wind He speaks with ma-jes-ty; though He's rul-ing o-ver land and sea, what is that to me? I will ce-le-brate na-ti-vi-ty, for it has a place in his-to-ry,

In the stars His handiwork I see,
on the wind He speaks with majesty;
though He's ruling over land and sea,
what is that to me?
I will celebrate nativity,
for it has a place in history,
sure, Christ came to set His people free.
What is that to me?

Then by faith I met Him face to face,
and I felt the wonder of His grace.
Then I knew that He was more than just a god
who didn't care, who lived away up there.
And now He lives within me day by day,
ever watching o'er me lest I stray,
helping me to find the narrow way.
He's everything to me.

113   I serve a risen Saviour

Words and music: Alfred Henry Ackley (1887–1960)

I serve a ris - en Sav - iour, He's in the world to - day;____ I know that He is liv - ing, what - ev - er men may say.____ I see His hand of mer - cy, I hear His voice of cheer;____ and

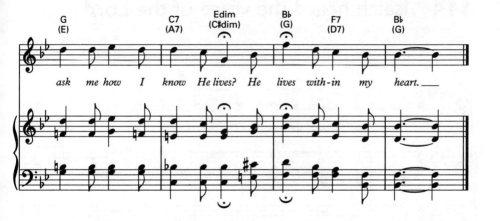

ask me how I know He lives? He lives with-in my heart. ____

1 I serve a risen Saviour,
   He's in the world today;
   I know that He is living,
   whatever men may say.
   I see His hand of mercy,
   I hear His voice of cheer;
   and just the time I need Him,
   He's always near.
      He lives, He lives,
      Christ Jesus lives today!
      He walks with me and talks with me
      along life's narrow way.
      He lives, He lives,
      salvation to impart!
      You ask me how I know He lives?
      He lives within my heart.

2 In all the world around me
   I see His loving care,
   and though my heart grows weary
   I never will despair;
   I know that He is leading,
   through all the stormy blast,
   the day of His appearing
   will come at last.
      He lives . . .

3 Rejoice, rejoice, O Christian,
   lift up your voice and sing
   eternal hallelujahs
   to Jesus Christ the King!
   The hope of all who seek Him,
   the help of all who find,
   none other is so loving,
   so good and kind.
      He lives . . .

114 Isaiah heard the voice of the Lord

Words and music: Anon
Music arranged Andy Silver

I-saiah heard the voice of the Lord and he said, 'Here am I, send me!' He loved to do the will of the Lord, so he said, 'Here am I, send me; here am I, send me a-ny-where for

Thee.' So when I hear the voice of the Lord I will say, 'Here am I, send me!'

Isaiah heard the voice of the Lord
and he said, 'Here am I, send me!'
He loved to do the will of the Lord,
so he said, 'Here am I, send me;
here am I, send me anywhere for Thee.'
So when I hear the voice of the Lord
I will say, 'Here am I, send me!'

115 I sing a song of the saints of God

Grand Isle Irregular

Words: L Scott (b1898)
Music: John Henry Hopkins (1861–1945)

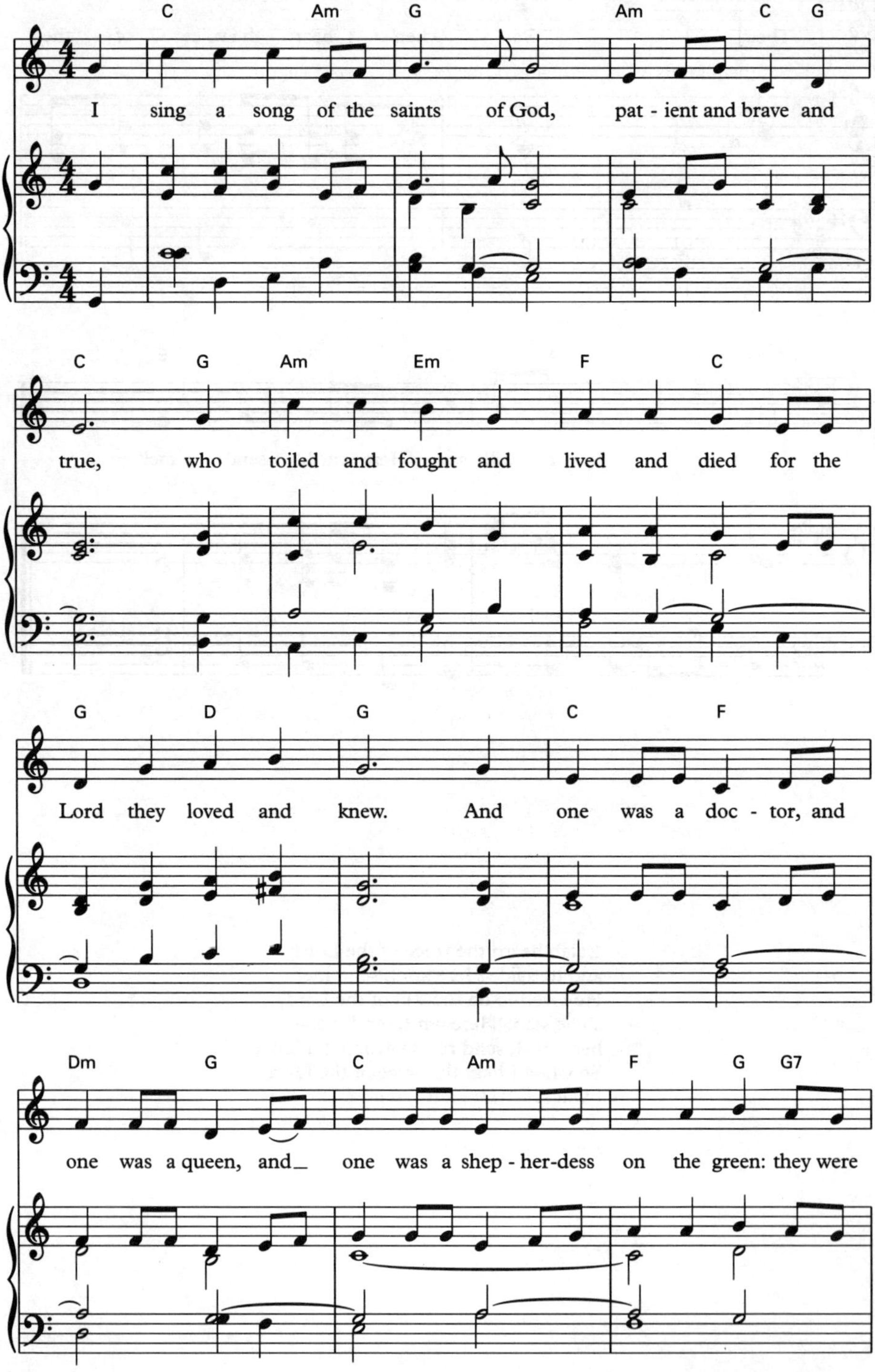

C Am G Am C G
I sing a song of the saints of God, pat - ient and brave and
C G Am Em F C
true, who toiled and fought and lived and died for the
G D G C F
Lord they loved and knew. And one was a doc - tor, and
Dm G C Am F G G7
one was a queen, and_ one was a shep - her-dess on the green: they were

all of them saints of God; and I mean, God help-ing, to be one too.

1 I sing a song of the saints of God,
   patient and brave and true,
   who toiled and fought and lived and died
   for the Lord they loved and knew.
   And one was a doctor, and one was a queen,
   and one was a shepherdess on the green:
   they were all of them saints of God; and I mean,
   God helping, to be one too.

2 They loved their God so good and dear,
   and His love made them strong;
   and they followed the right, for Jesus' sake,
   the whole of their good lives long.
   And one was a soldier, and one was a priest,
   and one was slain by a fierce wild beast:
   and there's not any reason, no, not in the least,
   why I shouldn't be one too.

3 They lived not only in ages past,
   there are hundreds of thousands still;
   the world is bright with the joyous saints
   who love to do Jesus' will.
   You can meet them in school, or in lanes, or at sea,
   in church, or in trains, or in shops, or at tea,
   for the saints of God began just like me,
   and I mean to be one too.

116   It came upon the midnight clear

NOEL   86 86 D

Words: Edward Hamilton Sears (1810–76)
in this version Jubilate Hymns
Music: English traditional melody
arranged Arthur Seymour Sullivan (1842–1900)

It came upon the midnight clear, that glorious song of old, from angels bending near the earth to touch their harps of gold: 'Peace on the earth, good-

- will to men from heaven's all - gra - cious King!' The world in sol - emn still - ness lay to__ hear the an - gels sing.

1 It came upon the midnight clear,
   that glorious song of old,
   from angels bending near the earth
   to touch their harps of gold:
   'Peace on the earth, goodwill to men
   from heaven's all-gracious King!'
   The world in solemn stillness lay
   to hear the angels sing.

2 With sorrow brought by sin and strife
   the world has suffered long,
   and, since the angels sang, have passed
   two thousand years of wrong;
   for man at war with man hears not
   the love-song which they bring:
   O hush the noise, you men of strife,
   and hear the angels sing!

3 And those whose journey now is hard,
   whose hope is burning low,
   who tread the rocky path of life
   with painful steps and slow:
   O listen to the news of love
   which makes the heavens ring!
   O rest beside the weary road
   and hear the angels sing!

4 And still the days are hastening on –
   by prophets seen of old –
   towards the fulness of the time
   when comes the age foretold:
   then earth and heaven renewed shall see
   the Prince of peace, their King;
   and all the world repeat the song
   which now the angels sing.

117   It is a thing most wonderful

BROOKFIELD   LM

Words: William Walsham How (1823–97)
in this version Jubilate Hymns
Music: Thomas Bishop Southgate (1814–68)

It is a thing most won - der - ful, al -
- most too won - der - ful to be, that
God's own Son should come from heaven and
die___ to save___ a child___ like me.

1 It is a thing most wonderful,
   almost too wonderful to be,
   that God's own Son should come from heaven
   and die to save a child like me.

2 And yet I know that it is true;
   He came to this poor world below
   and wept, and toiled, and mourned, and died,
   only because He loved us so.

3 I cannot tell how He could love
   a child so weak and full of sin;
   His love must be so wonderful,
   if He could die my love to win.

4 I sometimes think about the cross,
   and shut my eyes and try to see
   the cruel nails and crown of thorns,
   and Jesus crucified for me.

5 But even could I see Him die,
   I could but see a little part
   of that great love, which, like a fire,
   is always burning in His heart.

6 How wonderful it is to know
   His love for me so free and sure;
   but yet more wonderful to see
   my love for Him so faint and poor.

7 And yet I want to love You, Lord;
   O teach me how to grow in grace,
   that I may love You more and more,
   until I see You face to face.

118   It's a happy day

Words and music: Gary Pfeiffer

It's a hap-py day___ and I praise God for the weath - er.___ It's a hap-py day,___ liv - ing it for my Lord. It's a hap-py day, ___ things are going to get bet - ter,___

liv - ing each day by the pro - mis-es in God's word.

word.

1 It's a happy day and I praise God for the weather.
It's a happy day, living it for my Lord.
It's a happy day, things are going to get better,
living each day by the promises in God's word.

2 It's a grumpy day and I can't stand the weather.
It's a grumpy day, living it for myself.
It's a grumpy day and things aren't going to get better,
living each day with my Bible up on my shelf.

3 It's a happy day and I praise God for the weather.
It's a happy day, living it for my Lord.
It's a happy day, things are going to get better,
living each day by the promises in God's word.

119 It's me, it's me

Words and music: Traditional

It's me, it's me, it's me, O Lord, stand-in' in the need of prayer. It's me, it's me, it's me, O Lord, stand-in' in the need of prayer.

Not my bro-ther or my sis-ter, but it's me, O Lord,

stand-in' in the need of prayer. Not my bro-ther or my sis-ter, but it's

D.C. al Fine

me, O Lord, stand - in' in the need of prayer.

It's me, it's me, it's me, O Lord,
standin' in the need of prayer.
It's me, it's me, it's me, O Lord,
standin' in the need of prayer.

1 Not my brother or my sister, but it's me, O Lord,
standin' in the need of prayer.
Not my brother or my sister, but it's me, O Lord,
standin' in the need of prayer.
It's me, it's me . . .

2 Not my mother or my father, but it's me, O Lord,
standin' in the need of prayer.
Not my mother or my father, but it's me, O Lord,
standin' in the need of prayer.
It's me, it's me . . .

3 Not my stranger or my neighbour, but it's me, O Lord,
standin' in the need of prayer.
Not my stranger or my neighbour, but it's me, O Lord,
standin' in the need of prayer.
It's me, it's me . . .

120 I've got peace like a river

Words and music: Spiritual
Music arranged Roland Fudge

Quietly

I've got peace like a river, peace like a ri - ver, I've got peace like a ri - ver in my soul; _____ I've got peace like a ri - ver, peace like a ri - ver, I've got

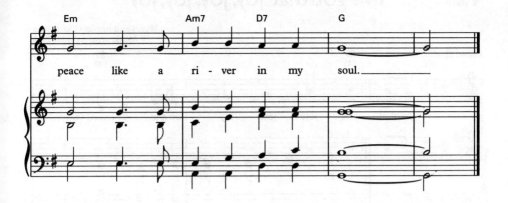

peace like a ri - ver in my soul.

Alternative version

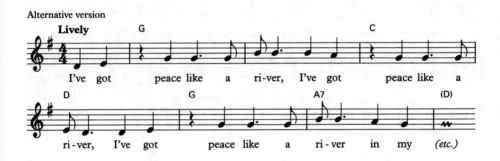

I've got peace like a ri - ver, I've got peace like a
ri - ver, I've got peace like a ri - ver in my *(etc.)*

I've got peace like a river, peace like a river,
I've got peace like a river in my soul;
I've got peace like a river, peace like a river,
I've got peace like a river in my soul.

121   I've got that joy, joy, joy, joy

Words and music: G W Cooke
Music arranged Phil Burt

Capo 1(E)

I've got that joy, joy, joy, joy down in my heart, (where?) down in my heart, (where?) down in my heart. I've got that joy, joy, joy, joy down in my heart, (where?) down in my heart to stay. *And I'm so hap - py, so ve-ry hap - py, I've got the love of Je-sus in my*

1 I've got that joy, joy, joy, joy
   down in my heart, (where?)
   down in my heart, (where?)
   down in my heart.
   I've got that joy, joy, joy, joy
   down in my heart, (where?)
   down in my heart to stay.
   And I'm so happy,
   so very happy,
   I've got the love of Jesus in my heart,
   and I'm so happy,
   so very happy,
   I've got the love of Jesus in my heart.

2 I've got the peace that passes understanding
   down in my heart, (where?)
   down in my heart, (where?)
   down in my heart.
   I've got the peace that passes understanding
   down in my heart, (where?)
   down in my heart to stay.
   And I'm so happy . . .

122   I want to live for Jesus every day

Words and music: Anon
Music arranged Jeanne Harper

1 I want to live for Jesus every day
  (every day).
I want to live for Jesus, come what may
  (come what may).
Take the world and all its pleasure,
I've got a more enduring treasure.
I want to live for Jesus every day.

2 I'm gonna live for Jesus every day
  (every day).
I'm gonna live for Jesus, come what may
  (come what may).
Take the world and all its pleasure,
I've got a more enduring treasure.
I'm gonna live for Jesus every day.

123   I will make you fishers of men

Words and music: Harry D Clarke

124 I want to walk with Jesus

Words: C Simmonds
Music: Swiss folk melody
arranged Phil Burt

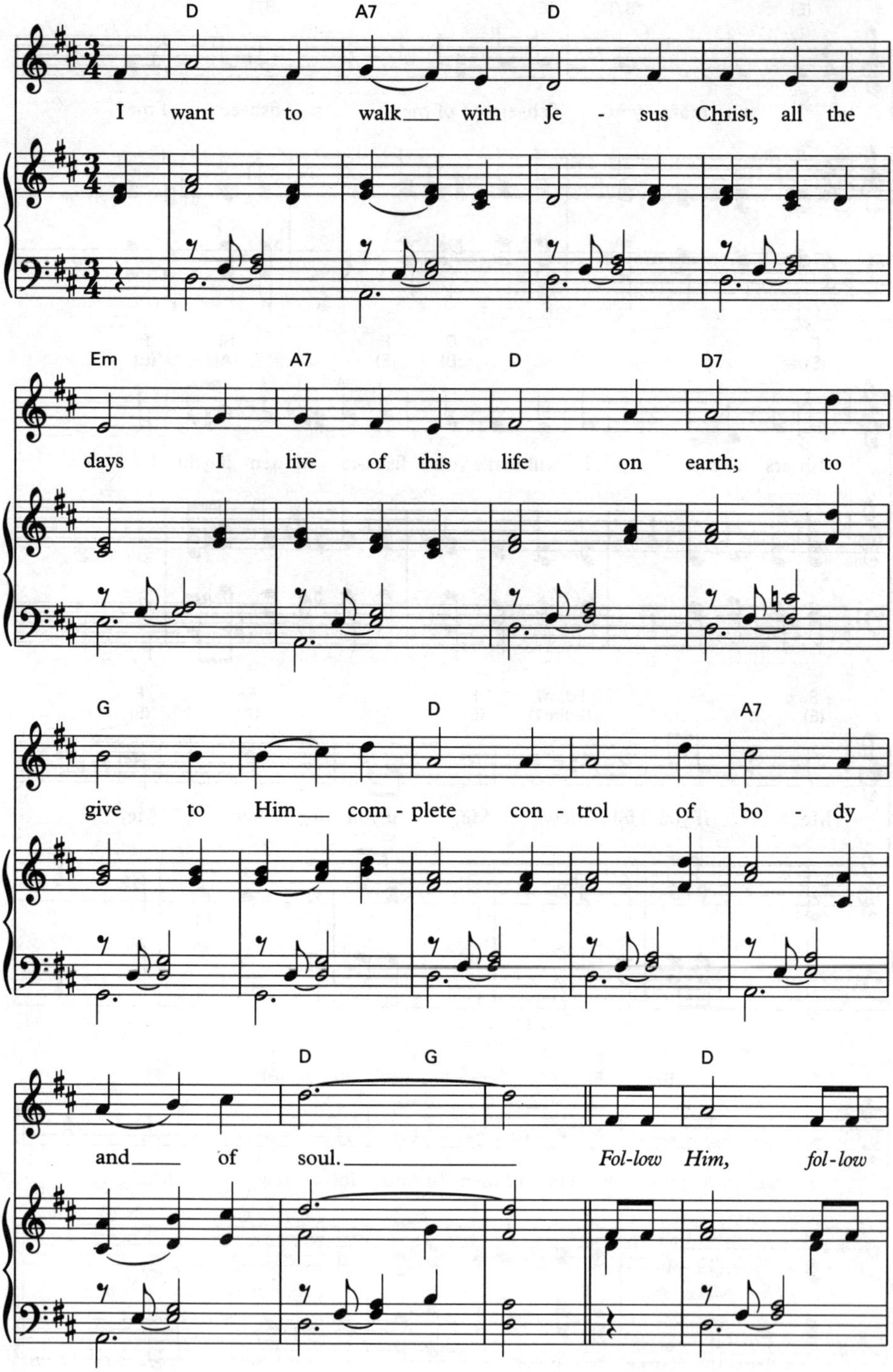
D
A7
D
I want to walk with Je - sus Christ, all the
Em
A7
D
D7
days I live of this life on earth; to
G
D
A7
give to Him com - plete con - trol of bo - dy
D
G
D
and of soul.
Fol-low Him, fol-low

Him, yield your life to Him – He has con - quered death, He is
King of kings; ac - cept the joy which He gives to
those who yield their lives____ to Him.____

1 I want to walk with Jesus Christ,
all the days I live of this life on earth;
to give to Him complete control
of body and of soul.
Follow Him, follow Him,
yield your life to Him –
He has conquered death,
He is King of kings;
accept the joy which He gives to those
who yield their lives to Him.

2 I want to learn to speak to Him,
to pray to Him, confess my sin,
to open my life and let Him in,
for joy will then be mine.
Follow Him, follow Him . . .

3 I want to learn to speak of Him –
my life must show that He lives in me;
my deeds, my thoughts, my words must speak
all of His love for me.
Follow Him, follow Him . . .

4 I want to learn to read His word,
for this is how I know the way
to live my life as pleases Him,
in holiness and joy.
Follow Him, follow Him . . .

5 O Holy Spirit of the Lord,
enter now into this heart of mine;
take full control of my selfish will
and make me wholly Thine!
Follow Him, follow Him . . .

125 I was lost but Jesus found me

A two-part round

Words and music: Anon
Music arranged Phil Burt

I was lost but Je-sus found me, found the sheep that went a-stray,— threw His lov-ing arms a-round me, drew me back in-to His way. (I was) Al - le - lu - ia, al - le - lu - ia, al - le -

1 I was lost but Jesus found me,
found the sheep that went astray,
threw His loving arms around me,
drew me back into His way.
   Alleluia, alleluia,
   alleluia, alleluia.

2 Glory, glory, alleluia,
come and bless the Lord our King.
Glory, glory, alleluia,
with His praise all heaven rings.
   Alleluia . . .

126 I will sing, I will sing

Words and music: Max Dyer

Liltingly

I will sing, I will sing a song____ un-to the Lord, I will

sing, I will sing a song___ un-to the Lord, I will sing, I will sing a song

___ un-to the Lord, al - le - lu - ia, glo - ry to the Lord.

Al - le - lu, al - le - lu - ia, glo - ry to the Lord, al - le -

-lu, al-le-lu - ia, glo - ry to the Lord, al-le-lu, al-le-lu - ia, glo-ry to the Lord, al - le - lu - ia, glo - ry to the Lord.

1 I will sing, I will sing a song unto the Lord, (*3 times*)
alleluia, glory to the Lord.
Allelu, alleluia, glory to the Lord,
allelu, alleluia, glory to the Lord,
allelu, alleluia, glory to the Lord,
alleluia, glory to the Lord.

2 We will come, we will come as one before the Lord, (*3 times*)
alleluia, glory to the Lord.
Allelu, alleluia . . .

3 If the Son, if the Son shall make you free, (*3 times*)
you shall be free indeed.
Allelu, alleluia . . .

4 They that sow in tears shall reap in joy, (*3 times*)
alleluia, glory to the Lord!
Allelu, alleluia . . .

5 Every knee shall bow and every tongue confess, (*3 times*)
that Jesus Christ is Lord.
Allelu, alleluia . . .

6 In His name, in His name we have the victory. (*3 times*)
Alleluia, glory to the Lord.
Allelu, alleluia . . .

127   I will sing the wondrous story

HYFRYDOL   87 87 D

Words: Francis Harold Rawley (1854–1952)
Music: Rowland Hugh Prichard (1811–87)

I will sing the won - drous sto - ry of the Christ who died for me – how He left the realms of glo - ry for the cross on Cal - va - ry. Yes, I'll sing the

won - drous sto - ry of the Christ__ who died__ for me – sing__ it with__ His saints__ in glo - ry, gath - ered by__ the crys - tal sea.

1 I will sing the wondrous story
of the Christ who died for me –
how He left the realms of glory
for the cross on Calvary.
Yes, I'll sing the wondrous story
of the Christ who died for me –
sing it with His saints in glory,
gathered by the crystal sea.

2 I was lost: but Jesus found me,
found the sheep that went astray,
raised me up and gently led me
back into the narrow way.
Days of darkness still may meet me,
sorrow's path I oft may tread;
but His presence still is with me,
by His guiding hand I'm led.

3 He will keep me till the river
rolls its waters at my feet:
then He'll bear me safely over,
made by grace for glory meet.
Yes, I'll sing the wondrous story
of the Christ who died for me –
sing it with His saints in glory,
gathered by the crystal sea.

128 Jesus bids us shine

10 11 10 10

Words: Susan Warner (1819–85)
Music: Edwin Othello Excell (1851–1921)

1 Jesus bids us shine
with a pure, clear light,
like a little candle
burning in the night.
In this world is darkness,
so let us shine,
you in your small corner
and I in mine.

2 Jesus bids us shine
first of all for Him.
Well He sees and knows it,
if our light grows dim.
He looks down from heaven
to see us shine,
you in your small corner
and I in mine.

3 Jesus bids us shine, then,
for all around;
many kinds of darkness
in the world are found –
sin and want and sorrow –
so we must shine,
you in your small corner
and I in mine.

129   Jesus Christ is alive today

Words and music: Anon
Music arranged Roland Fudge

Je - sus Christ is a - live to-day, I know, I know it's true.

Sove-reign of the u - ni-verse, I give Him hom-age due.

Seat-ed there at God's right hand, I am with Him in the pro-mised land.

Je - sus lives and reigns in me, that's how I know it's true.

130   Jesus Christ is risen today

EASTER HYMN   77 77 with Hallelujahs

Words and music: *Lyra Davidica*, 1708
Music arranged William Henry Monk (1823–89)

Je - sus Christ is risen to - day,— *hal - le - lu - jah!*

our tri-umph-ant ho - ly day,— *hal - le - lu - jah!*

who did once u - pon the cross, *hal - le - lu - jah!*

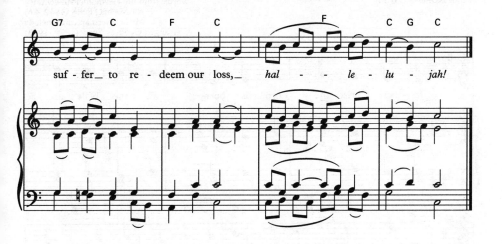

suf-fer_ to re-deem our loss,_ hal - - le - lu - jah!

1 Jesus Christ is risen today, *hallelujah!*
   our triumphant holy day, *hallelujah!*
   who did once upon the cross, *hallelujah!*
   suffer to redeem our loss, *hallelujah!*

2 Hymns of praise then let us sing, *hallelujah!*
   unto Christ our heavenly King, *hallelujah!*
   who endured the cross and grave, *hallelujah!*
   sinners to redeem and save, *hallelujah!*

3 But the pains which He endured, *hallelujah!*
   our salvation have procured, *hallelujah!*
   now in heaven above He's King, *hallelujah!*
   Where the angels ever sing, '*hallelujah!*'

131 Jesus Christ the Lord is born

Puer Nobis   76 77

Words: from the German (15th century)
Michael Perry (1942–96)
Music: German carol melody
arranged Geoffrey Shaw (1879–1943)

1 Jesus Christ the Lord is born,
all the bells are ringing!
Angels greet the Holy One
and shepherds hear them singing,
and shepherds hear them singing.

2 'Go to Bethlehem today,
find your King and Saviour:
glory be to God on high,
to earth His peace and favour,
to earth His peace and favour!'

3 Held within a cattle stall,
loved by love maternal,
see the Master of us all,
our Lord of lords eternal
our Lord of lords eternal!

4 Soon shall come the wise men three,
rousing Herod's anger;
mothers' hearts shall broken be
and Mary's Son in danger,
and Mary's Son in danger.

5 Death from life and life from death,
our salvation story;
let all living things give breath
to Christmas songs of glory,
to Christmas songs of glory!

Music: from the Oxford Book of Carols
by permission of Oxford University Press

132 Jesus died for all the children

Words and music: Anon

Jesus died for all the children,
all the children of the world.
Red and yellow, black and white,
all are precious in His sight:
Jesus died for all the children of the world.

133

Jesus, how lovely You are

Words and music: David Bolton

Je - sus,___ how love - ly You are!___

You are so gen - tle, so pure___ and kind,___

You___ shine___ like the morn - ing star:___

Je - sus,___ how love - ly You are.___

Jesus, how lovely You are!
You are so gentle, so pure and kind,
You shine like the morning star:
Jesus, how lovely You are.

1 Alleluia, Jesus is my Lord and King;
  alleluia, Jesus is my everything.
    Jesus, how lovely . . .

2 Alleluia, Jesus died and rose again;
  alleluia, Jesus forgave all my sin.
    Jesus, how lovely . . .

3 Alleluia, Jesus is meek and lowly;
  alleluia, Jesus is pure and holy.
    Jesus, how lovely . . .

4 Alleluia, Jesus is the bridegroom;
  alleluia, Jesus will take His bride soon.
    Jesus, how lovely . . .

134 Jesus' hands were kind hands

Words: Margaret Cropper
Music: French traditional melody

Je-sus' hands were kind hands, do-ing good to all, heal-ing pain and
sick - ness, bless-ing child-ren small, wash-ing tir - ed feet and
sav-ing those who fall; Je - sus' hands were kind hands do-ing good to all.

1 Jesus' hands were kind hands,
   doing good to all,
   healing pain and sickness,
   blessing children small,
   washing tired feet
   and saving those who fall;
   Jesus' hands were kind hands
   doing good to all.

2 Take my hands, Lord Jesus,
   let them work for You,
   make them strong and gentle,
   kind in all I do.
   Let me watch You, Jesus,
   till I'm gentle too,
   till my hands are kind hands,
   quick to work for You.

135 Jesus is knocking

Words and music: Gordon Brattle (1917–91)

Jesus is knocking, patiently waiting,
outside your heart's closed door.
Do not reject Him, simply accept Him,
now and for evermore.

136   Jesus is a friend of mine

Words and music: Paul Mazak
Music arranged Judith Barnard

1 Jesus is a friend of mine,
   praise Him!
   Jesus is a friend of mine,
   praise Him!
   Praise Him! Praise Him!
   Jesus is a friend of mine,
   praise Him!

2 Jesus died to set us free,
   praise Him!
   Jesus died to set us free,
   praise Him!
   Praise Him! Praise Him!
   Jesus died to set us free,
   praise Him!

3 Jesus is the King of kings,
   praise Him!
   Jesus is the King of kings,
   praise Him!
   Praise Him! Praise Him!
   Jesus is the King of kings,
   praise Him!

137

Jesus is Lord

Words and music: David J Mansell

With majesty

Capo 1(G)

Je-sus is Lord! Cre-a-tion's voice pro-claims it,

for by His power each tree and flower was planned and made.

Je-sus is Lord! The u-ni-verse de-clares it;

sun, moon and stars in hea-ven cry: 'Je-sus is Lord!'

1 Jesus is Lord! Creation's voice proclaims it,
   for by His power each tree and flower was planned and made.
   Jesus is Lord! The universe declares it;
   sun, moon and stars in heaven cry: 'Jesus is Lord!'
      Jesus is Lord! Jesus is Lord!
      Praise Him with hallelujahs, for Jesus is Lord!

2 Jesus is Lord! Yet from His throne eternal
   in flesh He came to die in pain on Calvary's tree.
   Jesus is Lord! From Him all life proceeding,
   yet gave His life a ransom thus setting us free.
      Jesus is Lord . . .

3 Jesus is Lord! O'er sin the mighty conqueror,
   from death He rose and all His foes shall own His name.
   Jesus is Lord! God sends His Holy Spirit
   to show by works of power that Jesus is Lord.
      Jesus is Lord . . .

138   Jesus, I will come with You

Words and music: Roger Jones
Music arranged: Phil Burt

A two-part round

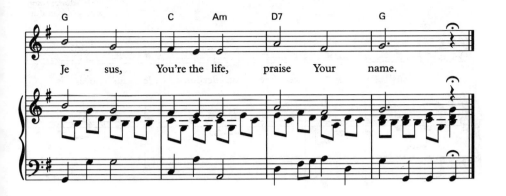

Jesus, I will come with You,
I will follow in Your way.
I will trust You,
I will bring You all I have today.
Jesus, You're the way,
Jesus, You're the truth,
Jesus, You're the life,
praise Your name.

139   Jesus' love is very wonderful

Words: H W Rattle
Music: Anon
arranged Phil Burt

Je-sus' love is ve-ry won-der-ful, Je-sus' love is

ve-ry won-der-ful, Je-sus' love is ve-ry won-der-ful,

O won-der-ful love! So high you

can't get o-ver it, so low you can't get un-der it,

so wide you can't get round it, O won-der-ful love!

Jesus' love is very wonderful,
Jesus' love is very wonderful,
Jesus' love is very wonderful,
O wonderful love!
So high you can't get over it,
so low you can't get under it,
so wide you can't get round it,
O wonderful love!

140 Jesus loves me

77 77 with chorus

Words: Anna Warner (1827–1915)
Music: William Batchelder Bradbury (1816–68)

Yes, Je-sus loves me! The Bi - ble tells me so.

1 Jesus loves me! this I know,
   for the Bible tells me so.
   Little ones to Him belong;
   they are weak, but He is strong.
   Yes, Jesus loves me!
   Yes, Jesus loves me!
   Yes, Jesus loves me!
   The Bible tells me so.

2 Jesus loves me! He who died,
   heaven's gate to open wide;
   He will wash away my sin,
   let His little child come in.
   Yes, Jesus loves me . . .

3 Jesus loves me! He will stay
   close beside me all the way;
   then His little child will take
   up to heaven, for His dear sake.
   Yes, Jesus loves me . . .

141 Jesus, name above all names

Words and music: Naida Hearn
Music arranged Roland Fudge

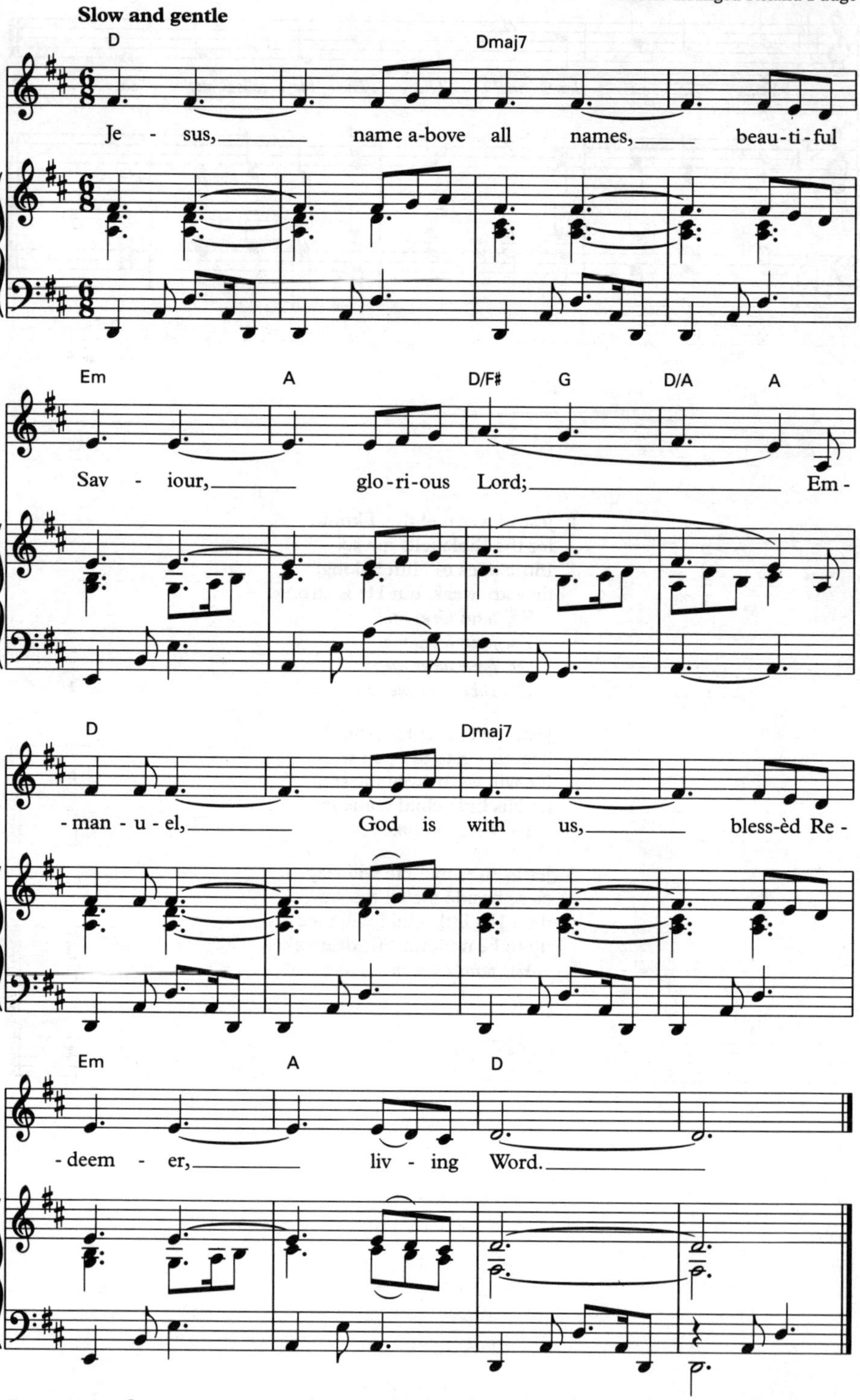

Slow and gentle
D
Dmaj7
Je - sus, name a-bove all names, beau-ti-ful
Em
A
D/F#
G
D/A
A
Sav - iour, glo-ri-ous Lord; Em-
D
Dmaj7
-man - u - el, God is with us, bless-èd Re-
Em
A
D
-deem - er, liv - ing Word.

142   Jesus said that whosoever will

Words and music: Anon
Music arranged Andy Silver

1 Jesus said that whosoever will,
whosoever will, whosoever will,
Jesus said that whosoever will,
whosoever will may come.

2 I'm so glad that He included me,
He included me, He included me,
I'm so glad that He included me,
when Jesus said that whosoever will may come.

143   Joshua fit the battle of Jericho

Words and music: Spiritual

Josh-ua fit the bat-tle of___ Je - ri - cho,___ Je - ri - cho,___

Je - ri - cho,___ Josh-ua fit the bat-tle of___ Je - ri - cho___ and the

walls came tumb - ling   down.   You may   talk a-bout your king of

Gi - de-on, you may talk a-bout your man of Saul, but there's none like good old

Joshua fit the battle of Jericho,
Jericho, Jericho,
Joshua fit the battle of Jericho
and the walls came tumbling down.

1 You may talk about your king of Gideon,
   you may talk about your man of Saul,
   but there's none like good old Joshua
   at the battle of Jericho.

2 Up to the walls of Jericho
   he marched with spear in hand.
   'Go, blow them ram-horns,' Joshua cried,
   ''cause the battle am in my hand!'

3 Then the ram-sheep's horns began to blow,
   trumpets began to sound.
   Joshua commanded the children to shout
   and the walls came tumbling down that morning.
       Joshua fit the battle . . .

144

Joy is the flag

Words and music: Anon
Music arranged E J Hume

Joy is the flag flown high from the cas-tle of my heart, from the
cas-tle of my heart, from the cas-tle of my heart, joy is the
flag flown high from the cas-tle of my heart when the
King is in re-si-dence there._____ So let it fly in the sky, let the

Joy is the flag flown high from the castle of my heart,
from the castle of my heart,
from the castle of my heart,
joy is the flag flown high from the castle of my heart
when the King is in residence there.
　　So let it fly in the sky, let the whole world know,
　　let the whole world know,
　　let the whole world know,
　　so let it fly in the sky, let the whole world know
　　that the King is in residence there.

145

Jubilate, everybody

From Psalm 100
Words and music: Fred Dunn (1909–79)

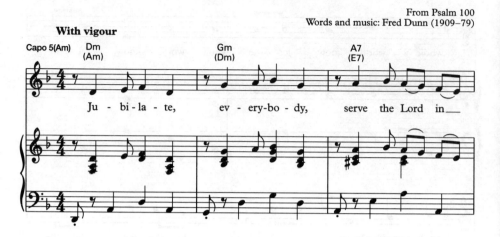

Ju - bi - la - te, ev - ery - bo - dy, serve the Lord in_

all your ways, and come be-fore His pre - sence sing - ing:

en - ter now_ His_ courts with praise. For the Lord our

God is gra-cious, and His mer-cy ev-er-last-ing.

Ju-bi-la-te, ju-bi-la-te, ju-bi-la-te De-o!

Jubilate, everybody,
serve the Lord in all your ways, and
come before His presence singing:
enter now His courts with praise.
For the Lord our God is gracious,
and His mercy everlasting.
Jubilate, jubilate,
jubilate Deo!

146 Just as I am

JUST AS I AM   888 6

Words: Marianne Farningham (1834–1909)
altered Horrobin/Leavers
Music: Joseph Barnby (1838–96)

Just as I am, Your child to be, friend of the young, who died for me, to give my life whole-heart-ed-ly, O Je-sus Christ, I come.

1 Just as I am, Your child to be,
  friend of the young, who died for me,
  to give my life wholeheartedly,
  O Jesus Christ, I come.

2 While I am still a child today,
  I give my life, my work and play
  to Him alone, without delay,
  with all my heart I come.

3 I see in Jesus Christ the light,
  with Him as Lord, and in His might
  I turn from sin to what is right,
  My Lord, to You I come.

4 Lord, take my dreams of fame and gold,
  I accept now a life controlled
  by faith in You, as days unfold,
  with my whole life I come.

5 Just as I am, young, strong and free,
  to be the best that I can be,
  that others may see You in me,
  Lord of my life, I come.

147 Keep me shining, Lord

Words and music: Kate Barclay Wilkinson (1859–1928)

Keep me shin-ing, Lord, keep me shin-ing, Lord, in all I say or do, that the world may see Christ lives in me, and learn to love Him too.

Keep me shining, Lord,
keep me shining, Lord,
in all I say or do,
that the world may see
Christ lives in me,
and learn to love Him too.

148   King of kings and Lord of lords

Words: Sophie Conty and Naomi Batya
Music: Hebrew folk melody

A two-part round

Brightly with increasing pace

King of kings and Lord of lords,
   glory, hallelujah!
King of kings and Lord of lords,
   glory, hallelujah!
Jesus, Prince of peace,
   glory, hallelujah!
Jesus, Prince of peace,
   glory, hallelujah!

Kum ba yah

Words and music: Traditional

1 Kum ba yah, my Lord, kum ba yah,
kum ba yah, my Lord, kum ba yah,
kum ba yah, my Lord, kum ba yah,
O Lord, kum ba yah.

2 Someone's crying, Lord . . .

3 Someone's singing, Lord . . .

4 Someone's praying, Lord . . .

5 Hear our prayer, O Lord, hear our prayer.
Keep our friends, O Lord, in Your care,
keep our friends, O Lord, in Your care,
O Lord, kum ba yah.

150   Let's talk about Jesus

Words and music: H Buffum Jr
Music arranged Phil Burt

Let's talk a-bout Je - sus, the King of kings is He,

the Lord of lords, su-preme through all e-ter-ni-ty,

the great I AM, the way, the truth, the life, the door.

Let's talk a-bout Je - sus, more and more.

151

Led like a lamb

Words and music: Graham Kendrick

Led like a lamb to the slaugh - ter, in si-lence and shame,

there on Your back You car - ried a world of vio-lence and pain.

Bleed-ing, dy-ing, bleed-ing, dy-ing. You're a -

- live, You're a-live, You have ris-en! Al-le-lu-ia! _ (al-le-lu-ia! al-le-lu-ia!) _ And the

power and the glo-ry is gi-ven, Al-le-lu-ia! _ (al-le-lu-ia! al-le-lu-ia!) Je-sus, to

1.2. You.

3. You.

1 Led like a lamb to the slaughter,
in silence and shame,
there on Your back You carried a world
of violence and pain.
Bleeding, dying, bleeding, dying.
You're alive,
You're alive,
You have risen!
Alleluia!
And the power
and the glory
is given,
Alleluia!
Jesus, to You.

2 At break of dawn, poor Mary,
still weeping she came,
when through her grief
she heard Your voice,
now speaking her name.
Mary! Master! Mary! Master!
You're alive . . .

3 At the right hand of the Father,
now seated on high,
You have begun Your eternal reign
of justice and joy.
Glory, glory, glory, glory.
You're alive . . .

152 Let us praise God together

Words: James E Seddon (1915–83)
Music: Calhoun melody
arranged David Wilson

Let us praise God to - geth - er, let us praise. Let us praise God to - geth - er, Him pro - claim. He is faith - ful in all His ways, He is worth - y of all our

1 Let us praise God together,
  let us praise.
  Let us praise God together,
  Him proclaim.
  He is faithful in all His ways,
  He is worthy of all our praise,
  His name be exalted on high.

2 Let us seek God together,
  let us pray.
  Let us seek His forgiveness
  as we pray.
  He will cleanse us from all sin,
  He will help us the fight to win,
  His name be exalted on high.

3 Let us serve God together,
  let us serve.
  Let our lives show His goodness
  as we work.
  Christ the Lord is the world's true light,
  let us serve Him with all our might.
  His name be exalted on high.

153   Live, live, live

Words and music: Marcus Uzilevsky

Fast

Live, live, live, live, live, live, Je - sus is liv - ing in my
soul. _____ Live, live, live, live, live, live,
Je - sus is liv - ing in my soul.
Hang-ing on the tree _____ He prayed for you and me.

Live, live, live,
live, live, live,
Jesus is living in my soul.
Live, live, live,
live, live, live,
Jesus is living in my soul.

1 Hanging on the tree
   He prayed for you and me.
   Jesus is living in my soul.
   To His spirit yield –
   by His stripes we're healed.
   Jesus is living in my soul.
       Live, live, live . . .

2 He took me out of darkness
   and He set me free.
   Jesus is living in my soul.
   Once I was blind,
   now I can see.
   Jesus is living in my soul.
       Live, live, live . . .

3 Gonna shout and sing,
   let the hallelujah ring.
   Jesus is living in my soul.
   I'm gonna shout and sing,
   there's healing in His wing.
   Jesus is living in my soul.
       Live, live, live . . .

154 Let us with a gladsome mind

Monkland   77 77

Words: John Milton (1608–74)
Music: John Antes (1740–1811)
arranged John Wilkes (1785–1869)

Let us with a glad-some mind praise the Lord for He is kind; For His mer-cies still en-dure, ev-er faith-ful, ev-er sure.

* This item appears in the key of C in the first edition of *Junior Praise*.

1 Let us with a gladsome mind
   praise the Lord for He is kind;
   For His mercies still endure,
   ever faithful, ever sure.

2 He, with all-commanding might,
   filled the new-made world with light:
   For His mercies . . .

3 All things living He does feed,
   His full hand supplies their need:
   For His mercies . . .

4 Let us then with gladsome mind,
   praise the Lord for He is kind!
   For His mercies . . .

155 Lord, dismiss us

DISMISSAL 87 87 87

Words: John Fawcett (1740–1817)
Altered Horrobin/Leavers
Music: William Letton Viner (1790–1856)

Lord, dis - miss us with Your bless-ing, fill our hearts with joy and peace.

Let us_ each, Your love pos-ses-sing, tri - umph in re - deem-ing grace.

O re - fresh us, O re-fresh us as to_ serve we leave this place.

1 Lord, dismiss us with Your blessing,
fill our hearts with joy and peace.
Let us each, Your love possessing,
triumph in redeeming grace.
O refresh us, O refresh us
as to serve we leave this place.

2 Thanks we give and adoration
for Your gospel's joyful sound;
may the fruits of Your salvation
in our hearts and lives abound;
so Your presence, so Your presence
will with us be always found.

156

Lord Jesus Christ

LIVING LORD   98 88 83

Words and music: Patrick Appleford

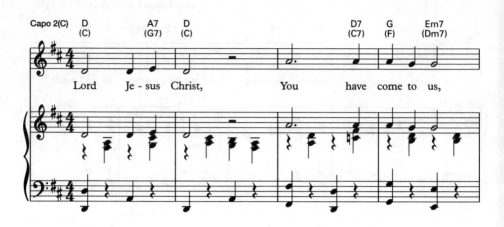

Lord Je - sus Christ, You have come to us,

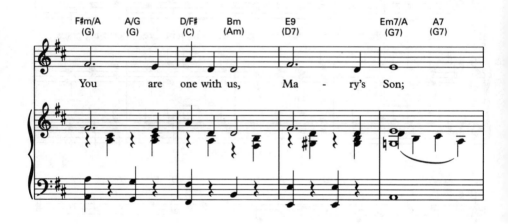

You are one with us, Ma - ry's Son;

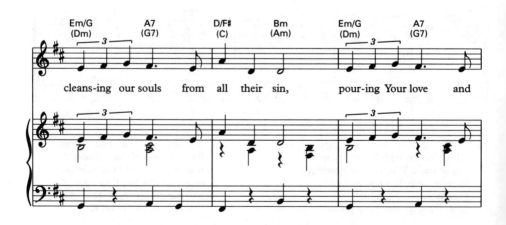

cleans-ing our souls from all their sin, pour-ing Your love and

good - ness in: Je - sus, our love for You we sing –

liv - ing Lord! Lord!

1 Lord Jesus Christ, You have come to us,
   You are one with us, Mary's Son;
   cleansing our souls from all their sin,
   pouring Your love and goodness in:
   Jesus, our love for You we sing –
       living Lord!

2 Lord Jesus Christ, now and every day
   teach us how to pray, Son of God;
   You have commanded us to do
   this in remembrance, Lord, of You:
   into our lives Your power breaks through –
       living Lord!

3 Lord Jesus Christ, You have come to us,
   born as one of us, Mary's Son;
   led out to die on Calvary,
   risen from death to set us free:
   living Lord Jesus, help us see
       You are Lord!

4 Lord Jesus Christ, I would come to You,
   live my life for You, Son of God;
   all Your commands I know are true,
   Your many gifts will make me new:
   into my life Your power breaks through –
       living Lord!

157 Lord of all hopefulness

SLANE   10 11 11 12 (Irregular)

Words: Jan Struther (1901–53)
Music: Irish traditional melody
arranged Martin Shaw (1875–1958)

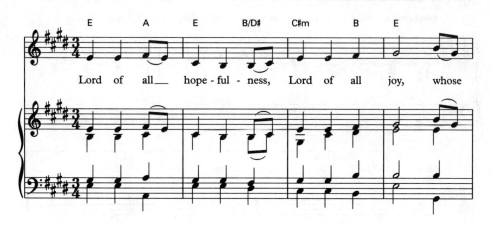

Lord of all__ hope-ful - ness, Lord of all joy, whose

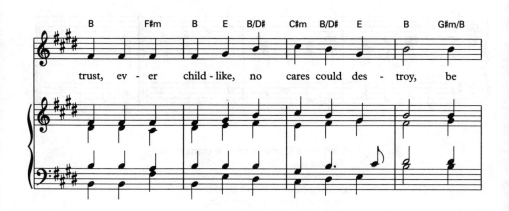

trust, ev - er child - like, no cares could des - troy, be

there at__ our__ wak - ing, and give us, we pray, Your

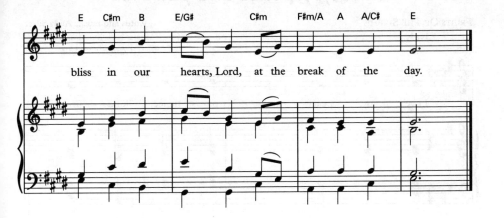

bliss　in　our　hearts, Lord,　at the　break　of　the　day.

1　Lord of all hopefulness, Lord of all joy,
　　whose trust, ever childlike, no cares could destroy,
　　be there at our waking, and give us, we pray,
　　Your bliss in our hearts, Lord, at the break of the day.

2　Lord of all eagerness, Lord of all faith,
　　whose strong hands were skilled at the plane and the lathe,
　　be there at our labours, and give us, we pray,
　　Your strength in our hearts, Lord, at the noon of the day.

3　Lord of all kindliness, Lord of all grace,
　　Your hand swift to welcome, Your arms to embrace,
　　be there at our homing, and give us, we pray,
　　Your love in our hearts, Lord, at the eve of the day.

4　Lord of all gentleness, Lord of all calm,
　　whose voice is contentment, whose presence is balm,
　　be there at our sleeping, and give us, we pray,
　　Your peace in our hearts, Lord, at the end of the day.

158 Love, joy, peace and patience

FRUITS OF THE SPIRIT

Words and music: Andy Silver

Love, joy, peace and pa - tience, kind - ness,

good - ness, meek - ness, faith, self-con - trol.__

These are the fruit of God's Ho - ly Spi - rit and a-

- gainst such there is no law.__ Those who be-long to Christ

Love, joy, peace and patience, kindness,
goodness, meekness, faith, self-control.
These are the fruit of God's Holy Spirit
and against such there is no law.
Those who belong to Christ should now live this way,
walking in the Spirit each day,
so praise Him, praise Him, give Him all the glory,
walking in the Spirit each day.

159   Low in the grave He lay

CHRIST AROSE   65 64 with refrain   Words and music: Robert Lowry (1826–99)

Low in the grave He lay, Je - sus, my Sav - iour; wait - ing the com - ing day, Je - sus, my Lord.

Up from the grave He a - rose, with a migh - ty tri - umph o'er His foes; He a - rose a vic - tor from the dark do - main, and He

1 Low in the grave He lay,
Jesus, my Saviour;
waiting the coming day,
Jesus, my Lord.
   Up from the grave He arose,
   with a mighty triumph o'er His foes;
   He arose a victor from the dark domain,
   and He lives for ever with His saints to reign:
   He arose! He arose! Hallelujah! Christ arose!

2 Vainly they watch His bed,
Jesus, my Saviour;
vainly they seal the dead,
Jesus, my Lord.
   Up from the grave . . .

3 Death cannot keep his prey,
Jesus, my Saviour,
He tore the bars away,
Jesus, my Lord.
   Up from the grave . . .

160 Majesty

Words and music: Jack Hayford

Majestically

Ma - jes - ty,_____ wor-ship His ma - jes - ty;_____ un - to Je - sus be glo - ry, hon-our and praise._____ Ma - jes - ty,_____ king-dom au - tho - ri - ty,_____ flows from His throne un - to His own, His an-them raise. So ex -

161 Make me a channel of Your peace

ST FRANCIS

Words and music: Sebastian Temple
Music arranged Betty Pulkingham

Flowing

Make me a chan-nel of Your peace.___ Where
there is hat-red let me bring Your love;___ where
there is in-ju-ry, Your par-don, Lord;___ and
where there's doubt, true faith in You.___ O

1 Make me a channel of Your peace.
   Where there is hatred let me bring Your love;
   where there is injury, Your pardon, Lord;
   and where there's doubt, true faith in You.
   O Master, grant that I may never seek
   so much to be consoled as to console;
   to be understood as to understand;
   to be loved, as to love with all my soul.

2 Make me a channel of Your peace.
   Where there's despair in life let me bring hope;
   where there is darkness, only light;
   and where there's sadness, ever joy.
   O Master . . .

3 Make me a channel of Your peace.
   It is in pardoning that we are pardoned,
   in giving to all men that we receive;
   and in dying that we're born to eternal life.

162 Make me a servant

Words and music: Kelly Willard

Sustained

Make me a ser-vant, hum-ble and meek.

Lord, let me lift up those who are weak.

And may the prayer of my heart al-ways be:

'Make me a ser-vant, make me a ser-vant,

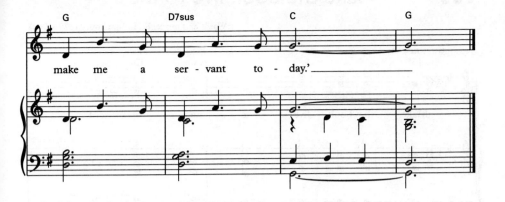

make me a ser - vant to - day.'

Make me a servant, humble and meek.
Lord, let me lift up those who are weak.
And may the prayer of my heart always be:
'Make me a servant, make me a servant,
make me a servant today.'

163   Make the book live to me

Words and music: R Hudson Pope (1879–1967)

Make the book live to me, O Lord,
show me Yourself with-in Your word,
show me my-self and
show me my Sav-iour and make the book live to me.

Make the book live to me, O Lord,
show me Yourself within Your word,
show me myself and show me my Saviour
and make the book live to me.

Mary had a little baby

Words and music: Andy Silver

Mary— had a lit - tle ba - by,— Ma - ry— had a lit - tle ba - by;— here and there and ev - ery-where the an - gels sang: 'Praise the Lord!'— Ma - ry— had a lit - tle ba - by,— Ma - ry—

Mary had a little baby, Mary had a little baby;
here and there and everywhere the angels sang:
'Praise the Lord!'
Mary had a little baby, Mary had a little baby;
here and there and everywhere the angels sang:
'Praise the Lord!'

Glory, glory, glory, glory,
everybody sing the song.
Glory, glory, glory, glory,
God's Son has come to earth.

Mary had a little baby, Mary had a little baby;
here and there and everywhere the angels sang:
'Praise the Lord!'

165   May the mind of Christ my Saviour

St Leonards   87 85

Words: Kate Barclay Wilkinson (1859–1928)
Music: Arthur Cyril Barham Gould (1891–1953)

1 May the mind of Christ my Saviour
live in me from day to day,
by His love and power controlling
all I do or say.

2 May the word of God dwell richly
in my heart from hour to hour,
so that all may see I triumph
only through His power.

3 May the peace of God my Father
rule my life in everything,
that I may be calm to comfort
sick and sorrowing.

4 May the love of Jesus fill me,
as the waters fill the sea;
Him uplifting, self denying,
this is victory.

5 May I run the race before me,
strong and brave onward I go,
looking only unto Jesus,
as in Him I grow.

166 Morning has broken

BUNESSAN 10 9 10 9

Words: Eleanor Farjeon (1881–1965)
Music: Gaelic melody
arranged Noël Tredinnick

Morn-ing has bro - ken like the first morn - ing;

black-bird has spo - ken like the first bird. Praise for the sing - ing!

Praise for the morn - ing! Praise for them, spring - ing fresh from the Word!

1 Morning has broken
like the first morning;
blackbird has spoken
like the first bird.
Praise for the singing!
Praise for the morning!
Praise for them, springing
fresh from the Word!

2 Mine is the sunlight!
Mine is the morning,
here in the bright light
of this fair day!
Praise with elation,
praise every morning
God's re-creation
of the new day!

Words: © David Higham Associates Ltd,
5–8 Lower John Street, Golden Square, London W1R 4HA
from *The Children's Bells*
published by Oxford University Press

Music arrangement: © Noël Tredinnick/Jubilee Hymns

167   Mister Noah built an ark

Words and music: Anon
Music arranged Phil Burt

Mis - ter No - ah built an ark, the peo - ple thought it such a lark. Mis - ter No - ah plead - ed so, but in - to the ark they would not go. *Down came the rain in tor - rents (splish, splash), down came the rain in tor - rents (splish, splash),*

down came the rain in tor - rents, and o - nly eight were saved.

1 Mister Noah built an ark,
  the people thought it such a lark.
  Mister Noah pleaded so,
  but into the ark they would not go.
   Down came the rain in torrents (splish, splash),
   down came the rain in torrents (splish, splash),
   down came the rain in torrents,
   and only eight were saved.

2 The animals went in two by two,
  elephant, giraffe and kangaroo.
  All were safely stowed away
  on that great and awful day.
   Down came the rain . . .

   Whenever you see a rainbow,
   whenever you see a rainbow,
   whenever you see a rainbow,
   remember God is love.

168 My faith is like a staff of oak

8 6 8 6 888 6

Words: Thomas Toke Lynch (1818–71)
Altered Horrobin/Leavers
Music: Swiss traditional melody

My faith is like a staff of oak, the tra-vel-ler's well-loved aid; my faith, it is a wea-pon strong, the sol-dier's trust-y blade. I'll tra-vel on, and still be stirred to

ac - tion at___ my___ Mas - ter's word; by all life's_ pe - rils___ un - de - terred, a sol - dier_ un - a - fraid.

1 My faith is like a staff of oak,
   the traveller's well-loved aid;
   my faith, it is a weapon strong,
   the soldier's trusty blade.
   I'll travel on, and still be stirred
   to action at my Master's word;
   by all life's perils undeterred,
   a soldier unafraid.

2 My faith is like a staff of oak,
   O let me on it lean!
   My faith, it is a sharpened sword,
   may falsehood find it keen!
   Now fill me with Your Spirit, Lord,
   teach and change me through Your word,
   and by Your love may I be stirred,
   as all true saints have been.

169 My God is so big

Words and music: Anon
Music arranged Phil Burt

My God is so big, so strong and so
migh-ty there's noth-ing that He can-not do.
The ri-vers are His, the
moun-tains are His, the stars are His han-di-work too.

1 My God is so big, so strong and so mighty
there's nothing that He cannot do.
My God is so big, so strong and so mighty
there's nothing that He cannot do.
The rivers are His, the mountains are His,
the stars are His handiwork too.
My God is so big, so strong and so mighty
there's nothing that He cannot do.

2 My God is so big, so strong and so mighty
there's nothing that He cannot do.
My God is so big, so strong and so mighty
there's nothing that He cannot do.
He's called you to live for Him every day
in all that you say and you do.
My God is so big, so strong and so mighty,
He can do all things through you.

170 My Lord is higher than a mountain

Words and music: Ian Smale
Music arranged: Phil Burt

My Lord is high-er than a moun-tain, He is strong-er than an ar-my, He is wi-ser than a-ny man can tell. My Lord is fast-er than a rock-et, can see more than a te-le-scope, is big-ger than the u-ni-verse as well. His love is

warm - er than the burn - ing sun, clos - er than the near - est friend, more real than a - ny truth can be. My Lord, He knows a-bout the past, and He knows a-bout the fu-ture, and He al - so knows all a-bout me.

My Lord is higher than a mountain,
He is stronger than an army,
He is wiser than any man can tell.
My Lord is faster than a rocket,
can see more than a telescope,
is bigger than the universe as well.
His love is warmer than the burning sun,
closer than the nearest friend,
more real than any truth can be.
My Lord, He knows about the past,
and He knows about the future,
and He also knows all about me.

171 New every morning

Melcombe LM

Words: John Keble (1792–1866)
Music: Samuel Webbe (1740–1816)

New ev - ery morn - ing is the love our
wak - ing and up - ris - ing prove: through sleep and dark - ness
safe - ly brought, re - stored to life and power and thought.

1 New every morning is the love
  our waking and uprising prove:
  through sleep and darkness safely brought,
  restored to life and power and thought.

2 New mercies, each returning day,
  surround Your people as they pray:
  new dangers past, new sins forgiven,
  new thoughts of God, new hopes of heaven.

3 If in our daily life our mind
  be set to honour all we find,
  new treasures still, of countless price,
  God will provide for sacrifice.

4 The trivial round, the common task,
  will give us all we ought to ask:
  room to deny ourselves, a road
  to bring us daily nearer God.

5 Prepare us, Lord, in Your dear love
  for perfect rest with You above,
  and help us, this and every day,
  to grow more like You as we pray.

172   Now be strong

Words and music: J H Cansdale (d 1995)
Words altered Horrobin/Leavers

Now be strong and very courageous, for I have commanded you. Be not afraid, be not dismayed; you will have victory. I will be with you unto the end, captain and leader, guide and friend.

Now be strong and very courageous,
for I have commanded you.
Be not afraid,
be not dismayed;
you will have victory.
I will be with you unto the end,
captain and leader,
guide and friend.

173 Now the day is over

Eudoxia 65 65

Words and music: Sabine Baring-Gould (1834–1924)
Words altered Horrobin/Leavers

1 Now the day is over,
    night will soon be here,
    help me to remember
    You are always near.

2 As the darkness gathers,
    stars shine overhead,
    creatures, birds and flowers
    rest their weary heads.

3 Father, give all people
    calm and peaceful rest;
    through Your gracious presence
    may our sleep be blessed.

4 Comfort every sufferer
    watching late in pain;
    those who plan some evil
    from their sin restrain.

5 When the morning wakes me,
    ready for the day,
    help me, Lord, to serve You,
    walking in Your way.

6 Glory to the Father,
    glory to the Son,
    and to the Holy Spirit,
    blessing everyone.

174   Now the green blade riseth
(Love is come again)

NOËL NOUVELET

Words: J M C Crum (1872–1958)
Music: French melody
arranged Martin Shaw (1875–1958)

Now the green blade ris - eth from the bu - ried grain,
wheat that in the dark earth ma - ny days has lain.
Love lives a - gain, that with the dead has been.

Love is come a - gain, like wheat that spring-eth green.

1 Now the green blade riseth from the buried grain,
   wheat that in the dark earth many days has lain.
   Love lives again, that with the dead has been.
   Love is come again, like wheat that springeth green.

2 In the grave they laid Him, Love whom men had slain,
   thinking that never He would wake again.
   Laid in the earth like grain that sleeps unseen,
   Love is come again, like wheat that springeth green.

3 Forth He came at Easter, like the risen grain,
   He that for three days in the grave had lain.
   Quick from the dead my risen Lord is seen;
   Love is come again, like wheat that springeth green.

4 When our hearts are wintry, grieving or in pain,
   Your touch can call us back to life again.
   Fields of our hearts that dead and bare have been;
   Love is come again, like wheat that springeth green.

175 Now thank we all our God

NUN DANKET   67 67 66 66

Words: Martin Rinkart (1586–1649)
tr. Catherine Winkworth (1829–78)
altered Horrobin/Leavers
Music: Johann Crüger (1598–1662)

Now thank we all our God, with hearts, and hands, and

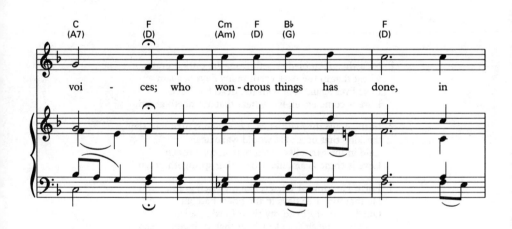

voi - ces; who won - drous things has done, in

whom His world re - joi - ces; who, from our mo - thers'

arms, has blessed us on our way with

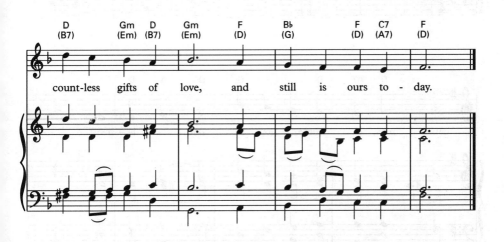

count-less gifts of love, and still is ours to - day.

1 Now thank we all our God,
with hearts, and hands, and voices;
who wondrous things has done,
in whom His world rejoices;
who, from our mothers' arms,
has blessed us on our way
with countless gifts of love,
and still is ours today.

2 We thank You, then, O God
that through our life You're near us,
for joy that fills our hearts,
which, with Your peace, restores us.
Lord, keep us in Your grace,
and guide us when perplexed,
that we may love Your ways,
in this world and the next.

3 All praise and thanks to God
the Father now be given,
the Son, and Him who reigns
with Them in highest heaven;
the one eternal God,
whom earth and heaven adore;
for thus it was, is now,
and shall be evermore.

176 O come, all you faithful

<small>ADESTE FIDELES Irregular</small>

<small>Words: Latin (18th century)
tr. Frederick Oakley (1802–80)
altered Horrobin/Leavers
Music: John Francis Wade (1711–86)
arranged William Henry Monk (1823–89)</small>

O come, all you faith-ful, joy-ful and tri-umph-ant, O come now, O come_ now to Beth - le -hem; come and be -hold Him, born the King of an-gels: O

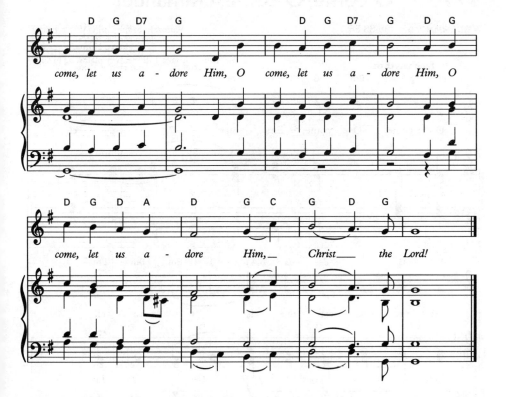

1 O come, all you faithful,
    joyful and triumphant,
    O come now, O come now to Bethlehem;
    come and behold Him,
    born the King of angels:
        O come, let us adore Him,
        O come, let us adore Him,
        O come, let us adore Him,
        Christ the Lord!

2 True God of true God,
    light of light eternal,
    He, who abhors not the virgin's womb;
    Son of the Father,
    begotten not created:
        O come, let us adore Him ...

3 Sing like the angels,
    sing in exultation,
    sing with the citizens of heaven above,
    'Glory to God,
    glory in the highest':
        O come, let us adore Him ...

4 Yes, Lord, we greet You,
    born that happy morning,
    Jesus, to You be glory given!
    Word of the Father,
    then in flesh appearing:
        O come, let us adore Him ...

177 O come, O come, Emmanuel

Veni Immanuel   88 88 88

Words: from the Latin (12th century)
tr. John Mason Neale (1818–66)
in this version Jubilate Hymns
Music: from a 15th-century plainsong melody

In free rhythm

O come, O come, Em-man - u - el,
and ran - som cap - tive Is - ra - el,
who mourns in lone - ly ex - ile here
un - til the Son of God draws near.

Re - joice, re - joice! Em - man - - - u - el

shall come to you, O Is - - ra - el.

1 O come, O come, Emmanuel,
   and ransom captive Israel,
   who mourns in lonely exile here
   until the Son of God draws near.
      Rejoice, rejoice! Emmanuel
      shall come to you, O Israel.

2 O come, true Branch of Jesse, free
   Your children from this tyranny;
   from depths of hell Your people save,
   to rise victorious from the grave.
      Rejoice, rejoice . . .

3 O come, bright Daybreak, come and cheer
   our spirits by Your advent here;
   dispel the long night's lingering gloom
   and pierce the shadows of the tomb.
      Rejoice, rejoice . . .

4 O come, strong key of David, come
   and open wide our heavenly home;
   make safe the path that leads on high,
   and close the path to misery.
      Rejoice, rejoice . . .

5 O come, O come, great Lord of might,
   who long ago on Sinai's height
   gave all Your tribes the ancient law
   in cloud and majesty and awe.
      Rejoice, rejoice . . .

178

O happy day

Words: Philip Dodderidge (1702–51),
altered Horrobin/Leavers
Music: Ron Jones

O hap-py day!____ that fixed my choice____ on You, my Sav-iour and my God!____ Well may this grate - ful heart re - joice,____ and tell of Christ's re - deem - ing blood.____ *O hap-py day!____ O hap-py day!*__ *when Je-sus washed my sins a - way;* *He taught me how__ to watch and*

pray,___ and live re - joic - ing ev - ery day;___ hal - le - lu-jah! O hap-py

day!___ O hap-py day!___ when Je-sus washed my sins a - way.___

1 O happy day! that fixed my choice
on You, my Saviour and my God!
Well may this grateful heart rejoice,
and tell of Christ's redeeming blood.
   O happy day! O happy day!
   when Jesus washed my sins away;
   He taught me how to watch and pray,
   and live rejoicing every day; (hallelujah!)
   O happy day! O happy day!
   when Jesus washed my sins away.

2 It's done, the great transaction's done!
I am my Lord's and He is mine!
He led me, and I followed on,
responding to the voice divine.
   O happy day . . .

3 Now rest, my long-divided heart,
in Jesus Christ who loves you, rest;
and never from your Lord depart,
enriched by Him, by Him possessed.
   O happy day . . .

4 So God, who heard the solemn vow,
in daily prayer shall hear my voice,
till in my final breath I bow,
and bless the day that fixed my choice.
   O happy day . . .

179 O Lord my God!

HOW GREAT THOU ART

From a Russian hymn
Words and music: Stuart Wesley Keene Hine (1899–1989)

O Lord my God! when I in awe-some won-der___ con-sid-er all the works Thy hand hath made, I see the stars, I hear the migh-ty thun-der,___ the power through-out the u-ni-verse dis-played; Then sings my soul, my Sav-iour God, to Thee, how great Thou

1 O Lord my God! when I in awesome wonder
   consider all the works Thy hand hath made,
   I see the stars, I hear the mighty thunder,
   the power throughout the universe displayed;
       Then sings my soul, my Saviour God, to Thee,
       how great Thou art, how great Thou art!
       Then sings my soul, my Saviour God, to Thee,
       how great Thou art, how great Thou art!

2 When through the woods and forest glades I wander
   and hear the birds sing sweetly in the trees;
   when I look down from lofty mountain grandeur,
   and hear the brook, and feel the gentle breeze;
       Then sings my soul . . .

3 And when I think that God, His Son not sparing,
   sent Him to die – I scarce can take it in,
   that on the cross my burden gladly bearing,
   He bled and died to take away my sin:
       Then sings my soul . . .

4 When Christ shall come with shout of acclamation
   and take me home – what joy shall fill my heart!
   Then shall I bow in humble adoration
   and there proclaim, my God, how great Thou art!
       Then sings my soul . . .

180   O! O! O! how good is the Lord

Words and music: Anon
Music arranged Jeanne Harper

With joyful abandon

O! O! O! how good is the Lord, O! O! O! how good is the Lord, O! O! O! how good is the Lord, I ne-ver will for-get what He has done for me.

He gives me sal-va-tion, how good is the Lord, He

gives me sal-va-tion, how good is the Lord, He gives me sal-va-tion, how

good is the Lord, I ne-ver will for-get what He has done for me.

O! O! O! how good is the Lord,
O! O! O! how good is the Lord,
O! O! O! how good is the Lord,
I never will forget what He has done for me.

1 He gives me salvation, how good is the Lord,
  He gives me salvation, how good is the Lord,
  He gives me salvation, how good is the Lord,
  I never will forget what He has done for me.
    O! O! O! ...

2 He gives me His blessings ...
    O! O! O! ...

3 He gives me His Spirit ...
    O! O! O! ...

4 He gives me His healing ...
    O! O! O! ...

5 He gives me His glory ...
    O! O! O! ...

OTHER SUITABLE VERSES MAY BE ADDED
He gives us each other ...
He gives us His body ...
He gives us His freedom ... *etc.*

181 O the love that drew salvation's plan

Words: William Reed Newell (1868–1956)
Music: Daniel Brink Towner (1850–1919)

O the love that drew sal - va - tion's plan!

O the grace that brought it down to man! O the migh - ty gulf that

God did span at Cal - va - ry.

Mer - cy there was great and grace was free,

par - don there was mul - ti - plied to me, there my bur-dened soul found

lib - er - ty, at Cal - va - ry.

O the love that drew salvation's plan!
O the grace that brought it down to man!
O the mighty gulf that God did span at Calvary.
Mercy there was great and grace was free,
pardon there was multiplied to me,
there my burdened soul found liberty, at Calvary.

182 O little town of Bethlehem

FOREST GREEN   DCM (Irregular)

Words: Phillips Brooks (1835–93)
Music: English traditional melody
collected and arranged Ralph Vaughan Williams (1872–1958)

O lit - tle town of Beth - le - hem, how still we__ see you lie! A - bove your deep and dream - less__ sleep the si - lent__ stars go by: yet__ in your dark__ streets

Music: from the *English Hymnal*
by permission of Oxford University Press

shin - ing is ev - er - last - ing light; the

hopes and fears of all__ the years are met in__ you to - night.

1 O little town of Bethlehem,
how still we see you lie!
Above your deep and dreamless sleep
the silent stars go by:
yet in your dark streets shining
is everlasting light;
the hopes and fears of all the years
are met in you tonight.

2 For Christ is born of Mary;
and, gathered all above,
while mortals sleep, the angels keep
their watch of wondering love.
O morning stars, together
proclaim the holy birth,
and praises sing to God the King,
and peace to men on earth.

3 How silently, how silently,
the wondrous gift is given!
So God imparts to human hearts
the blessings of His heaven.
No ear may hear His coming;
but in this world of sin,
where meek souls will receive Him, still
the dear Christ enters in.

4 O holy Child of Bethlehem,
descend to us, we pray;
cast out our sin, and enter in;
be born in us today.
We hear the Christmas angels
the great glad tidings tell;
O come to us, abide with us,
our Lord Immanuel.

183 On Calvary's tree

Words: A W Edsor
Music: A E Walton
arranged Norman Warren

On Cal-vary's tree He died for me, that I His love might know. _

To set me free He died for me – that's why I love Him so.

On Calvary's tree He died for me,
that I His love might know.
To set me free He died for me –
that's why I love Him so.

184 Oh, the Lord looked down

Words and music: Traditional

Oh, the Lord looked down from His win-dow in the sky, said, 'I cre-a-ted man but I can't re-mem-ber why! Noth-ing but fight-ing since cre-a-tion day. I'll send a lit-tle wa-ter and wash them all a-way.' Oh, the Lord came down and looked a-round a spell. There was Mis-ter Noah_ be-

1 Oh, the Lord looked down from His window in the sky,
   said, 'I created man but I can't remember why!
   Nothing but fighting since creation day.
   I'll send a little water and wash them all away.'
   Oh, the Lord came down and looked around a spell.
   There was Mr Noah behaving mighty well.
   And that is the reason, the Scriptures record,
   Noah found grace in the eyes of the Lord.
   Noah found grace in the eyes of the Lord,
   Noah found grace in the eyes of the Lord,
   Noah found grace in the eyes of the Lord,
   and He left him high and dry.

2 The Lord said, 'Noah, there's going to be a flood,
   there's going to be some water, there's going to be some mud.
   So take off your hat, Noah, take off your coat,
   get Shem and Ham and Japheth and build yourself a boat.'
   Noah said, 'Lord, I don't believe I could.'
   The Lord said, 'Noah, get yourself some wood.
   You never know what you can do till you try.
   Build it fifty cubits wide and thirty cubits high.'
   Noah found grace . . .

3 Noah said, 'There she is, there she is, Lord!'
   The Lord said, 'Noah, it's time to get aboard.
   Take of each creature a he and a she,
   and of course take Mrs Noah and the whole family.'
   Noah said, 'Lord, it's getting mighty dark.'
   The Lord said, 'Noah, get those creatures in the ark.'
   Noah said, 'Lord, it's beginning to pour.'
   The Lord said, 'Noah, hurry up and close the door.'
   Noah found grace . . .

4 The ark rose up on the bosom of the deep.
   After forty days Mr Noah took a peep.
   He said, 'We're not moving, Lord, where are we at?'
   The Lord said, 'You're sitting right on Mount Ararat.'
   Noah said, 'Lord, it's getting nice and dry.'
   The Lord said, 'Noah, see my rainbow in the sky.
   Take all your creatures and people the earth,
   and be sure you're not more trouble than you're worth.'
   Noah found grace . . .

185 Once in royal David's city

IRBY   87 87 77

Words: Cecil Frances Alexander (1818–95)
Music: Henry John Gauntlett (1805–76)

Once in roy - al Da - vid's— ci - ty, stood a
low - ly cat - tle— shed, where a mo - ther laid— her—
ba - by, in a man - ger for— His— bed. Ma - ry

was that mo-ther mild, Je - sus Christ her lit - tle__ child.

1 Once in royal David's city,
   stood a lowly cattle shed,
   where a mother laid her baby,
   in a manger for His bed.
   Mary was that mother mild,
   Jesus Christ her little child.

2 He came down to earth from heaven,
   who is God and Lord of all;
   and His shelter was a stable,
   and His cradle was a stall:
   with the poor and mean and lowly
   lived on earth our Saviour holy.

3 And through all His wondrous childhood
   He would honour and obey,
   love, and watch the lowly mother,
   in whose gentle arms He lay:
   Christian children all should be,
   kind, obedient, good as He.

4 For He is our childhood's pattern:
   day by day like us He grew;
   He was little, weak, and helpless,
   tears and smiles like us He knew;
   and He feels for all our sadness,
   and He shares in all our gladness.

5 And our eyes at last shall see Him,
   through His own redeeming love;
   for that child, so dear and gentle,
   is our Lord in heaven above;
   and He leads His children on
   to the place where He is gone.

6 Not in that poor lowly stable,
   with the oxen standing by,
   we shall see Him, but in heaven,
   set at God's right hand on high;
   there His children gather round,
   bright like stars, with glory crowned.

186 On Jordan's bank the Baptist's cry

WINCHESTER NEW   LM

Words: Charles Coffin (1676–1749)
tr. John Chandler (1806–76)
altered Horrobin/Leavers
Music: adapted from a chorale in
Musicalisches HandBuch, Hamburg, 1690
arranged William Henry Havergal (1793–1870)

On Jor-dan's bank the Bap-tist's cry an-noun-ces that the Lord is nigh; come then and list-en for he brings glad tid-ings from the King of kings.

1 On Jordan's bank the Baptist's cry
  announces that the Lord is nigh;
  come then and listen for he brings
  glad tidings from the King of kings.

2 Then cleansed be every heart from sin;
  make straight the way for God within;
  prepare we in our hearts a home,
  where such a mighty guest may come.

3 For You are our salvation, Lord,
  our refuge and our great reward;
  without Your grace we waste away,
  like flowers that wither and decay.

4 To Him who left the throne of heaven
  to save mankind, all praise be given;
  to God the Father, voices raise,
  and Holy Spirit, let us praise.

187 One day when heaven

Words: J Wilbur Chapman (1859–1918)
Music: Charles H Marsh (1886–1956)

One day when hea - ven was filled with His prais - es, one day when

sin was as black as could be,___ Je-sus came down to be born of a

vir - gin, lived a-mong men, my ex - am - ple is He!___

Liv - ing, He loved me; dy - ing, He saved me; bur - ied, He

car - ried my sins far a - way,___ ris-ing, He jus - ti-fied free-ly for

ev - er: one day He's com - ing: O glo - ri - ous day.___

1 One day when heaven was filled with His praises,
one day when sin was as black as could be,
Jesus came down to be born of a virgin,
lived among men, my example is He!
Living, He loved me; dying, He saved me;
buried, He carried my sins far away,
rising, He justified freely for ever:
one day He's coming: O glorious day.

2 One day they led Him up Calvary's mountain,
one day they nailed Him to die on the tree;
suffering anguish, despised and rejected;
bearing our sins, my Redeemer is He!
Living, He loved me . . .

3 One day they left Him alone in the garden,
one day He rested, from suffering free;
angels came down o'er His tomb to keep vigil;
hope of the hopeless, my Saviour is He!
Living, He loved me . . .

4 One day the grave could conceal Him no longer,
one day the stone rolled away from the door;
then He arose, over death He had conquered;
now is ascended, my Lord evermore!
Living, He loved me . . .

5 One day the trumpet will sound for His coming,
one day the skies with His glory will shine;
wonderful day, my beloved ones bringing;
glorious Saviour, this Jesus is mine!
Living, He loved me . . .

188 One more step along the world I go

Words and music: Sydney Carter
Music arranged Douglas Coombes

With a spring

One more step a-long the world I go, one more step a-long the world I go, from the old things to the new keep me tra-vel-ling a-long with You. *And it's from the old I tra-vel to the new, keep me tra-vel-ling a-long with You.*

1 One more step along the world I go,
   one more step along the world I go,
   from the old things to the new
   keep me travelling along with You.
   And it's from the old I travel to the new,
   keep me travelling along with You.

2 Round the corners of the world I turn,
   more and more about the world I learn.
   And the new things that I see
   You'll be looking at along with me.
   And it's from the old . . .

3 As I travel through the bad and good
   keep me travelling the way I should.
   Where I see no way to go
   You'll be telling me the way, I know.
   And it's from the old . . .

4 Give me courage when the world is rough,
   keep me loving, though the world is tough.
   Leap and sing in all I do,
   keep me travelling along with You.
   And it's from the old . . .

5 You are older than the world can be.
   You are younger than the life in me.
   Ever old and ever new,
   keep me travelling along with You.
   And it's from the old . . .

189 One, two, three, Jesus loves me

Words and music: Lisa Mazak

Happily

One, two, three, Je - sus loves me. One, two, Je - sus loves you. *1* Three, four, He loves you more than you've ev - er been loved be - fore. *2* Five, six, seven, we're go - ing to heaven. Eight, nine, it's tru - ly di - vine.

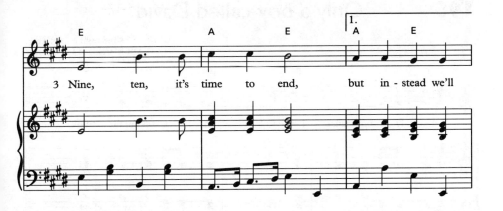

One, two, three, Jesus loves me.
One, two, Jesus loves you.

1 Three, four, He loves you more
  than you've ever been loved before.
  One, two, three . . .

2 Five, six, seven, we're going to heaven.
  Eight, nine, it's truly divine.
  One, two, three . . .

3 Nine, ten, it's time to end,
  but instead we'll sing it again
  LAST TIME
  (there's no time to sing it again).

190

Only a boy called David

Words and music: Anon
Music arranged J H Stringer

On - ly a boy called Da - vid, on - ly a rip - pling brook;

on - ly a boy called Da - vid, five lit - tle stones he took. Then

one lit - tle stone went in the sling, and the sling went round and round,

one lit - tle stone went in the sling, and the sling went round and round.

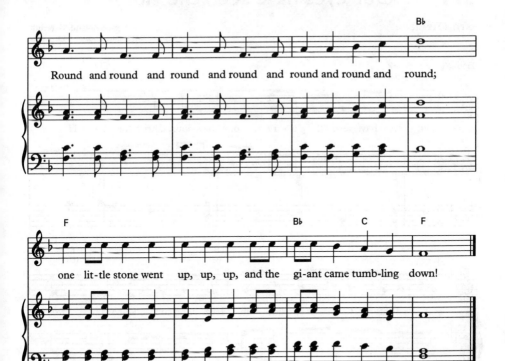

Round and round and round and round and round and round and round;

one lit-tle stone went up, up, up, and the gi-ant came tumb-ling down!

Only a boy called David,
only a rippling brook;
only a boy called David,
five little stones he took.
Then one little stone went in the sling,
and the sling went round and round,
one little stone went in the sling,
and the sling went round and round.
Round and round and round and round
and round and round and round;
one little stone went up, up, up,
and the giant came tumbling down!

191 Our eyes have seen the glory

BATTLE HYMN

Words: Roland Meredith
Music: American traditional melody
arranged Phil Burt

Our eyes have seen the glo-ry of our Sav-iour, Christ the Lord; He is seat-ed at His Fa-ther's side in love and full ac-cord; from there up-on the sons of men His Spi-rit is out-poured, all hail, as-cend-ed King!_____ *Glo- ry, glo-ry, hal-le-*

-lu - jah, glo - ry, glo - ry, hal - le - lu - jah,
glo - ry, glo - ry, hal - le - lu - jah, all hail, as - cend - ed King!

1 Our eyes have seen the glory
  of our Saviour, Christ the Lord;
  He is seated at His Father's side
  in love and full accord;
  from there upon the sons of men
  His Spirit is outpoured,
  all hail, ascended King!
    Glory, glory, hallelujah,
    glory, glory, hallelujah,
    glory, glory, hallelujah,
    all hail, ascended King!

2 He came to earth at Christmas
  and was made a man like us;
  He taught, He healed, He suffered –
  and they nailed Him to the cross;
  He rose again on Easter Day –
  our Lord victorious,
  all hail, ascended King!
    Glory, glory . . .

3 The good news of His kingdom
  must be preached to every shore,
  the news of peace and pardon,
  and the end of strife and war;
  the secret of His kingdom
  is to serve Him evermore,
  all hail, ascended King!
    Glory, glory . . .

4 His kingdom is a family
  of men of every race,
  they live their lives in harmony,
  enabled by His grace;
  they follow His example
  till they see Him face to face,
  all hail, ascended King!
    Glory, glory . . .

192   Our Father who is in heaven

CARIBBEAN LORD'S PRAYER   Music arrangement: Allen Percival

Our Fa-ther who is in hea-ven, *hal-lowed be Your name,* Your king-dom come, Your will be done, *hal-lowed be Your name.* *name.*

1 Our Father who is in heaven,
   hallowed be Your name,
   Your kingdom come, Your will be done,
   hallowed be Your name.

2 On earth as it is in heaven,
   hallowed be Your name,
   give us this day our daily bread,
   hallowed be Your name.

3 Forgive us all our trespasses,
   hallowed be Your name,
   as we forgive those who trespass against us,
   hallowed be Your name.

4 And lead us not into temptation,
   hallowed be Your name,
   but deliver us from all that is evil,
   hallowed be Your name.

5 For Yours is the kingdom, the power and the glory,
   hallowed be Your name,
   for ever and for ever and ever,
   hallowed be Your name.

6 Amen, amen, it shall be so,
   hallowed be Your name,
   amen, amen, it shall be so,
   hallowed be Your name.

193   # Our harvest day is over

Words: Eric A Thorn
Music: Roger Jones

Our har - vest day is o - ver for
yet an - oth - er year. The gifts we've brought to
Je - sus are now be - fore us here. Be -

1 Our harvest day is over for yet another year.
The gifts we've brought to Jesus are now before us here.
Before we go, again we raise our thanks to God above
for all that He provides us with from His great hand of love.

2 We thank God for providing fresh air for us to breathe.
Thirst-quenching water, also, to us He does bequeath.
Fresh fruit and daily bread as well are gifts from God above,
tinned foods, and eggs, and poultry come from our great God of love.

3 Our clothes and health come also from God's all-gracious hand;
our happiness is something which He again has planned.
But something more important still comes to us through God's love –
eternal life, through His dear Son; all praise to God above.
All praise to God above!

194   O sinner man

Words and music: Spiritual

O sinner man, where will you run to,
O sinner man, where will you run to,
O sinner man, where will you run to,
all on that day?

1 Run to the rocks, rocks, won't you hide me,
run to the rocks, rocks, won't you hide me,
run to the rocks, rocks, won't you hide me,
all on that day?
O sinner man . . .

2 Run to the sea, sea is a-boiling,
run to the sea, sea is a-boiling,
run to the sea, sea is a-boiling,
all on that day.
O sinner man . . .

3 Run to the Lord, Lord, won't you hide me,
run to the Lord, Lord, won't you hide me,
run to the Lord, Lord, won't you hide me,
all on that day?
O sinner man . . .

4 O sinner man, should bin a-praying,
O sinner man, should bin a-praying,
O sinner man, should bin a-praying,
all on that day.
O sinner man . . .

195   O when the saints go marching in

Words and music: Traditional
Music arranged David Wilson

1 O when the saints go marching in,
  O when the saints go marching in,
  O Lord, I want to be among the number
  when the saints go marching in!

2 O when they crown Him Lord of all,
  O when they crown Him Lord of all,
  O Lord, I want to be among the number
  when they crown Him Lord of all.

3 O when all knees bow at His name,
  O when all knees bow at His name,
  O Lord, I want to be among the number
  when all knees bow at His name.

4 O when they sing the Saviour's praise,
  O when they sing the Saviour's praise,
  O Lord, I want to be among the number
  when they sing the Saviour's praise.

5 O when the saints go marching in,
  O when the saints go marching in,
  O Lord, I want to be among the number
  when the saints go marching in!

196 Peace I give to you

Words and music: Graham Kendrick
Music arranged Christopher Norton

1 Peace I give to you, I give to you My peace;
   peace I give to you, I give to you My peace.
   Let it flow to one another,
   let it flow, let it flow;
   let it flow to one another,
   let it flow, let it flow.

2 Love I give to you, I give to you My love;
   love I give to you, I give to you My love.
   Let it flow . . .

3 Hope I give to you, I give to you My hope;
   hope I give to you, I give to you My hope.
   Let it flow . . .

4 Joy I give to you, I give to you My joy;
   joy I give to you, I give to you My joy.
   Let it flow . . .

197 Peter and James and John

Words and music: Anon
Music arranged Phil Burt

Pe-ter and James and John in a sail-boat, Pe-ter and James and John in a sail-boat,

Pe-ter and James and John in a sail-boat, out on the beau-ti-ful sea. be.

1 Peter and James and John in a sailboat,
   Peter and James and John in a sailboat,
   Peter and James and John in a sailboat,
   out on the beautiful sea.

2 They fished all night but they caught nothing,
   they fished all night but they caught nothing,
   they fished all night but they caught nothing,
   out on the beautiful sea.

3 Along came Jesus walking on the water,
   along came Jesus walking on the water,
   along came Jesus walking on the water,
   out on the beautiful sea.

4 He said, 'Throw your nets over on the other side!'
   He said, 'Throw your nets over on the other side!'
   He said, 'Throw your nets over on the other side!'
   out on the beautiful sea.

5 The nets were filled with great big fishes,
   the nets were filled with great big fishes,
   the nets were filled with great big fishes,
   out on the beautiful sea.

6 The lesson of this story is, 'listen to the Lord',
   the lesson of this story is, 'listen to the Lord',
   the lesson of this story is, 'listen to the Lord',
   wherever you may be.

198 Peter and John

Words and music: Anon
Music arranged Betty Pulkingham

Rollicking

Pe-ter and John went to pray,___ they met a lame man on the way; he asked for alms___ and held out his palms, and this is what Pe-ter did say:___ 'Sil-ver and gold have I none,___ but such as I have I give you. In the

199

Praise God

Words: Thomas Ken (1637–1711)
Music: Jimmy Owens

With movement

Praise God from whom all bless - ings flow; praise Him all crea - tures here be - low, praise Him a - bove, you hea - ven - ly hosts; praise Fa - ther, Son, and Ho - ly Ghost.

200   Praise Him on the trumpet

Words and music: John Kennett
Music arranged Christopher Norton

Rock 'n' roll

Praise Him on the trum - pet,_ the psalt - ery and harp;

praise Him on the tim - brel and the dance;___ praise Him

with stringed in - stru-ments too;___

praise Him on the loud cym-bals, praise Him on the loud

cym - bals; let ev - ery - thing that has breath praise the

Lord! Hal - le - lu - jah, praise the Lord;

hal - le - lu - jah, praise the Lord:_ let ev - ery-thing that has breath praise the

Lord!_____ breath praise the Lord!_____

8va bassa

201 Praise Him, praise Him, all you little children

Words: Anon, c1890
Music: E Rawdon Bailey (1859–1938)

He Is Love   10 6 10 6

1 Praise Him, praise Him, all you little children,
   God is love, God is love.
   Praise Him, praise Him, all you little children,
   God is love, God is love.

2 Love Him, love Him, all you little children,
   God is love, God is love.
   Love Him, love Him, all you little children,
   God is love, God is love.

3 Thank Him, thank Him, all you little children,
   God is love, God is love.
   Thank Him, thank Him, all you little children,
   God is love, God is love.

202 Praise Him, praise Him, praise Him in the morning

Words and music: Anon
Music arranged Phil Burt

1 Praise Him, praise Him,
  praise Him in the morning,
  praise Him in the noontime,
  praise Him, praise Him,
  praise Him as the sun goes down.

2 Thank Him . . .

3 Love Him . . .

4 Serve Him . . .

203 Praise Him, praise Him

PRAISE HIM! 12 10 12 10 11 10 12 10

Words: Frances van Alstyne (1820–1915)
(Fanny J Crosby), altered Horrobin/Leavers
Music: Chester G Allen (1838–78)

Praise Him, praise Him! Je-sus, our bless-èd Re-deem-er!

Sing, O earth— His won-der-ful love pro-claim!

Hail Him, hail Him! high-est arch-an-gels in glo-ry;

strength and hon-our give to his ho-ly name!

1 Praise Him, praise Him! Jesus, our blessèd Redeemer!
Sing, O earth – His wonderful love proclaim!
Hail Him, hail Him! highest archangels in glory;
strength and honour give to his holy name!
Like a shepherd, Jesus will guard His children,
in His arms He carries them all day long.
Praise Him, praise Him!
tell of His excellent greatness;
praise Him, praise Him
ever in joyful song!

2 Praise Him, praise Him! Jesus, our blessèd Redeemer!
For our sins He suffered, and bled, and died;
He – our rock, our hope of eternal salvation,
hail Him, hail Him! Jesus the crucified!
Sound His praises – Jesus who bore our sorrows,
love unbounded, wonderful, deep and strong.
Praise Him . . .

3 Praise Him, praise Him! Jesus, our blessèd Redeemer!
All in heaven, let their hosannas ring!
Jesus, Saviour, reigning for ever and ever:
crown Him, crown Him! Prophet, and Priest, and King!
Christ is coming, over the world victorious,
power and glory unto the Lord belong.
Praise Him . . .

204 Praise, my soul, the King of heaven

PRAISE, MY SOUL   87 87 87

Words: Henry Francis Lyte (1793–1847)
altered Horrobin/Leavers
Music: John Goss (1800–80)

Praise, my soul, the King of hea - ven; to His feet your wor - ship bring; ran - somed, healed, re - stored, for - giv - en, we do now His prais - es sing. Praise Him! Praise Him! Praise Him!

Praise Him! Praise the ev - er - last - ing King.

1 Praise, my soul, the King of heaven;
  to His feet your worship bring;
  ransomed, healed, restored, forgiven,
  we do now His praises sing.
    Praise Him! Praise Him!
    Praise Him! Praise Him!
  Praise the everlasting King.

2 Praise Him for His grace and favour
  to our fathers, in distress;
  praise Him, still the same for ever;
  merciful, He waits to bless.
    Praise Him! Praise Him!
    Praise Him! Praise Him!
  Glorious in His faithfulness.

3 Father-like He loves and spares us;
  well our weaknesses He knows;
  in His hands He gently bears us,
  rescues us from all our foes.
    Praise Him! Praise Him!
    Praise Him! Praise Him!
  Widely as His mercy flows.

4 Angels, help us to adore Him;
  you behold Him face to face;
  sun and moon, bow down before Him;
  dwellers all in time and space.
    Praise Him! Praise Him!
    Praise Him! Praise Him!
  Praise with us the God of grace.

205 Praise to the Lord our God

Words: Estelle White
Music: Anon

A four-part round

① F ... **C** ... **② F**

Praise to the Lord our_ God, let us sing to-geth-er, lift - ing our hearts and our

C ... **③ F** ... **C**

voi - ces____ to sing with joy and glad - ness.

④ F ... **C7** ... **F**

Come a-long, a - long, a-long and sing with Praise to the Lord our_

This song can be sung straight through with the accompaniment
or it can be sung unaccompanied as a four-part round.

Praise to the Lord our God, let us sing together,
lifting our hearts and our voices to sing
    with joy and gladness.
Come along, along, along and sing with praise.

206   Put your hand in the hand

This song has been withdrawn for copyright-related reasons

207 Remember all the people

TYROLESE   76 76 D

Words: Percy Dearmer (1867–1936)
Music: Tyrolese melody

Re - mem - ber all the peo - ple who live in far off lands, in strange and love - ly ci - ties, or roam the des - ert sands, or farm the moun - tain pas - tures, or till the end - less plains where

child-ren wade through rice___ fields and watch the cam - el trains.

1 Remember all the people
who live in far off lands,
in strange and lovely cities,
or roam the desert sands,
or farm the mountain pastures,
or till the endless plains
where children wade through rice fields
and watch the camel trains.

2 Some work in sultry forests
where apes swing to and fro,
some fish in mighty rivers,
some hunt across the snow.
Remember all God's children
who yet have never heard
the truth that comes from Jesus,
the glory of His word.

3 God bless the men and women
who serve Him oversea:
God raise up more to help them
to set the nations free,
till all the distant people
in every foreign place
shall understand His kingdom
and come into His grace.

208 Rejoice in the Lord always

Words: from Philippians 4
Music: traditional
arranged Evelyn Tanner

A four-part round

209 Ride on, ride on

WINCHESTER NEW   LM

Words: Henry Hart Milman (1791–1868)
in this version Jubilate Hymns
Music: adapted from a chorale in
Musicalisches HandBuch, Hamburg, 1690
arranged William Henry Havergal (1793–1870)

1 Ride on, ride on in majesty
   as all the crowds, 'Hosanna!' cry:
   through waving branches slowly ride,
   O Saviour, to be crucified.

2 Ride on, ride on in majesty,
   in lowly pomp ride on to die:
   O Christ, your triumph now begin
   with captured death and conquered sin!

3 Ride on, ride on in majesty –
   the angel armies of the sky
   look down with sad and wondering eyes
   to see the approaching sacrifice.

4 Ride on, ride on in majesty,
   the last and fiercest foe defy:
   the Father on His sapphire throne
   awaits His own anointed Son.

5 Ride on, ride on in majesty,
   in lowly pomp ride on to die:
   bow Your meek head to mortal pain,
   then take, O God, Your power and reign!

210

Rise and shine
(The arky, arky song)

Words and music: Traditional
Music arranged E J Hume

Rise_ and shine and give God His glo-ry, glo-ry, rise_ and shine and
give God His glo-ry, glo-ry, rise and shine and give God His glo-ry, glo-ry,
child-ren of the Lord. The Lord said to No-ah, 'There's
gon-na be a flood-y, flood-y.' Lord said to No-ah, 'There's

Rise and shine and give God His glory, glory,
rise and shine and give God His glory, glory,
rise and shine and give God His glory, glory,
children of the Lord.

1　The Lord said to Noah, 'There's gonna be a floody, floody.'
　Lord said to Noah, 'There's gonna be a floody, floody.
　Get those children out of the muddy, muddy,
　children of the Lord.'
　　Rise and shine . . .

2　The Lord told Noah to build Him an arky, arky,
　the Lord told Noah to build Him an arky, arky,
　build it out of gopher barky, barky,
　children of the Lord.
　　Rise and shine . . .

3　The animals, the animals, they came on by twosies, twosies,
　the animals, the animals, they came on by twosies, twosies,
　elephants and kangaroosies, 'roosies,
　children of the Lord.
　　Rise and shine . . .

4　It rained and poured for forty daysies, daysies,
　it rained and poured for forty daysies, daysies,
　almost drove those animals crazies, crazies,
　children of the Lord.
　　Rise and shine . . .

5　The sun came out and dried up the landy, landy,
　the sun came out and dried up the landy, landy.
　Everything was fine and dandy, dandy,
　children of the Lord.
　　Rise and shine . . .

211
Said Judas to Mary

Judas And Mary

Words and music: Sydney Carter

Said Ju-das to Ma-ry, 'Now what will you do with your oint-ment so rich and so rare?'_____ 'I'll pour it all o-ver the feet of the Lord and I'll wipe it a-way with my hair,' she said, 'I'll wipe it a-way with my hair.'_____ 'O - way.'_____

1 Said Judas to Mary, 'Now what will you do
with your ointment so rich and so rare?'
'I'll pour it all over the feet of the Lord
and I'll wipe it away with my hair,' she said,
'I'll wipe it away with my hair.'

2 'O Mary, O Mary, O think of the poor –
this ointment it could have been sold,
and think of the blankets and think of the bread
you could buy with the silver and gold,' he said,
'you could buy with the silver and gold.'

3 'Tomorrow, tomorrow I'll think of the poor,
tomorrow,' she said, 'not today;
for dearer than all of the poor of the world
is my love who is going away,' she said,
'is my love who is going away.'

4 Said Jesus to Mary, 'Your love is so deep,
today you may do as you will;
tomorrow, you say, I am going away,
but My body I leave with you still,' He said,
'My body I leave with you still.'

5 'The poor of the world are My body,' He said,
'to the end of the world they shall be;
the bread and the blankets you give to the poor
you'll find you have given to Me,' He said,
'you'll find you have given to Me.'

6 'My body will hang on the cross of the world
tomorrow,' He said, 'and today,
and Martha and Mary will find Me again
and wash all My sorrow away,' He said,
'and wash all my sorrow away.'

212   Search me, O God

This song has been withdrawn for copyright-related reasons

213   See, amid the winter snow

HUMILITY   77 77 with refrain

Words: Edward Caswall (1814–78)
altered Horrobin/Leavers
Music: John Goss (1800–80)

See, a-mid the win-ter snow, born for us on earth be-low;

see, the Son of God ap-pears, pro-mised from e-ter-nal years.

Hail, O ev-er-bless-èd morn! Hail, re-demp-tion's hap-py dawn!

Sing through all Je - ru - sa-lem, Christ is born in Beth - le - hem!

1 See, amid the winter snow,
born for us on earth below;
see, the Son of God appears,
promised from eternal years.
Hail, O ever-blessèd morn!
Hail, redemption's happy dawn!
Sing through all Jerusalem,
Christ is born in Bethlehem!

2 Low within a manger lies
He who built the starry skies,
He who, throned in heaven's height
reigns in power and glorious light.
Hail, O ever-blessèd morn . . .

3 Say, you humble shepherds, say,
what's your joyful news today?
Tell us why you left your sheep
on the lonely mountain steep:
Hail, O ever-blessèd morn . . .

4 'As we watched at dead of night,
all around us shone a light:
angels singing, "Peace on earth!"
told us of a Saviour's birth.'
Hail, O ever-blessèd morn . . .

5 Sacred baby, King most dear,
what a tender love was here!
Down He came from glory high
in a manger there to lie.
Hail, O ever-blessèd morn . . .

6 Holy Saviour, born on earth,
teach us by Your lowly birth;
grant that we may ever be
taught by such humility.
Hail, O ever-blessèd morn . . .

214   See Him lying on a bed of straw

Calypso Carol   Irregular

Words and music: Michael Perry (1942–96)
Music arranged Stephen Coates

See Him ly-ing on a bed of straw:_ a draugh-ty sta-ble with an o-pen door; Ma-ry cra-dl-ing the babe she bore — the Prince of glo-ry is His name.

O now car-ry me to Beth-le-hem___ to

1 See Him lying on a bed of straw:
  a draughty stable with an open door;
  Mary cradling the babe she bore –
  the Prince of glory is His name.
  O now carry me to Bethlehem
  to see the Lord appear to men –
  just as poor as was the stable then,
  the Prince of glory when He came.

2 Star of silver, sweep across the skies,
  show where Jesus in the manger lies;
  shepherds, swiftly from your stupor rise
  to see the Saviour of the world!
  O now carry . . .

3 Angels, sing the song that you began,
  bring God's glory to the heart of man;
  sing that Bethl'em's little baby can
  be salvation to the soul.
  O now carry . . .

4 Mine are riches, from Your poverty,
  from Your innocence, eternity;
  mine forgiveness by Your death for me,
  child of sorrow for my joy.
  O now carry . . .

215   Seek ye first

Words and music: Karen Lafferty
Music arranged Roland Fudge

Rich and broad

Seek ye first the kingdom of God, and His righteousness, and all these things shall be added unto you. Alleluia, alleluia.

1 Seek ye first the kingdom of God,
   and His righteousness,
   and all these things shall be added unto you.
   Allelu, alleluia.
   Seek ye first . . .

2 Man shall not live by bread alone,
   but by every word
   that proceeds from the mouth of God.
   Allelu, alleluia.
   Man shall not . . .

3 Ask and it shall be given unto you,
   seek and ye shall find;
   knock and the door shall be opened up to you.
   Allelu, alleluia.
   Ask and it shall . . .

216 Saviour of the world

Begin slowly – with increasing
excitement in verses 2 and 3

Words and music: Greg Leavers
Music arranged Phil Burt

Sav-iour of the world, thank You for dy-ing on the cross. All

praise to You, our ris-en Lord, hal-le-lu-jah! Je-sus.

In the gar-den of Geth-se-ma-ne Je-sus knelt and prayed;

for He knew the time was near when He would be be-trayed.

Saviour of the world,
thank You for dying on the cross.
All praise to You, our risen Lord,
hallelujah! Jesus.

1 In the garden of Gethsemane Jesus knelt and prayed;
   for He knew the time was near when He would be betrayed.
   God gave Him the strength to cope with all that people did to hurt Him;
   soldiers laughed and forced a crown of thorns upon His head.
       Saviour of the world . . .

2 On a cross outside the city they nailed Jesus high;
   innocent, but still He suffered as they watched Him die.
   Nothing that the soldiers did could make Him lose control, for Jesus
   knew the time to die, then, 'It is finished!' was His cry.
       Saviour of the world . . .

3 Three days later by God's power He rose up from the dead,
   for the tomb could not hold Jesus, it was as He'd said;
   victor over sin and death, He conquered Satan's power; so let us
   celebrate that Jesus is alive for evermore.
       Saviour of the world . . .

217   Shalōm, my friend

Words: Michael Lehr
Music: Michael Metcalf

Shalōm, my friend, shalōm, my friend,
shalōm, shalōm.
Till we meet again, till we meet again,
shalōm, shalōm.

218   Sing we the King

THE GLORY SONG   10 10 10 10 with refrain

Words: Charles Silvester Horne (1865–1914)
altered Horrobin/Leavers
Music: Charles Hutchinson Gabriel (1856–1932)

1 Sing we the King who is coming to reign,
glory to Jesus, the Lamb that was slain;
life and salvation His coming shall bring,
joy to the nations when Jesus is King.
Come let us sing: praise to our King.
Jesus our King, Jesus our King:
this is our song, who to Jesus belong:
glory to Jesus, to Jesus our King.

2 All men who dwell in His marvellous light,
races long severed His love shall unite;
justice and truth from His sceptre shall spring,
wrong shall be ended when Jesus is King.
Come let us sing . . .

3 All shall be well in His kingdom of peace,
freedom and wisdom and love shall not cease;
foe shall be friend when His triumph we sing,
sword shall be sickle when Jesus is King.
Come let us sing . . .

4 Souls shall be saved from the burden of sin;
doubt shall not darken his witness within;
hell has no terrors, and death has no sting;
love is victorious, when Jesus is King.
Come let us sing . . .

5 Kingdom of Christ, for your coming we pray;
hasten, O Father, the dawn of the day
when this new song Your creation shall sing,
Satan is conquered and Jesus is King.
Come let us sing . . .

219 Silent night

STILLE NACHT   Irregular

Words: Joseph Mohr (1792–1848)
tr. Stopford Augustus Brooke (1832–1916)
Music: Franz Gruber (1787–1863)

1 Silent night, holy night!
   Sleeps the world; hid from sight,
   Mary and Joseph in stable bare
   watched o'er the child belovèd and fair
      sleeping in heavenly rest,
      sleeping in heavenly rest.

2 Silent night, holy night!
   Shepherds first saw the light,
   heard resounding clear and long,
   far and near, the angel-song:
      'Christ the Redeemer is here,
      Christ the Redeemer is here.'

3 Silent night, holy night!
   Son of God, O how bright
   love is smiling from Your face!
   Strikes for us now the hour of grace,
      Saviour, since You are born,
      Saviour, since You are born.

220 Someone's brought a loaf of bread

Skip To My Lou

Words: Anon
Music: Traditional
Music arranged Phil Burt

1 Someone's brought a loaf of bread,
   someone's brought a loaf of bread,
   someone's brought a loaf of bread
   to put on the harvest table.

2 Someone's brought a jar of jam,
   someone's brought a jar of jam,
   someone's brought a jar of jam
   to put on the harvest table.

Other verses may be added

Last verse:

   Thank You, Lord, for all Your gifts,
   thank You, Lord, for all Your gifts,
   thank You, Lord, for all Your gifts
   to put on the harvest table.

221   Soon, and very soon

Words and music: Andraé Crouch

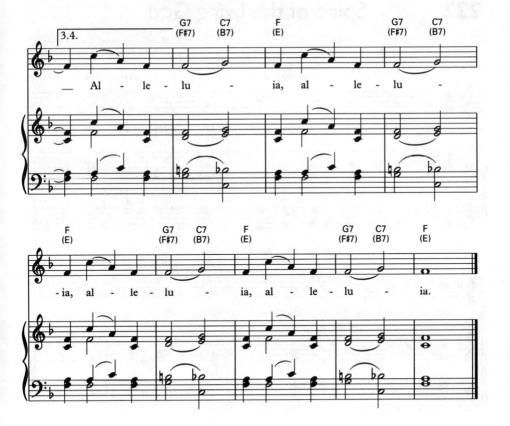

Al - le - lu - ia, al - le - lu -
-ia, al - le - lu - ia, al - le - lu - ia.

G7 (F#7) C7 (B7) F (E) G7 (F#7) C7 (B7)
F (E) G7 (F#7) C7 (B7) F (E) G7 (F#7) C7 (B7) F (E)

1 Soon, and very soon,
  we are going to see the King;
  soon, and very soon,
  we are going to see the King;
  soon, and very soon,
  we are going to see the King;
    alleluia, alleluia,
    we're going to see the King!

2 No more crying there . . .
    alleluia . . .

3 No more dying there . . .
    alleluia . . .
    Alleluia, alleluia, alleluia, alleluia.

4 Soon and very soon . . .
    alleluia . . .
    Alleluia, alleluia, alleluia, alleluia.

222 Spirit of the living God

Words and music: Daniel Iverson
Music arranged W G Hathaway

Spi - rit of the liv - ing God, fall a-fresh on me;

Spi - rit of the liv - ing God, fall a-fresh on me;

break me, melt me, mould me, fill me;

Spi - rit of the liv - ing God, fall a-fresh on me.

223 Surely goodness and mercy

Words and music: Alfred B Smith
and John W Peterson

good - ness and mer - cy shall fol - low___
me all the days, all the days of my life.___

Surely goodness and mercy shall follow me
all the days, all the days of my life;
surely goodness and mercy shall follow me
all the days, all the days of my life.
And I shall dwell in the house of the Lord forever,
and I shall feast at the table spread for me.
Surely goodness and mercy shall follow me
all the days, all the days of my life.

224 Stand up and bless the Lord

Words and music: Andy Silver

Stand up and bless the Lord your God, stand up and
bless the Lord; His name is ex-alt-ed a-bove all names; stand up
and bless the Lord. For our God is good to us,
al-ways rea-dy to for-give;

225   Stand up, clap hands

Words: Roger Dyer
Music: Alan Forest

I look a-round and then I think, 'Oh, my!' The world is such a

won-der-ful place, and all be-cause of the good Lord's grace. *Stand*

Stand up, clap hands, shout, 'Thank You, Lord,
thank You for the world I'm in.'
Stand up, clap hands, shout, 'Thank You, Lord,
for happiness and peace within.'

1 I look around and the sun's in the sky,
  I look around and then I think, 'Oh, my!'
  The world is such a wonderful place,
  and all because of the good Lord's grace.
  Stand up, clap hands . . .

2 I look around and the creatures I see,
  I look around and it amazes me
  that every fox and bird and hare
  must fit in a special place somewhere.
  Stand up, clap hands . . .

3 I look around at all the joy I've had,
  I look around and then it makes me glad
  that I can offer thanks and praise
  to Him who guides me through my days.
  Stand up, clap hands . . .

226 Stand up! stand up for Jesus

MORNING LIGHT 76 76 D

Words: George Duffield (1818–88)
in this version Jubilate Hymns
Music: George James Webb (1803–87)

Stand up! stand up for Jesus! you sol-diers of the cross,

lift high His roy-al ban-ner; it must not suf-fer loss.

From vic-tory un-to vic-tory His ar-my He shall lead,___

till ev-il is de-feat-ed and Christ is Lord in-deed.

1 Stand up! stand up for Jesus!
  you soldiers of the cross,
  lift high His royal banner;
  it must not suffer loss.
  From victory unto victory
  His army He shall lead,
  till evil is defeated
  and Christ is Lord indeed.

2 Stand up! stand up for Jesus!
  the trumpet-call obey;
  then join the mighty conflict
  in this His glorious day.
  Be strong in faith and serve Him
  against unnumbered foes;
  let courage rise with danger,
  and strength to strength oppose.

3 Stand up! stand up for Jesus!
  stand in His power alone;
  for human might will fail you,
  you dare not trust your own.
  Put on the gospel armour,
  keep watch with constant prayer;
  where duty calls, or danger,
  be never failing there.

4 Stand up! stand up for Jesus!
  the fight will not be long;
  this day the noise of battle,
  the next the victor's song.
  To everyone who conquers
  a crown of life shall be;
  we with the King of glory
  shall reign eternally.

227 Tell me the old, old story

TELL ME   76 76 D with refrain

Words: Arabella Catherine Hankey (1834–1911) altd.
Music: William Howard Doane (1832–1915)

Tell me the old, old sto - ry of un-seen things a - bove, of
Je - sus and His glo - ry, of Je - sus and His love.

Tell me the sto - ry sim - ply, as to a lit - tle child, for
I am weak and wea - ry, and help - less and de - filed.

1 Tell me the old, old story
of unseen things above,
of Jesus and His glory,
of Jesus and His love.
Tell me the story simply,
as to a little child,
for I am weak and weary,
and helpless and defiled.
Tell me the old, old story,
tell me the old, old story,
tell me the old, old story
of Jesus and His love.

2 Tell me the story slowly,
that I may take it in –
that wonderful redemption,
God's remedy for sin.
Tell me the story often,
for I forget so soon:
the early dew of morning
has passed away at noon.
Tell me the old . . .

3 Tell me the story softly,
with earnest tones and grave;
Remember! I'm the sinner
whom Jesus came to save.
Tell me the story always,
if you would really be,
in any time of trouble,
a comforter to me.
Tell me the old . . .

4 Tell me the same old story,
when you have cause to fear
that this world's empty glory
is costing me too dear.
Yes, and when that world's glory
is dawning on my soul,
tell me the old, old story;
'Christ Jesus makes you whole.'
Tell me the old . . .

228 Tell me the stories of Jesus

STORIES OF JESUS   84 84 54 54

Words: William Henry Parker (1845–1929)
verse 6 by Hugh Martin (1890–1964)
adapted Horrobin / Leavers
Music: Frederick A Challinor (1866–1952)

Tell me the sto-ries of Je-sus I love to hear;___ things I would ask Him to tell me if He were here;___ scenes by the way-side, tales of the sea,___ sto-ries of Je-sus, tell them to me.___

1 Tell me the stories of Jesus
  I love to hear;
  things I would ask Him to tell me
  if He were here;
  scenes by the wayside,
  tales of the sea,
  stories of Jesus,
  tell them to me.

2 First let me hear how the children
  stood round His knee;
  that I may know of His blessing
  resting on me;
  words full of kindness,
  deeds full of grace,
  signs of the love found
  in Jesus' face.

3 Tell me, in words full of wonder,
  how rolled the sea,
  tossing the boat in a tempest
  on Galilee.
  Jesus then doing
  His Father's will,
  ended the storm saying,
  'Peace, peace, be still.'

4 Into the city I'd follow
  the children's band,
  waving a branch of the palm-tree
  high in my hand;
  worshipping Jesus,
  yes, I would sing
  loudest hosannas,
  for He is King!

5 Show me that scene in the garden,
  of bitter pain;
  and of the cross where my Saviour
  for me was slain;
  and, through the sadness,
  help me to see
  how Jesus suffered
  for love of me.

6 Gladly I'd hear of His rising
  out of the grave,
  living and strong and triumphant,
  mighty to save:
  and how He sends us
  all men to bring
  stories of Jesus,
  Jesus, their King.

229(i)

Tell out, my soul

Go Forth   10 10 10 10

Words: Timothy Dudley-Smith
Music: Michael Baughen

With a swing

Tell out, my soul, the great-ness of the Lord;
un - num-bered bless - ings give my spi - rit voice;
ten - der to me the pro-mise of His word; in
God my Sav - iour shall my heart re - joice.

1 Tell out, my soul, the greatness of the Lord;
   unnumbered blessings give my spirit voice;
   tender to me the promise of His word;
   in God my Saviour shall my heart rejoice.

2 Tell out, my soul, the greatness of His name!
   Make known His might, the deeds His arm has done;
   His mercy sure, from age to age the same;
   His holy name – the Lord, the Mighty One.

3 Tell out, my soul, the greatness of His might!
   powers and dominions lay their glory by;
   proud hearts and stubborn wills are put to flight,
   the hungry fed, the humble lifted high.

4 Tell out, my soul, the glories of His word!
   firm is His promise, and His mercy sure:
   tell out, my soul, the greatness of the Lord
   to children's children and for evermore!

229(ii)

Tell out, my soul

WOODLANDS   10 10 10 10

Words: Timothy Dudley-Smith
Music: Walter Greatorex (1877–1949)

Tell out, my soul, the great-ness of the Lord;
un-num-bered bless-ings give my spi-rit voice;
ten-der to me the pro-mise of His word;
in God my Sav-iour shall my heart re-joice.

1 Tell out, my soul, the greatness of the Lord;
  unnumbered blessings give my spirit voice;
  tender to me the promise of His word;
  in God my Saviour shall my heart rejoice.

2 Tell out, my soul, the greatness of His name!
  Make known His might, the deeds His arm has done;
  His mercy sure, from age to age the same;
  His holy name – the Lord, the Mighty One.

3 Tell out, my soul, the greatness of His might!
  powers and dominions lay their glory by;
  proud hearts and stubborn wills are put to flight,
  the hungry fed, the humble lifted high.

4 Tell out, my soul, the glories of His word!
  firm is His promise, and His mercy sure:
  tell out, my soul, the greatness of the Lord
  to children's children and for evermore!

230

Thank You
(simplified version)

Words and music: M G Schneider
tr. and adpt. S Lonsdale and Michael Baughen

1 Thank You for every new good morning,
   thank You for every fresh new day,
   thank You that I may cast my burdens
   wholly on to You.

2 Thank You for every friend I have, Lord,
   thank You for everyone I know,
   thank You when I can feel forgiveness
   to my greatest foe.

3 Thank You for leisure and employment,
   thank You for every heartfelt joy,
   thank You for all that makes me happy
   and for melody.

4 Thank You for every shade and sorrow,
   thank You for comfort in Your word,
   thank You that I am guided by You
   everywhere I go.

5 Thank You for grace to know Your gospel,
   thank You for all Your Spirit's power,
   thank You for Your unfailing love
   which reaches far and near.

6 Thank You for free and full salvation,
   thank You for grace to hold it fast.
   Thank You, O Lord, I want to thank You
   that I'm free to thank!
   Thank You, O Lord, I want to thank You
   that I'm free to thank!

Thank You
(full version)

Words and music: M G Schneider
tr. and adpt. S Lonsdale and Michael Baughen

1 Thank You___ for ev-ery new good morn-ing, thank You___ for ev-ery fresh new day,
thank You___ that I may cast my bur-dens whol-ly on to You.

2 Thank You___ for ev-ery friend I have, Lord, thank You___ for ev-ery-one I know,
thank You___ when I can feel for-give-ness to my great-est foe.

231 Thank You, thank You, Jesus

Words and music: Anon
Music arranged Betty Pulkingham

Thank You, thank You, Je-sus, thank You, thank You, Je-sus,
thank You, thank You, Je-sus, in my heart.
Thank You, thank You, Je-sus, O thank You, thank You, Je-sus,
thank You, thank You, Je-sus, in my heart.

1 Thank You, thank You, Jesus,
   thank You, thank You, Jesus,
   thank You, thank You, Jesus, in my heart.
   Thank You, thank You, Jesus,
   O thank You, thank You, Jesus,
   thank You, thank You, Jesus, in my heart.

2 You can't make me doubt Him,
   you can't make me doubt Him,
   you can't make me doubt Him in my heart.
   You can't make me doubt Him,
   O you can't make me doubt Him,
   thank You, thank You, Jesus, in my heart.

3 I can't live without Him,
   I can't live without Him,
   I can't live without Him in my heart.
   I can't live without Him,
   O I can't live without Him,
   thank You, thank You, Jesus, in my heart.

4 Glory, hallelujah,
   glory, hallelujah,
   glory, hallelujah in my heart!
   Glory, hallelujah,
   O glory, hallelujah,
   thank You, thank You, Jesus, in my heart.

232 Thank You, Lord, for this fine day

Words and music: Diane Davis Andrew

Thank___ You, Lord, for this fine day, thank___ You, Lord, for this fine day, thank___ You, Lord, for this fine day, right___ where we are. Al - le - lu - ia, praise the Lord! Al - le - lu - ia, praise the Lord! Al -

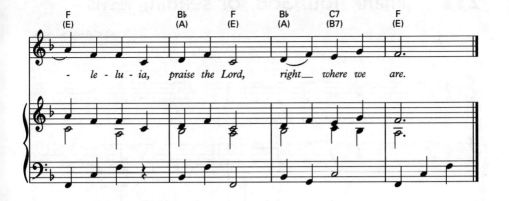

- le - lu - ia, praise the Lord, right___ where we are.

1 Thank You, Lord, for this fine day,
  thank You, Lord, for this fine day,
  thank You, Lord, for this fine day,
  right where we are.
    Alleluia, praise the Lord!
    Alleluia, praise the Lord!
    Alleluia, praise the Lord,
    right where we are.

2 Thank You, Lord, for loving us,
  thank You, Lord, for loving us,
  thank You, Lord, for loving us,
  right where we are.
    Alleluia . . .

3 Thank You, Lord, for giving us peace,
  thank You, Lord, for giving us peace,
  thank You, Lord, for giving us peace,
  right where we are.
    Alleluia . . .

4 Thank You, Lord, for setting us free,
  thank You, Lord, for setting us free,
  thank You, Lord, for setting us free,
  right where we are.
    Alleluia . . .

233 Thank You, God, for sending Jesus

Words and music: Anon
Music arranged Phil Burt

Thank You, God, for sending Jesus;
thank You, Jesus, that You came;
Holy Spirit, won't You tell us
more about His wondrous name?

234   The best book to read

Words and music: P Bilhorn (1865–1936)

The best book to read is the Bi - ble, the best book to read is the Bi - ble; if you read it ev-ery day it will help you on your way, Oh, the best book to read is the Bi - ble.

1 The best book to read is the Bible,
the best book to read is the Bible;
if you read it every day
it will help you on your way,
Oh, the best book to read is the Bible.

2 The best friend to have is Jesus,
the best friend to have is Jesus;
He will hear me when I call,
He will keep me lest I fall,
Oh, the best friend to have is Jesus.

3 The best thing to do is to trust Him,
the best thing to do is to trust Him;
and if you on Him depend,
He will keep you to the end;
Oh, the best thing to do is to trust Him.

235

Thank You, Jesus

Words and music: Alison Huntley
Music arranged Roland Fudge

Thank You, Je-sus,_____ thank You, Je-sus,_____ _ thank You, Lord,_____ for lov-ing me._____ Thank You, Je-sus,_____ thank You, Je-sus, thank You, Lord,_____ for lov-ing me._____ _

1 Thank You, Jesus, thank You, Jesus,
   thank You, Lord, for loving me.
   Thank You, Jesus . . .

2 You went to Calvary, there You died for me,
   thank You, Lord, for loving me.
   You went to Calvary . . .

3 You rose up from the grave, to me new life You gave,
   thank You, Lord, for loving me.
   You rose up from the grave . . .

4 You're coming back again, and we with You shall reign,
   thank You, Lord, for loving me.
   You're coming back again . . .

236   The day You gave us

St Clement   98 98

Words: John Ellerton (1826–93)
in this version Jubilate Hymns
Music: Clement Cotterill Scholefield (1839–1904)

The day You gave us, Lord, is end-ed, the sun is sink-ing in the west; to You our morn-ing hymns as-cend-ed, Your praise shall sanc-ti-fy our rest.

1 The day You gave us, Lord, is ended,
   the sun is sinking in the west;
   to You our morning hymns ascended,
   Your praise shall sanctify our rest.

2 We thank You that Your Church, unsleeping
   while earth rolls onward into light,
   through all the world her watch is keeping,
   and rests not now by day or night.

3 As to each continent and island
   the dawn proclaims another day,
   the voice of prayer is never silent,
   nor dies the sound of praise away.

4 The sun, that bids us rest, is waking
   Your church beneath the western sky;
   fresh voices hour by hour are making
   Your mighty deeds resound on high.

5 So be it, Lord, Your throne shall never,
   like earth's proud empires, pass away;
   Your kingdom stands, and grows for ever,
   until there dawns that glorious day.

237 The fields are white

Words and music: Michael Baughen

The fields are white un-to har-vest time, look up and
see, the fields are white un-to har-vest time, look
up and see! *Pray to the*
Lord of the har-vest, Christ says, 'Pray!'

Pray to the Lord for the work-ers which we need— in this day. The day.

1 The fields are white unto harvest time,
   look up and see,
   the fields are white unto harvest time,
   look up and see!
      Pray to the Lord of the harvest,
      Christ says, 'Pray!'
      Pray to the Lord for the workers
      which we need in this day.

2 The harvest truly is fit to reap
   but workers few,
   the harvest truly is fit to reap
   but workers few.
      Pray to the Lord . . .

3 Who else will go into all the world
   to preach the word?
   Who else will go into all the world
   to preach the word?
      Pray to the Lord . . .

4 The Lord's return may be very soon,
   the time is short,
   the Lord's return may be very soon,
   the time is short!
      Pray to the Lord . . .

238   The first nowell

THE FIRST NOWELL   Irregular

Words: Anon (17th century)
in this version Jubilate Hymns
Music: English traditional carol
arranged David Willcocks

The_ first_____ no - well the_ an - gel did say, was to Beth - le - hem's shep-herds in fields as they lay; in_ fields_____ where they lay_ keep - ing their sheep on a cold win - ter's night_ that was_ so deep:

No - well,_____ no - well, no - well, no - well, born is the King_____ of Is - ra - el!

1 The first nowell the angel did say,
   was to Bethlehem's shepherds in fields as they lay;
   in fields where they lay keeping their sheep
   on a cold winter's night that was so deep:
       Nowell, nowell, nowell, nowell,
       born is the King of Israel!

2 Then wise men from a country far
   looked up and saw a guiding star;
   they travelled on by night and day
   to reach the place where Jesus lay:
       Nowell, nowell . . .

3 At Bethlehem they entered in,
   on bended knee they worshipped Him;
   they offered there in His presence
   their gold and myrrh and frankincense:
       Nowell, nowell . . .

4 Then let us all with one accord
   sing praises to our heavenly Lord;
   for Christ has our salvation wrought
   and with His blood mankind has bought:
       Nowell, nowell . . .

239   The greatest thing

Words and music: Mark Pendergrass

The great-est thing___ in all my life is know-ing You;___ the great-est thing___ in all my life is know-ing You;___ I want to know You

more; I want to know You more. The

great-est thing___ in all my life is know - ing You.

1 The greatest thing in all my life
   is knowing You;
 the greatest thing in all my life
   is knowing You;
 I want to know You more;
   I want to know You more.
 The greatest thing in all my life
   is knowing You.

2 The greatest thing in all my life
   is loving You;
 the greatest thing in all my life
   is loving You;
 I want to love You more;
   I want to love You more.
 The greatest thing in all my life
   is loving You.

3 The greatest thing in all my life
   is serving You;
 the greatest thing in all my life
   is serving You;
 I want to serve You more;
   I want to serve You more.
 The greatest thing in all my life
   is serving You.

240 The joy of the Lord is my strength

Words and music: Alliene Vale
Music arranged Norman Warren

1 The joy of the Lord is my strength,
the joy of the Lord is my strength,
the joy of the Lord is my strength,
the joy of the Lord is my strength.

2 If you want joy you must sing for it,
if you want joy you must sing for it,
if you want joy you must sing for it,
the joy of the Lord is my strength.

3 If you want joy you must shout for it,
if you want joy you must shout for it,
if you want joy you must shout for it,
the joy of the Lord is my strength.

4 If you want joy you must jump for it,
if you want joy you must jump for it,
if you want joy you must jump for it,
the joy of the Lord is my strength.

241 The King of love

DOMINUS REGIT ME   87 87

Words: Henry Williams Baker (1821–77)
in this version Jubilate Hymns
Music: John Bacchus Dykes (1823–76)

The King of love my shep-herd is, whose good-ness fails me ne - ver; I no-thing lack if I am His and He is mine for ev - er.

1 The King of love my shepherd is,
whose goodness fails me never;
I nothing lack if I am His
and He is mine for ever.

2 Where streams of living water flow,
a ransomed soul, He leads me;
and where the fertile pastures grow
with food from heaven feeds me.

3 Perverse and foolish I have strayed;
but in His love He sought me,
and on His shoulder gently laid,
and home, rejoicing, brought me.

4 In death's dark vale I fear no ill
with You, dear Lord, beside me;
Your rod and staff my comfort still,
Your cross before to guide me.

5 You spread a banquet in my sight
of love beyond all knowing,
and O the gladness and delight
from Your pure chalice flowing!

6 And so through all the length of days
Your goodness fails me never;
Good Shepherd, may I sing Your praise
within Your house for ever!

242   The Lord has need of me

Words and music: Cecil J Allen (1886–1973)
Music arranged Phil Burt

The Lord has need of me, His sol - dier I will
be; He gave Him - self my life to win, and
so I mean to fol - low Him, and serve Him faith - ful -
- ly. So al - though the fight be fierce and long, I'll

The Lord has need of me,
His soldier I will be;
He gave Himself my life to win,
and so I mean to follow Him,
and serve Him faithfully.
So although the fight be fierce and long,
I'll carry on: He makes me strong;
and then one day His face I'll see,
and O the joy when He says to me,
'Well done, my brave crusader!'

243 The Lord's my shepherd

CRIMOND CM

Words: Francis Rous (1579–1659)
revised for *Scottish Psalter*, 1650
altered Horrobin/Leavers
Music: melody by Jessie Seymour Irvine (1836–87)

The Lord's my shep - herd, I'll not want;
He makes me down to lie
in pas - tures green; He's lead - ing me

the   qui - et   wa - ters   by.

1 The Lord's my shepherd, I'll not want;
   He makes me down to lie
   in pastures green; He's leading me
   the quiet waters by.

2 My soul He does restore again,
   and me to walk does make
   within the paths of righteousness,
   e'en for His own name's sake.

3 Yes, though I walk through death's dark vale,
   yet will I fear no ill;
   for You are with me, and Your rod
   and staff me comfort still.

4 My table You have furnishèd
   in presence of my foes;
   my head You now with oil anoint,
   and my cup overflows.

5 Goodness and mercy all my life
   shall surely follow me;
   and in God's house for evermore
   my dwelling-place shall be.

244   The Lord is my shepherd

A two-part round

Words: from Psalm 23
Music: Anon
arranged Andy Silver

The Lord is my___ shep-herd, I'll trust in Him al-ways. He leads me by still wa-ters, I'll trust in Him al-ways. Al - ways, al - ways, I'll trust in Him al-ways. Al - ways, al - ways, I'll trust in Him al - ways.

245 There is a green hill

HORSLEY CM

Words: Cecil Frances Alexander (1818–95)
Music: William Horsley (1774–1858)

1 There is a green hill far away
   outside a city wall,
   where the dear Lord was crucified,
   who died to save us all.

2 We may not know, we cannot tell
   what pains He had to bear;
   but we believe it was for us
   He hung and suffered there.

3 He died that we might be forgiven,
   He died to make us good,
   that we might go at last to heaven,
   saved by His precious blood.

4 There was no other good enough
   to pay the price of sin;
   He only could unlock the gate
   of heaven, and let us in.

5 O dearly, dearly has He loved,
   and we must love Him too,
   and trust in His redeeming blood,
   and try His works to do.

246 There are hundreds of sparrows

Words: J Gowans
Music: J Larsson

There are hun - dreds of spar - rows, thou - sands, mil - lions, they're
two a pen - ny, far too ma - ny there must be; there are
hun - dreds and thou - sands, mil - lions of spar - rows, but
God knows ev - ery one and God knows me.

but God knows ev - ery one and God knows me.

1 There are hundreds of sparrows, thousands, millions,
   they're two a penny, far too many there must be;
   there are hundreds and thousands, millions of sparrows,
   but God knows every one and God knows me.

2 There are hundreds of flowers, thousands, millions,
   and flowers fair the meadows wear for all to see;
   there are hundreds and thousands, millions of flowers,
   but God knows every one and God knows me.

3 There are hundreds of planets, thousands, millions,
   way out in space each has a place by God's decree;
   there are hundreds and thousands, millions of planets,
   but God knows every one and God knows me.

4 There are hundreds of children, thousands, millions,
   and yet their names are written on God's memory;
   there are hundreds and thousands, millions of children,
   but God knows every one and God knows me,
   but God knows every one and God knows me.

247   There's a song of exaltation

Words and music: Anon
Music arranged Andy Silver

ALL There's a song of ex-al-ta-tion full of joy and in-spi-ra-tion ech-oed down through all cre-a-tion, sing hal-le-lu-jah, sing.

PART 1 Sing hal-le-lu-jah, PART 2 sing hal-le-lu-jah,

ALL   There's a song of exaltation
full of joy and inspiration
echoed down through all creation,
sing hallelujah, sing.

PART 1   Sing hallelujah,
PART 2   sing hallelujah,
PART 1   sing hallelujah,
PART 2   sing hallelujah,
PART 1   sing hallelujah,
PART 2   sing hallelujah,
ALL   sing hallelujah, sing.

248 There's a way back

Words and music: E H Swinstead (d1976)

There's a way back to God from the dark paths of sin; there's a door that is o-pen and you may go in: at Cal-va-ry's cross is where you be-gin, when you come as a sin-ner to Je - sus.

There's a way back to God
  from the dark paths of sin;
there's a door that is open
  and you may go in:
at Calvary's cross is where you begin,
when you come as a sinner to Jesus.

249   There's new life in Jesus

Words and music: Anon
Music arranged Andy Silver

1 There's new life in Jesus, lift up your heart,
   there's new life in Jesus, lift up your heart.
   Lift up your heart, lift up your heart,
   there's new life in Jesus, lift up your heart.

2 There is healing in His love, lift up your heart,
   there is healing in His love, lift up your heart.
   Lift up your heart ...

3 There is joy in serving Him, lift up your heart,
   there is joy in serving Him, lift up your heart.
   Lift up your heart ...

250   The steadfast love

Words and music: Edith McNeill

The stead-fast love of the Lord ne-ver ceas - es, His mer-cies ne - ver_ come to an end; they are new ev-ery morn-ing, new ev - ery morn-ing: great is Your faith - ful -

* This item appears in the key of E♭ in the first edition of *Junior Praise*.

The guitar chords and piano arrangement are not designed to be used together.

Words and music: © 1974 Celebration, administered in Europe and the British
Commonwealth (excl Canada, Australasia and Africa) by Kingsway's Thankyou Music,
PO Box 75, Eastbourne, East Sussex BN23 6NW, UK. Used by permission

-ness, O Lord, great is Your faith - ful - ness.

The steadfast love of the Lord never ceases,
His mercies never come to an end;
they are new every morning, new every morning:
great is Your faithfulness, O Lord,
great is Your faithfulness.

251   The virgin Mary had a baby boy

Words: Anon
Music: melody from the Edric Connor Collection
arranged D J Crawshaw

The vir-gin Ma-ry had a baby boy,___ the vir-gin Ma-ry had a baby boy,___ the vir-gin Ma-ry had a baby boy___ and they said that His name was Je-sus.

He come___ from the glo - ry,

1 The virgin Mary had a baby boy,
the virgin Mary had a baby boy,
the virgin Mary had a baby boy
and they said that His name was Jesus.
He come from the glory,
He come from the glorious kingdom,
He come from the glory,
He come from the glorious kingdom.
O yes, believer,
O yes, believer,
He come from the glory,
He come from the glorious kingdom.

2 The angels sang when the baby was born,
the angels sang when the baby was born,
the angels sang when the baby was born,
and proclaimed Him the Saviour Jesus.
He come from the glory . . .

3 The wise men saw where the baby was born,
the wise men saw where the baby was born,
the wise men saw where the baby was born,
and they saw that His name was Jesus.
He come from the glory . . .

The wise man built his house upon the rock

Words and music: Anon
Music arranged Phil Burt

The wise man built his house up-on the rock,___ the
wise man built his house up - on the rock,___ the
wise man built his house up-on the rock and the rain came tum - bling
down.___ And the rain came down and the floods came up,___ the

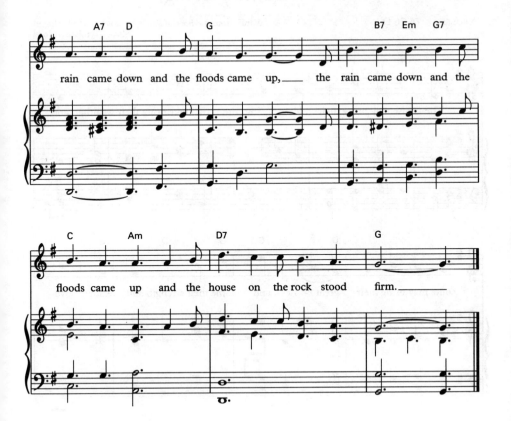

rain came down and the floods came up,___ the rain came down and the floods came up and the house on the rock stood firm.___

1 The wise man built his house upon the rock,
   the wise man built his house upon the rock,
   the wise man built his house upon the rock
   and the rain came tumbling down.
   And the rain came down and the floods came up,
   the rain came down and the floods came up,
   the rain came down and the floods came up
   and the house on the rock stood firm.

2 The foolish man built his house upon the sand,
   the foolish man built his house upon the sand,
   the foolish man built his house upon the sand
   and the rain came tumbling down.
   And the rain came down and the floods came up,
   the rain came down and the floods came up,
   the rain came down and the floods came up
   and the house on the sand fell flat.

253 The wise may bring

TYROLESE   76 76 D

Words: from the *Book of Praise for Children*, 1881, altered
Music: Tyrolese melody

The wise may bring their learn— ing, the rich may bring their wealth, and
some may bring their great - ness, and some their strength and health. We
too would bring our trea - sures to of - fer to the King; we
have no wealth or lear - ning, what gifts then shall we bring?

Music arrangement: from the *BBC Hymnbook,* 1951
by permission of Oxford University Press

1 The wise may bring their learning,
the rich may bring their wealth,
and some may bring their greatness,
and some their strength and health.
We too would bring our treasures
to offer to the King;
we have no wealth or learning,
what gifts then shall we bring?

2 We'll bring the many duties
we have to do each day.
We'll try our best to please Him
at home, at school, at play,
and better are these treasures
to offer to the King
than richest gifts without them,
yet these we all may bring.

3 We'll bring Him hearts that love Him,
we'll bring Him thankful praise,
and lives for ever striving
to follow in His ways,
and these shall be the treasures
we offer to the King,
and these are gifts that ever
our grateful hearts may bring.

254 Think of a world without any flowers

Words: Doreen Newport
Music: Graham Westcott
arranged Douglas Coombes

Think of a world with - out a - ny flo - wers, think of a world with - out a - ny trees, think of a sky with - out a - ny sun - shine, think of the air with - out a - ny breeze. We thank You, Lord, for flowers and trees and sun-shine, we thank You, Lord, and praise Your ho - ly name.

1 Think of a world without any flowers,
   think of a world without any trees,
   think of a sky without any sunshine,
   think of the air without any breeze.
   We thank You, Lord, for flowers and trees and sunshine,
   we thank You, Lord, and praise Your holy name.

2 Think of a world without any animals,
   think of a field without any herd,
   think of a stream without any fishes,
   think of a dawn without any bird.
   We thank You, Lord, for all Your living creatures,
   we thank You, Lord, and praise Your holy name.

3 Think of a world without any people,
   think of a street with no-one living there,
   think of a town without any houses,
   no-one to love and nobody to care.
   We thank You, Lord, for families and friendships,
   we thank You, Lord, and praise Your holy name.

255

This is the day

Words: Les Garrett
Music: Fiji Island folk melody
Music arranged Roland Fudge

1 This is the day,
  this is the day that the Lord has made,
  that the Lord has made.
  We will rejoice,
  we will rejoice and be glad in it,
  and be glad in it.
  This is the day that the Lord has made,
  we will rejoice and be glad in it.
  This is the day,
  this is the day that the Lord has made.

2 This is the day,
  this is the day when He rose again,
  when He rose again.
  We will rejoice,
  we will rejoice and be glad in it,
  and be glad in it.
  This is the day when He rose again,
  we will rejoice and be glad in it.
  This is the day,
  this is the day when He rose again.

3 This is the day,
  this is the day when the Spirit came,
  when the Spirit came.
  We will rejoice,
  we will rejoice and be glad in it,
  and be glad in it.
  This is the day when the Spirit came,
  we will rejoice and be glad in it.
  This is the day,
  this is the day when the Spirit came.

256   This joyful Eastertide

VRUECHTEN

Words: Fred Pratt Green
Music: 17th-century Dutch melody

This joy-ful Eas-ter-tide, what need is there for griev - - ing? Cast all your care a-side and be not un-be-liev - - ing: *Come, share our Eas-ter joy that death could*

not im-pri-son, nor a-ny power des-troy, our

Christ, who is a-ris-en, a-ris-en, a-ris-en, a-ris-en!

1 This joyful Eastertide,
   what need is there for grieving?
   Cast all your care aside
   and be not unbelieving:
       Come, share our Easter joy
       that death could not imprison,
       nor any power destroy,
       our Christ, who is arisen,
       arisen, arisen, arisen!

2 No work for Him is vain,
   no faith in Him mistaken,
   for Easter makes it plain
   His kingdom is not shaken:
       Come, share our Easter joy ...

3 Then put your trust in Christ,
   in waking or in sleeping.
   His grace on earth sufficed;
   He'll never quit His keeping:
       Come, share our Easter joy ...

257 Though the world has forsaken God
(They are watching you)

Words and music: Richard Bewes
Music arranged Christian Strover

Though the world has for - sa - ken God, treads a diff - erent path, lives a diff - erent way, __ I walk the road that the Sav - iour trod, __ and all may know I live un - der Je - sus' sway. *They are watch - ing you, __ mark - ing all you do,*

hear-ing the things you say; let them see the Sav - iour as He shines in you, let His power con-trol you ev - ery day.

1 Though the world has forsaken God,
   treads a different path, lives a different way,
   I walk the road that the Saviour trod,
   and all may know I live under Jesus' sway.
   They are watching you, marking all you do,
   hearing the things you say;
   let them see the Saviour as He shines in you,
   let His power control you every day.

2 Men will look at the life I lead,
   see the side I take and the things I love;
   they judge my Lord by my every deed –
   Lord, set my affections on things above.
   They are watching you . . .

3 When assailed in temptation's hour
   by besetting sins, by the fear of man,
   then I can know Jesus' mighty power,
   and become like Him in His perfect plan.
   They are watching you . . .

4 Here on earth people walk in the night;
   with no lamp to guide they are dead in sin.
   I know the Lord who can give them light,
   I live, yet not I, but Christ within.
   They are watching you . . .

258 This little light of mine

Words and music: Traditional

The light that shines is the light of love,_

lights the dark - ness from a - bove. It shines on me and it

shines on you,_ and shows what the pow - er of

love can do. I'm gon-na shine my light both far and near, I'm gon-na

shine my light both bright and clear. Where there's a dark cor - ner

in this land _ I'm gon - na let my lit - tle light shine.

D.C. al Fine

This little light of mine, I'm gonna let it shine,
this little light of mine, I'm gonna let it shine.
This little light of mine, I'm gonna let it shine,
let it shine, let it shine, let it shine.

1 The light that shines is the light of love,
  lights the darkness from above.
  It shines on me and it shines on you,
  and shows what the power of love can do.
  I'm gonna shine my light both far and near,
  I'm gonna shine my light both bright and clear.
  Where there's a dark corner in this land
  I'm gonna let my little light shine.
    This little light of mine . . .

2 On Monday, He gave me the gift of love,
  Tuesday, peace came from above.
  On Wednesday He told me to have more faith,
  on Thursday He gave me a little more grace.
  Friday, He told me just to watch and pray,
  Saturday, He told me just what to say.
  On Sunday He gave me the power divine
  to let my little light shine.
    This little light of mine . . .

259

To God be the glory!

Words: Frances van Alstyne (1820–1915)
(Fanny J Crosby)
Music: William Howard Doane (1832–1916)

To God be the glo-ry! great things He has done; so loved He the world that He gave us His Son; who yield - ed His life an a - tone-ment for sin, and o - pened the life gate that all may go in.

1 To God be the glory! great things He has done;
   so loved He the world that He gave us His Son;
   who yielded His life an atonement for sin,
   and opened the life gate that all may go in.
     Praise the Lord, praise the Lord!
     let the earth hear His voice;
     praise the Lord, praise the Lord!
     let the people rejoice:
     O come to the Father,
     through Jesus the Son
     and give Him the glory;
     great things He has done!

2 O perfect redemption, the purchase of blood!
   to every believer the promise of God;
   the vilest offender who truly believes,
   that moment from Jesus a pardon receives.
     Praise the Lord . . .

3 Great things He has taught us, great things He has done,
   and great our rejoicing through Jesus the Son;
   but purer, and higher, and greater will be
   our wonder, our rapture, when Jesus we see.
     Praise the Lord . . .

260 Turn your eyes upon Jesus

Words and music: Helen H Lemmel (1864–1961)

1 Turn your eyes upon Jesus,
  look full in His wonderful face;
  and the things of earth will grow strangely dim
  in the light of His glory and grace.

2 Keep your eyes upon Jesus,
  let nobody else take His place;
  so that hour by hour you will know His power
  till at last you have run the great race.

261   Twelve men went to spy

Words and music: Hugh Mitchell
Music arranged Andy Silver

Twelve men went to spy in Ca-naan, ten were bad, two were good.

What did they see when they spied in Ca-naan? Ten were bad, two were good.

Some saw gi-ants tough and tall, some saw grapes in clus-ters fall,

some saw God was in it all,___ ten were bad, two were good.

262

Two little eyes

Words and music: C C Kerr

Two lit-tle eyes to look to God, two lit-tle ears to hear His word,

two lit-tle feet to walk in His ways, two lit-tle lips to sing His praise,

two lit-tle hands to do His will, and one lit-tle heart to love Him still.

Two little eyes to look to God,
two little ears to hear His word,
two little feet to walk in His ways,
two little lips to sing His praise,
two little hands to do His will,
and one little heart to love Him still.

263   Unto us a boy is born!

Puer Nobis   76 77

Words: German (15th century)
tr. Percy Dearmer (1867–1936)
Music: German carol melody
arranged Geoffrey Shaw (1879–1943)

1 Unto us a boy is born!
  King of all creation,
  came He to a world forlorn,
    the Lord of every nation,
    the Lord of every nation.

2 Cradled in a stall was He
  with sleepy cows and asses;
  but the very beasts could see
    that He all men surpasses,
    that He all men surpasses.

3 Herod then with fear was filled:
  'A Prince,' he said, 'in Jewry!'
  All the little boys he killed
    at Bethlehem in his fury,
    at Bethlehem in his fury.

4 Now may Mary's Son, who came
  so long ago to love us,
  lead us all with hearts aflame
    unto the joys above us,
    unto the joys above us.

5 Alpha and Omega He!
  Let the organ thunder,
  while the choir with peals of glee
    doth rend the air asunder,
    doth rend the air asunder!

264 We have a king who rides a donkey

WHAT SHALL WE DO

Words: Fred Kaan
Music: Traditional

1 We have a king who rides a donkey,
   we have a king who rides a donkey,
   we have a king who rides a donkey
   and His name is Jesus.
   Jesus the King is risen,
   Jesus the King is risen,
   Jesus the King is risen
   early in the morning.

2 Trees are waving a royal welcome,
   trees are waving a royal welcome,
   trees are waving a royal welcome
   for the king called Jesus.
   Jesus the King is risen . . .

3 We have a king who cares for people,
   we have a king who cares for people,
   we have a king who cares for people
   and His name is Jesus.
   Jesus the King is risen . . .

4 What shall we do with our life this morning,
   what shall we do with our life this morning,
   what shall we do with our life this morning?
   Give it up in service!
   Jesus the King is risen . . .

265   We love to praise You

Words: Margaret Westworth
Music: Phil Burt

1 We love to praise You, Jesus,
we love to tell You
that You are Lord, that You are Lord.

2 We love to know You, Jesus,
we love to hear You,
say we are Yours, say we are Yours.

3 We want to thank You, Jesus,
for giving Your life
so we can live, so we can live.

266   We have heard a joyful sound

LIMPSFIELD   73 73 77 73

Words: Priscilla Jane Owens (1829–1907)
altered Horrobin/Leavers
Music: Josiah Booth (1852–1929)

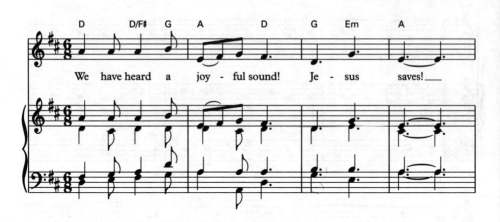

We have heard a joy - ful sound! Je - sus saves!___

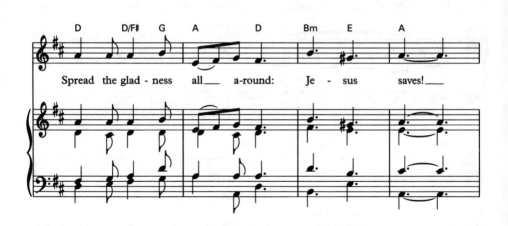

Spread the glad - ness all___ a-round: Je - sus saves!___

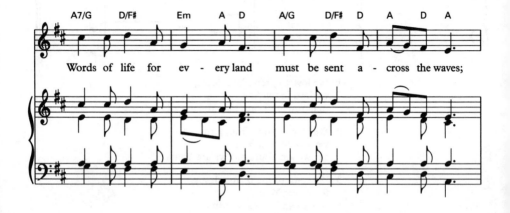

Words of life for ev - ery land must be sent a - cross the waves;

on - ward! 'tis our Lord's com-mand: Je - sus saves!___

1 We have heard a joyful sound!
 Jesus saves!
 Spread the gladness all around:
 Jesus saves!
 Words of life for every land
 must be sent across the waves;
 onward! 'tis our Lord's command:
 Jesus saves!

2 Sing above the toils of life:
 Jesus saves!
 He is with us in the strife:
 Jesus saves!
 Sing the truth, He died yet lives,
 strengthening me through all my days.
 Sing in triumph! Life He gives:
 Jesus saves!

3 Let the nations hear God's voice:
 Jesus saves!
 So that they can then rejoice:
 Jesus saves!
 Shout salvation full and free
 that every land may hear God's praise –
 this our song of victory:
 Jesus saves!

267   We plough the fields

WIR PFLÜGEN   76 76 D with refrain

Words: Matthias Claudius (1740–1815)
tr. Jane Montgomery Campbell (1817–78)
altered Horrobin/Leavers
Music: Jonathan Abraham Peter Schulz (1747–1800)

We plough the fields and scat - ter the good seed on the land,

but it is fed and wa - tered by God's al - migh - ty hand;

He sends the snow in win - ter, the warmth to swell the grain,

the breez - es and the sun - shine and soft re - fresh - ing rain.

All good gifts a-round us are sent from heaven a-bove,

then thank the Lord, O thank the Lord, for all____ His love.

1 We plough the fields and scatter
  the good seed on the land,
  but it is fed and watered
  by God's almighty hand;
  He sends the snow in winter,
  the warmth to swell the grain,
  the breezes and the sunshine
  and soft refreshing rain.
    All good gifts around us
    are sent from heaven above,
    then thank the Lord, O thank the Lord,
    for all His love.

2 He only is the maker
  of all things near and far;
  He paints the wayside flower,
  He lights the evening star;
  the wind and waves obey Him,
  by Him the birds are fed;
  much more to us, His children,
  He gives our daily bread.
    All good gifts . . .

3 We thank You then, O Father,
  for all things bright and good,
  the seed-time and the harvest,
  our life, our health, our food.
  Accept the gifts we offer
  for all Your love imparts;
  we come now, Lord, to give You
  our humble, thankful hearts.
    All good gifts . . .

268 We really want to thank You, Lord

Words: Ed Baggett
verse 3 after Thomas Ken (1637–1711)
Music: Ed Baggett, arranged Betty Pulkingham

With a swing

Capo 2(C)

We real - ly want to thank You, Lord, we real - ly want to bless Your name: hal - le - lu - jah! Je - sus is___ our King!___

We thank You, Lord,_ for Your gift to us,___ Your

life so rich be-yond com-pare, the gift of Your bo-dy here on earth of which we sing and share.

⊕ CODA

D.C. al Coda

King!

We really want to thank You, Lord,
we really want to bless Your name:
hallelujah! Jesus is our King!

1 We thank You, Lord, for Your gift to us,
   Your life so rich beyond compare,
   the gift of Your body here on earth
   of which we sing and share.
      We really want ...

2 We thank You, Lord, for our life together,
   to live and move in the love of Christ,
   Your tenderness which sets us free
   to serve You with our lives.
      We really want ...

3 Praise God from whom all blessings flow,
   praise Him all creatures here below,
   praise Him above, you heavenly host,
   praise Father, Son and Holy Ghost.
      We really want ...

Were you there?

American folk hymn
Music arranged Francis Brotherton Westbrook (1903–75)

Were you there when they cru - ci - fied my Lord?_____
_____ Were you there when they cru - ci - fied my
Lord?_____ Oh!_____

Some-times it caus - es me to trem-ble, trem-ble, trem - ble; Were you there when they cru - ci - fied my Lord?

1 Were you there when they crucified my Lord?
  Were you there when they crucified my Lord?
  Oh! Sometimes it causes me to tremble, tremble, tremble;
  Were you there when they crucified my Lord?

2 Were you there when they nailed Him to the tree?
  Were you there when they nailed Him to the tree?
  Oh! Sometimes it causes me to tremble, tremble, tremble;
  Were you there when they nailed Him to the tree?

3 Were you there when they laid Him in the tomb?
  Were you there when they laid Him in the tomb?
  Oh! Sometimes it causes me to tremble, tremble, tremble;
  Were you there when they laid Him in the tomb?

4 Were you there when God raised Him from the dead?
  Were you there when God raised Him from the dead?
  Oh! Sometimes it causes me to tremble, tremble, tremble;
  Were you there when God raised Him from the dead?

270   We shall overcome

This song has been withdrawn for copyright-related reasons

271 We three kings of Orient are

Words and music: John H Hopkins (1820–91)
Words altered Horrobin/Leavers

roy - al beau - ty bright, *west - ward lead - ing, still pro - ceed - ing, guide us to the per - fect light.*

1 We three kings of Orient are,
   bearing gifts we travel afar,
   field and fountain, moor and mountain,
   following yonder star:
     O star of wonder, star of night,
     star with royal beauty bright,
     westward leading, still proceeding,
     guide us to the perfect light.

2 Born a King on Bethlehem plain,
   gold I bring to crown Him again:
   King for ever, ceasing never,
   over us all to reign.
     O star of wonder . . .

3 Frankincense for Jesus have I,
   God on earth yet Priest on high;
   prayer and praising all men raising:
   worship is earth's reply.
     O star of wonder . . .

4 Myrrh is mine: its bitter perfume
   tells of His death and Calvary's gloom;
   sorrowing, sighing, bleeding, dying,
   sealed in a stone-cold tomb.
     O star of wonder . . .

5 Glorious now, behold Him arise,
   King, and God, and sacrifice!
   Heaven sings, 'Alleluia!',
   'Alleluia!' the earth replies.
     O star of wonder . . .

272 We've a story to tell

MESSAGE 10 8 87 with refrain

Words: Colin Sterne (1862–1926)
altered Horrobin/Leavers
Music: Henry Ernest Nichol (1862–1926)

We've a sto-ry to tell to the na - tions, that shall turn their hearts to the right; a sto-ry of truth and sweet - ness, a sto-ry of peace and light,____ a sto-ry of peace and light:

For the dark - ness shall turn to dawn - ing, and the

1 We've a story to tell to the nations,
   that shall turn their hearts to the right;
   a story of truth and sweetness,
   a story of peace and light,
   a story of peace and light:
       For the darkness shall turn to dawning,
       and the dawning to noon-day bright,
       and Christ's great kingdom shall come on earth,
       the kingdom of love and light.

2 We've a song to be sung to the nations,
   that shall lift their hearts to the Lord;
   a song that shall conquer evil,
   so love will replace the sword,
   so love will replace the sword.
       For the darkness . . .

3 We've a message to give to the nations,
   that the Lord who's reigning above
   has sent us His Son to save us,
   and show us that God is love,
   and show us that God is love:
       For the darkness . . .

4 We've a Saviour to show to the nations,
   who the path of sorrow has trod,
   that all of the world may listen
   and learn of the truth of God,
   and learn of the truth of God:
       For the darkness . . .

273   What a friend we have in Jesus

CONVERSE   87 87 D

Words: Joseph Scriven (1819–86)
altered Horrobin/Leavers
Music: Charles Crozat Converse (1832–1918)

What a friend we have in Je - sus, all our sins and griefs to bear!

What a pri-vi-lege to car - ry ev - ery-thing to God in prayer!

O what peace we of-ten for - feit, O what need-less pain we bear –

all be-cause we do not car - ry ev - ery-thing to God in prayer!

1 What a friend we have in Jesus,
all our sins and griefs to bear!
What a privilege to carry
everything to God in prayer!
O what peace we often forfeit,
O what needless pain we bear –
all because we do not carry
everything to God in prayer!

2 Have we trials and temptations?
Is there trouble anywhere?
We should never be discouraged:
take it to the Lord in prayer!
Can we find a friend so faithful,
who will all our sorrows share?
Jesus knows our every weakness –
take it to the Lord in prayer!

3 Are we weak and heavy-laden,
cumbered with a load of care?
Jesus only is our refuge!
Take it to the Lord in prayer!
Do your friends despise, forsake you?
Take it to the Lord in prayer!
In His arms He'll take and shield you,
you will find His comfort there.

274   What a wonderful Saviour

Words and music: Anon
Music arranged Betty Pulkingham

Brightly

What a won-der-ful Sav-iour is Je-sus,_____ what a

won - der-ful friend is He,   for He

left all the glo-ry of hea-ven,_____ came to

earth to die on Cal-va-ry:

1 What a wonderful Saviour is Jesus,
what a wonderful friend is He,
for He left all the glory of heaven,
came to earth to die on Calvary:
Sing hosanna, sing hosanna,
sing hosanna to the King of kings!
Sing hosanna, sing hosanna,
sing hosanna to the King.

2 He arose from the grave, hallelujah!
and He lives never more to die,
at the Father's right hand interceding,
He will hear and heed our faintest cry:
Sing hosanna ...

3 He is coming some day to receive us,
we'll be caught up to heaven above,
what a joy it will be to behold Him,
sing for ever of His grace and love.
Sing hosanna ...

275 When I needed a neighbour

NEIGHBOURS

Words and music: Sydney Carter

When I need-ed a neigh-bour, were you there, were you there? When I need - ed a neigh-bour were you there? *And the creed and the col - our and the name won't mat-ter, were you there?* I was

1 When I needed a neighbour, were you there, were you there?
  When I needed a neighbour, were you there?
  And the creed and the colour and the name won't matter,
  were you there?

2 I was hungry and thirsty, were you there, were you there?
  I was hungry and thirsty, were you there?
  And the creed . . .

3 I was cold, I was naked, were you there, were you there?
  I was cold, I was naked, were you there?
  And the creed . . .

4 When I needed a shelter, were you there, were you there?
  When I needed a shelter, were you there?
  And the creed . . .

5 When I needed a healer, were you there, were you there?
  When I needed a healer, were you there?
  And the creed . . .

6 Wherever you travel, I'll be there, I'll be there,
  Wherever you travel, I'll be there.
  And the creed . . .

276 When Israel was in Egypt's land

Go Down Moses

Words and music: Spiritual, adapted Peter D Smith
Music arranged Michael Metcalf

1 When Israel was in Egypt's land,
   let my people go;
   oppressed so hard they could not stand,
   let my people go.
   Go down, Moses, way down in Egypt's land,
   tell old Pharaoh to let my people go.

2 The Lord told Moses what to do,
   let my people go;
   to lead the children of Israel through,
   let my people go.
   Go down ...

3 Your foes shall not before you stand,
   let my people go;
   and you'll possess fair Canaan's land,
   let my people go.
   Go down ...

4 O let us from all bondage flee,
   let my people go;
   and let us all in Christ be free,
   let my people go.
   Go down ...

5 I do believe without a doubt,
   let my people go;
   that a Christian has a right to shout,
   let my people go.
   Go down ...

277 When I survey

ROCKINGHAM   LM

Words: Isaac Watts (1674–1748)
Music: Edward Miller (1731–1807)

1 When I survey the wondrous cross
   on which the Prince of glory died,
   my richest gain I count but loss,
   and pour contempt on all my pride.

2 Forbid it, Lord, that I should boast,
   save in the death of Christ my God:
   all the vain things that charm me most,
   I sacrifice them to His blood.

3 See from His head, His hands, His feet,
   sorrow and love flow mingled down:
   did e'er such love and sorrow meet,
   or thorns compose so rich a crown?

4 Were the whole realm of nature mine,
   that were an offering far too small,
   love so amazing, so divine,
   demands my soul, my life, my all.

278 When morning gilds the skies

LAUDES DOMINI   666 D

Words: tr. from the German by
Edward Caswall (1814–78)
in this version Jubilate Hymns
Music: Joseph Barnby (1838–96)

When morn-ing gilds the skies,___ my heart a-waken-ing cries:___ May
Je - sus Christ be praised! A - like at work and prayer___ I
know my Lord is there:___ may Je - sus Christ be praised!

1 When morning gilds the skies,
   my heart awakening cries:
      May Jesus Christ be praised!
   Alike at work and prayer
   I know my Lord is there:
      May Jesus Christ be praised!

2 When sadness fills my mind
   my strength in Him I find –
      may Jesus Christ be praised!
   When earthly hopes grow dim
   my comfort is in Him –
      may Jesus Christ be praised!

3 The night becomes as day
   when from the heart we say:
      May Jesus Christ be praised!
   The powers of darkness fear,
   when this glad song they hear:
      May Jesus Christ be praised!

4 Be this, while life is mine,
   my canticle divine:
      May Jesus Christ be praised!
   Be this the eternal song
   through all the ages long:
      May Jesus Christ be praised!

279 When the road is rough and steep

Words and music: Norman J Clayton

When the road is rough and steep, fix your eyes up-on Je - sus,
He a - lone has power to keep, fix your eyes up-on Him.
Je - sus is a gra-cious friend, one on whom you can de-pend,
He is faith-ful to the end, fix your eyes up-on Him.

280 When the Lord in glory comes

GLORIOUS COMING 77 77 77 D

Words: Timothy Dudley-Smith
Music: Michael Baughen
and David Wilson

When the Lord in glo-ry comes, not the trum-pets, not the drums, not the an-them, not the psalm, not the thun - der, not the calm, not the shout the hea-vens raise, not the cho-rus, not the praise,

1 When the Lord in glory comes,
  not the trumpets, not the drums,
  not the anthem, not the psalm,
  not the thunder, not the calm,
  not the shout the heavens raise,
  not the chorus, not the praise,
  not the silences sublime,
  not the sounds of space and time,
  but His voice when He appears
  shall be music to my ears;
    but His voice when He appears
    shall be music to my ears.

2 When the Lord is seen again,
  not the glories of His reign,
  not the lightnings through the storm,
  not the radiance of His form,
  not His pomp and power alone,
  not the splendours of His throne,
  not His robe and diadems,
  not the gold and not the gems,
  but His face upon my sight
  shall be darkness into light;
    but His face upon my sight
    shall be darkness into light.

3 When the Lord to human eyes
  shall bestride our narrow skies,
  not the child of humble birth,
  not the carpenter of earth,
  not the man by all denied,
  not the victim crucified,
  but the God who died to save,
  but the victor of the grave,
  He it is to whom I fall,
  Jesus Christ, my all in all;
    He it is to whom I fall,
    Jesus Christ, my all in all.

281   When the trumpet of the Lord

ROLL CALL

Words and music: James M Black (1856–1938)

When the trum-pet of the Lord shall sound, and time shall be no more, and the

morn-ing breaks, e-ter-nal, bright, and fair; when the saved of earth shall gath-er o-ver

on the oth-er shore, and the roll is called up yon-der, I'll be there.

When the roll_____ is called up yon - der, when the

roll_____ is called up yon - der, when the roll_____ is called up
yon - der, when the roll is called up yon - der I'll be there.

1 When the trumpet of the Lord shall sound, and time shall be no more,
   and the morning breaks, eternal, bright, and fair;
   when the saved of earth shall gather over on the other shore,
   and the roll is called up yonder, I'll be there.
     When the roll is called up yonder,
     when the roll is called up yonder,
     when the roll is called up yonder,
     when the roll is called up yonder I'll be there.

2 On that bright and cloudless morning when the dead in Christ shall rise,
   and the glory of His resurrection share;
   when His chosen ones shall gather to their home beyond the skies,
   and the roll is called up yonder, I'll be there.
     When the roll is called . . .

3 Let us labour for the Master from the dawn till setting sun,
   let us talk of all His wondrous love and care;
   then when all of life is over, and our work on earth is done,
   and the roll is called up yonder, I'll be there.
     When the roll is called . . .

282 Wherever I am

Words and music: Anon
Music arranged David Peacock

Quite fast

Wher-ev-er I am, I'll praise Him, when-ev-er I can, I'll praise Him; for His love sur-rounds me like_ a sea;_____ _ I'll praise the name of Je-sus, lift up the name of Je-sus, for the name of Je-sus lift-ed me._____

283 Wherever I am I will praise You

Words: Margaret Westworth
Music: Greg Leavers
arranged Phil Burt

1 Wherever I am I will praise You, Lord,
praise You, Lord.
Wherever I am
Your Spirit fills my life with song.

2 Whenever I can I will tell You, Lord,
I love You.
Wherever I am
Your Spirit fills my heart with love.

3 Wherever I go I will serve You, Lord,
serve You, Lord.
Wherever I am
Your Spirit fills my life with power.

4 Whatever I do I will need You, Lord,
need You, Lord.
Wherever I am
Your Spirit lives Your life through me.

284 Whether you're one

Words and music: Graham Kendrick
Music arranged Phil Burt

Whe-ther you're one or whe-ther you're two or three or four or five, six or seven or eight or nine, it's good to be a-live. It real-ly does-n't mat-ter how old you are, Je-sus loves you who-ev-er you are.

La, la, la, la, la, la, la, la, la, — Je - sus loves us all.

La, la, la, la, la, la, la, la, la, — Je - sus loves us all.

1 Whether you're one or whether you're two
   or three or four or five,
   six or seven or eight or nine,
   it's good to be alive.
   It really doesn't matter how old you are,
   Jesus loves you whoever you are.
     La, la, la, la, la, la, la, la, la,
     Jesus loves us all.
     La, la, la, la, la, la, la, la, la,
     Jesus loves us all.

2 Whether you're big or whether you're small
   or somewhere in between,
   first in the class or middle or last,
   we're all the same to Him.
   It really doesn't matter how clever you are,
   Jesus loves you whoever you are.
     La, la, la, la . . .

285   While shepherds watched

WINCHESTER OLD   CM

Words: Nahum Tate (1652–1715)
Music: Tate's *Psalms*, 1592

1 While shepherds watched their flocks by night,
   all seated on the ground,
   the angel of the Lord came down
   and glory shone around.

2 'Fear not,' said he for mighty dread
   had seized their troubled mind –
   'Glad tidings of great joy I bring
   to you and all mankind:

3 'To you in David's town this day
   is born of David's line,
   a Saviour, who is Christ the Lord.
   And this shall be the sign:

4 'The heavenly babe you there shall find
   to human view displayed,
   all meanly wrapped in swaddling bands,
   and in a manger laid.'

5 Thus spake the angel; and forthwith
   appeared a shining throng
   of angels praising God, who thus
   addressed their joyful song:

6 'All glory be to God on high,
   and to the earth be peace;
   goodwill henceforth from heaven to men
   begin and never cease!'

286   Who took fish and bread?

ONLY JESUS

Words and music: Betty Lou Mills and Russell J Mills

Who took fish and bread, hun - gry peo - ple fed?

Who changed wa - ter in - to wine?

Who made well the sick, who made see the blind?

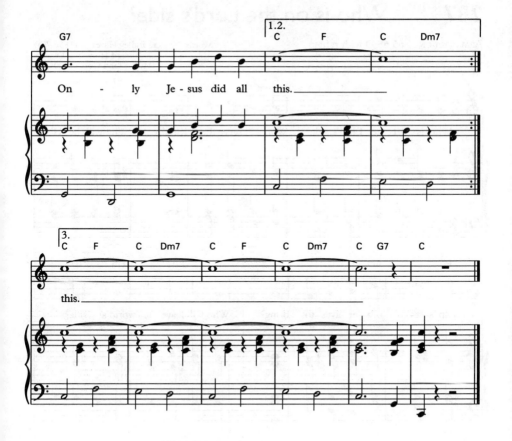

On - ly Je - sus did all this.

this.

1 Who took fish and bread, hungry people fed?
   Who changed water into wine?
   Who made well the sick, who made see the blind?
   Who touched earth with feet divine?
   Only Jesus, only Jesus, only He has done this:
   Who made live the dead? Truth and kindness spread?
   Only Jesus did all this.

2 Who walked dusty road? Cared for young and old?
   Who sat children on His knee?
   Who spoke words so wise? Filled men with surprise?
   Who gave all but charged no fee?
   Only Jesus, only Jesus, only He has done this:
   Who in death and grief spoke peace to a thief?
   Only Jesus did all this.

3 Who soared through the air? Joined His Father there?
   He has you and me in view:
   He who this has done is God's only Son,
   and He's interested in you.
   Only Jesus, only Jesus, only He has done this:
   He can change a heart, give a fresh new start,
   only He can do all this.

287 Who is on the Lord's side?

ARMAGEDDON 65 65 D with refrain

Words: Frances Ridley Havergal (1836–79)
altered Horrobin/Leavers
Music: John Goss (1800–80)

Who is on the Lord's side? Who will serve the King? Who will be His
help - ers oth - er lives to bring? Who will leave the world's side?
Who will face the foe? Who is on the Lord's side? Who for
Him will go? By His call of mer - cy, now our lives we

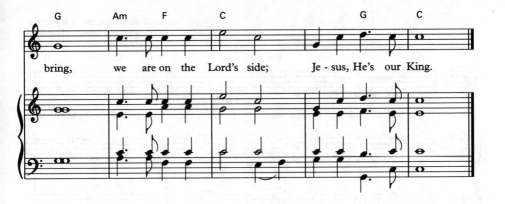

bring,   we   are on   the   Lord's side;   Je - sus, He's   our   King.

1   Who is on the Lord's side?
    Who will serve the King?
    Who will be His helpers
    other lives to bring?
    Who will leave the world's side?
    Who will face the foe?
    Who is on the Lord's side?
    Who for Him will go?
    By His call of mercy,
    now our lives we bring,
    we are on the Lord's side;
    Jesus, He's our King.

2   Fierce may be the conflict,
    strong may be the foe,
    but the King's own army
    none can overthrow.
    Round His standard ranging,
    victory is secure,
    for His truth unchanging
    makes the triumph sure.
    Joyfully enlisting,
    now our lives we bring,
    we are on the Lord's side;
    Jesus, He's our King.

3   Chosen to be soldiers
    in an alien land,
    chosen, called, and faithful,
    for our captain's band;
    in the service royal
    let us not grow cold;
    let us be right loyal,
    noble, true and bold.
    Master, You will keep us,
    serving You we sing:
    'Always on the Lord's side,
    Jesus, always King!'

288 Who put the colours in the rainbow?

Words and music: J A P Booth
Music arranged Douglas Coombes

Who put the col-ours in the rain - bow? Who put the salt in-to the sea? Who put the cold in-to the snow - flake? Who made you and me? Who put the hump up-on the cam - el? Who put the neck on the gir-affe? Who put the tail up-on the

mon - key? Who made hy-e-nas laugh? Who made whales and

snails and quails? Who made hogs and dogs and frogs?

Who made bats and rats and cats? Who made ev - ery-thing?

1 Who put the colours in the rainbow?
Who put the salt into the sea?
Who put the cold into the snowflake?
Who made you and me?
Who put the hump upon the camel?
Who put the neck on the giraffe?
Who put the tail upon the monkey?
Who made hyenas laugh?
Who made whales and snails and quails?
Who made hogs and dogs and frogs?
Who made bats and rats and cats?
Who made everything?

2 Who put the gold into the sunshine?
Who put the sparkle in the stars?
Who put the silver in the moonlight?
Who made Earth and Mars?
Who put the scent into the roses?
Who taught the honey bee to dance?
Who put the tree inside the acorn?
It surely can't be chance!
Who made seas and leaves and trees?
Who made snow and winds that blow?
Who made streams and rivers flow?
God made all of these!

289   Who's the king of the jungle?

Words and music: Annie Bush
Music arranged Andy Silver

Who's the king_ of the jun - gle? Who's the king_ of the sea? Who's the king_ of the u - ni - verse and who's the king of me? I'll tell you J - E - S - U - S is,

He's the king_ of me, He's the king_ of the u - ni - verse, the jun - gle and the sea.

Who's the king of the jungle?
Who's the king of the sea?
Who's the king of the universe
and who's the king of me?
I'll tell you J-E-S-U-S is,
He's the king of me,
He's the king of the universe,
the jungle and the sea.

290 Will your anchor hold

Words: Priscilla Jane Owens (1829–1907)
Music: William James Kirkpatrick (1838–1921)

Will your an - chor hold in the storms of life, when the clouds un - fold their

wings of strife? When the strong tides lift, and the ca - bles strain, will your

an - chor drift, or__ firm re - main? *We have an - chor that keeps the soul*

1 Will your anchor hold in the storms of life,
when the clouds unfold their wings of strife?
When the strong tides lift, and the cables strain,
will your anchor drift, or firm remain?
We have an anchor that keeps the soul
steadfast and sure while the billows roll;
fastened to the rock which cannot move,
grounded firm and deep in the Saviour's love!

2 Will your anchor hold in the straits of fear,
when the breakers roar and the reef is near?
While the surges rage, and the wild winds blow,
shall the angry waves then your life o'erflow?
We have an anchor . . .

3 Will your anchor hold in the floods of death,
when the waters cold chill your final breath?
On the rising tide you can never fail,
while your anchor holds within the veil.
We have an anchor . . .

4 Will your eyes behold through the morning light,
the city of gold and the harbour bright?
Will you anchor safe by the heavenly shore,
when life's storms are past for evermore?
We have an anchor . . .

291 With Jesus in the boat

Words and music: Anon
Music arranged Phil Burt

sail - ing home, with Je - sus in the boat we can smile at the storm as we go sail - ing home.

With Jesus in the boat we can smile at the storm,
smile at the storm, smile at the storm,
with Jesus in the boat we can smile at the storm
as we go sailing home.
Sailing, sailing home,
sailing, sailing home,
with Jesus in the boat we can smile at the storm
as we go sailing home.

292   Wide, wide as the ocean

Words and music: C Austin Miles (1865–1946)

293
Yes, God is good

WILLIAMS   LM

Words: John Hampden Gurney (1802–62)
Music: from *Templi Carmina*, 1829

1 Yes, God is good – in earth and sky,
   from ocean depths and spreading wood,
   ten thousand voices seem to cry:
   'God made us all, and God is good!'

2 The sun that keeps his trackless way,
   and downward pours his golden flood,
   night's sparkling hosts, all seem to say
   in accents clear that God is good.

3 The joyful birds prolong the strain,
   their song with every spring renewed;
   the air we breathe, and falling rain,
   each softly whispers: 'God is good!'

4 I hear it in the rushing breeze;
   the hills that have for ages stood,
   the echoing sky and roaring seas,
   all swell the chorus: 'God is good!'

5 Yes, God is good, all nature says,
   by God's own hand with speech endued;
   and man, in louder notes of praise,
   should sing for joy that God is good.

6 For all Your gifts we bless You, Lord,
   but chiefly for our heavenly food,
   Your pardoning grace, Your quickening word,
   these prompt our song, that God is good.

294 Yesterday, today, for ever

Words: Albert B Simpson (1843–1919)
Music: James H Burke (19th century)

Yes-ter-day,_ to-day, for ev-er, Je-sus is__ the same;_ all may change, but Je-sus ne-ver, glo-ry to His name!_

Glo-ry to His name!_____ Glo-ry to__ His name!_

All may change, but Je-sus ne-ver, glo-ry to His name!_

295   Your ways are higher than mine

Words and music: Georgian Banov

Brightly

Your ways are high-er than mine,_ Your ways are high-er than mine, Your ways are high-er than mine, much high-er._____ Your ways are high-er than mine, Your ways are high-er than mine, Your ways are high-er than mine, much high-

Hal - le - lu - jah, hal - le - lu - jah, hal - le - lu - jah, hal - le - lu.

1 Your ways are higher than mine,
  Your ways are higher than mine,
  Your ways are higher than mine,
  much higher.
  Your ways are higher than mine,
  Your ways are higher than mine,
  Your ways are higher than mine,
  much higher.
  Higher, higher, much much higher,
  higher, higher, much higher.
  Higher, higher, much much higher,
  higher, higher, much higher.

2 Your thoughts are wiser . . .

3 Your strength is greater . . .

  Hallelujah, hallelujah,
  hallelujah, hallelu.
  Hallelujah, hallelujah,
  hallelujah, hallelu.

296 You are the King of glory

Words and music: Mavis Ford

You are the King of glo-ry, You are the Prince of peace,
You are the Lord of heaven and earth, You're the Son of right-eous-ness.
An-gels bow down be-fore_ You, wor-ship and a-dore, for You have the words of e-ter-nal life,_

You are Je-sus Christ the Lord.___ Ho-san-na to the Son of Da-vid!___ Ho-

-san-na to the King of___ kings! Glo-ry in the high-est

hea - ven, for Je-sus the Mes-si - ah reigns!

You are the King of glory,
You are the Prince of peace,
You are the Lord of heaven and earth,
You're the Son of righteousness.
Angels bow down before You,
worship and adore,
for You have the words of eternal life,
You are Jesus Christ the Lord.
Hosanna to the Son of David!
Hosanna to the King of kings!
Glory in the highest heaven,
for Jesus the Messiah reigns!

297 You can't stop rain from falling down

Words: John Gowans
Music: John Larsson

keep the day from dawn - ing; you can't stop God from lov - ing you, His love is new each morn - ing.

1 You can't stop rain from falling down,
   prevent the sun from shining,
   you can't stop spring from coming in,
   or winter from resigning,
   or still the waves or stay the winds,
   or keep the day from dawning;
   you can't stop God from loving you,
   His love is new each morning.

2 You can't stop ice from being cold,
   you can't stop fire from burning,
   or hold the tide that's going out,
   delay its sure returning,
   or halt the progress of the years,
   the flight of fame and fashion;
   you can't stop God from loving you,
   His nature is compassion.

3 You can't stop God from loving you,
   though you may disobey Him.
   You can't stop God from loving you,
   however you betray Him.
   From love like this no power on earth
   the human heart can sever.
   You can't stop God from loving you,
   not God, not now, not ever.

298   Your hand, O God, has guided

THORNBURY   76 76 D

Words: Edward Hayes Plumptre (1821–91)
Music: Basil Harwood (1859–1949)

Your hand, O God, has guid - ed Your flock, from age — to age; Your faith - ful - ness is writ - ten on his - tory's o - pen page; our fa - thers knew Your good - ness, and we — their deeds re -

1 Your hand, O God, has guided
   Your flock, from age to age;
   Your faithfulness is written
   on history's open page;
   our fathers knew Your goodness,
   and we their deeds record;
   and both to this bear witness:
   One Church, one faith, one Lord.

2 Your heralds brought the gospel
   to greatest as to least;
   they summoned men to hasten
   and share the great King's feast;
   and this was all their teaching
   in every deed and word;
   to all alike proclaiming:
   One Church, one faith, one Lord.

3 Through many days of darkness,
   through many scenes of strife,
   the faithful few fought bravely
   to guard the nation's life.
   Their gospel of redemption,
   sin pardoned, man restored,
   was all in this enfolded:
   One Church, one faith, one Lord.

4 Your mercy will not fail us,
   nor leave Your work undone;
   with Your right hand to help us,
   the victory shall be won;
   and then by earth and heaven
   Your name shall be adored,
   and this shall be their anthem:
   One Church, one faith, one Lord.

299 Yours be the glory

MACCABAEUS   10 11 11 11 with refrain

Words: Edmond Budry (1854–1932)
in this version Jubilate Hymns
tr. R Birch Hoyle (1875–1939)
Music: George Frideric Handel (1685–1759)

Yours be the glo - ry, ri - sen,_ con-quering Son,
end - less_ is the vic - tory o - ver_ death You won;
an - gels robed in splen - dour rolled the stone a - way,
kept_ the_ fold - ed grave - clothes where Your bo - dy lay.

1 Yours be the glory, risen, conquering Son,
   endless is the victory over death You won;
   angels robed in splendour rolled the stone away,
   kept the folded grave-clothes where Your body lay.
     Yours be the glory, risen, conquering Son,
     endless is the victory over death You won.

2 See! Jesus meets us, risen from the tomb;
   lovingly He greets us, scatters fear and gloom;
   let the Church with gladness hymns of triumph sing,
   for her Lord is living; death has lost its sting.
     Yours be the glory . . .

3 No more we doubt You, glorious Prince of life;
   what is life without You? Aid us in our strife;
   make us more than conquerors, through Your deathless love:
   bring us safe through Jordan to Your home above.
     Yours be the glory . . .

300   Zacchaeus was a very little man

Words and music: Anon
Music arranged J W

Zac - chae - us was a ve -ry lit-tle man, and a ve -ry lit-tle man was
he. He climbed up in - to a sy - ca-more tree for the
Sav-iour he want-ed to see. And when the Sav - iour
passed that way He looked in - to the tree and

(spoken)

said, 'Now, Zac-chae-us, you come down, for I'm com-ing to your house to tea.'

Zacchaeus was a very little man,
and a very little man was he.
He climbed up into a sycamore tree
for the Saviour he wanted to see.
And when the Saviour passed that way
He looked into the tree
and said, 'Now, Zacchaeus, you come down,
for I'm coming to your house to tea.'

301 Lord, we ask now

Words: Peter Horrobin
Music: Phil Burt, Peter Horrobin and Greg Leavers

Lord, we ask now to re-ceive Your bless-ing,
Lord, we ask now to re-ceive Your love,
Come, we pray, come, we pray and
lead us hour by hour.

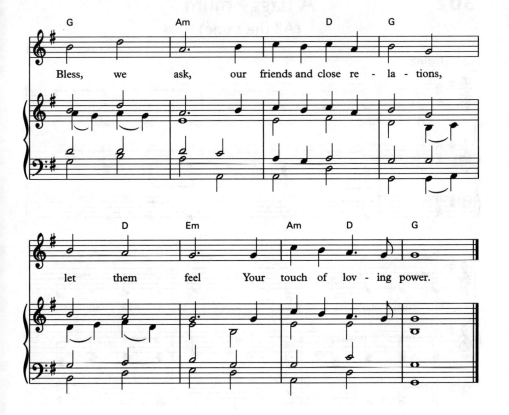

Bless, we ask, our friends and close re - la - tions,
let them feel Your touch of lov - ing power.

1 Lord, we ask now to receive Your blessing,
Lord, we ask now to receive Your love,
Come, we pray, come, we pray
and lead us hour by hour.
Bless, we ask, our friends and close relations,
let them feel Your touch of loving power.

2 Lord, we trust You to give us Your blessing,
Lord, we trust You to give us Your love.
As we give, as we give
our lives afresh to You.
Take, we ask, all that we have and are, Lord,
let them now be used in service true.

3 Lord, we give to others now Your blessing,
Lord, we give to others now Your love.
As we share, as we share
with them the life You've given.
Yes, we will, in harmony with You, Lord,
let them see in us a touch of heaven.

302

A naggy mum
(All the same)

Words and music: Paul Field

A nag - gy mum, a grum - py dad, a bro - ther who's a pain. A sis - ter who takes toys and ne - ver gives them back a - gain. *All the same, all the same, in sun-shine and in rain. No*

mat - ter who we are,___ you know, God loves us all the same.

1 A naggy mum, a grumpy dad, a brother who's a pain.
A sister who takes toys and never gives them back again.
All the same, all the same,
in sunshine and in rain.
No matter who we are, you know,
God loves us all the same.

2 An auntie who cooks sprouts for tea and makes you eat them all.
A grandad who tells terrible jokes and drives you up the wall.
All the same ...

3 An uncle who forgets about your birthday when it comes.
A teacher who gets cross with you and makes you do more sums.
All the same ...

303 A new commandment

From John 13
Words and music: Roy Crabtree
Music arranged Christopher Hayward

With feeling

A new com-mand-ment that I give to you, is to love one an-oth-er as I have loved you, is to love one an-oth-er as I have loved you. By this shall all men know that you are My dis-ci-ples, if

A new commandment that I give to you,
is to love one another as I have loved you,
is to love one another as I have loved you.

By this shall all men know that you are My disciples,
if you have love one for another;
by this shall all men know that you are My disciples,
if you have love one for another.

304

A purple robe

A PURPLE ROBE   8 6 8 6 Triple

Words: Timothy Dudley-Smith
Music: David Wilson
Music arranged Noël Tredinnick

1 A purple robe, a crown of thorn, a reed in His right hand; before the soldiers' spite and scorn I see my Saviour stand.

v 4

2 He bears between the Roman guard the weight of all our woe; a

v 5

1 A purple robe, a crown of thorn,
   a reed in His right hand;
   before the soldiers' spite and scorn
   I see my Saviour stand.

2 He bears between the Roman guard
   the weight of all our woe;
   a stumbling figure bowed and scarred
   I see my Saviour go.

3 Fast to the cross's spreading span,
   high in the sunlit air,
   all the unnumbered sins of man
   I see my Saviour bear.

4 He hangs, by whom the world was made,
   beneath the darkened sky;
   the everlasting ransom paid,
   I see my Saviour die.

5 He shares on high His Father's throne,
   who once in mercy came;
   for all His love to sinners shown
   I sing my Saviour's name.

305

A special star

Words: Laura and Heather Bradley
Music: Laura Bradley
Music arranged Christopher Hayward

A spe - cial star_ is in the sky_ to lead the way_ (to lead the way); a ti - ny sta - ble cold and lone - ly where they can stay_ (where they can stay). *But our hearts have been warm, since the day_ Je - sus*

Christ was born, and that's the way it shall stay, be-cause He is the way, the truth and the life, (the truth and the life).

1 A special star is in the sky
to lead the way (to lead the way);
a tiny stable cold and lonely
where they can stay (where they can stay).
But our hearts have been warm,
since the day Jesus Christ was born,
and that's the way it shall stay,
because He is the way, the truth and the life,
(the truth and the life).

2 The shepherds left their flocks behind
to see the Babe (to see the Babe);
the angel told them to bring a gift so
a lamb they gave (a lamb they gave).
But our hearts . . .

3 The wise men came from lands afar,
on camels they rode, (on camels they rode);
the gifts they offered were frankincense,
myrrh and gold (myrrh and gold).
But our hearts . . .

306   A wiggly waggly worm
(Wiggly waggly song)

Words and music: Paul Field

A wig-gly wag-gly worm, a slip-pery sli-my slug, a cree-py craw-ly buz-zy thing, a tick-ly wick-ly bug. Of all the things to be, I'm hap-py that I'm me. Thank you, Lord, I'm hap-py that I'm me. I'm hap-py that I'm me,

1 A wiggly waggly worm, a slippery slimy slug,
  a creepy crawly buzzy thing, a tickly wickly bug.
  Of all the things to be, I'm happy that I'm me.
  Thank you, Lord, I'm happy that I'm me.

  I'm happy that I'm me, happy that I'm me.
  There's no-one else in all the world that I would rather be.
  A wiggly waggly worm, a slippery slimy slug,
  a creepy crawly buzzy thing, a tickly wickly bug.

2 A prickly porcupine, a clumsy kangaroo,
  A croaky frog, a hairy hog, a monkey in a zoo.
  Of all the things to be, I'm happy that I'm me.
  Thank you, Lord, I'm happy that I'm me.

  I'm happy that I'm me, happy that I'm me.
  There's no-one else in all the world that I would rather be.
  A prickly porcupine, a clumsy kangaroo,
  a croaky frog, a hairy hog, a monkey in a zoo.

307
All you have to do

Words: Paul Field and Ralph Chambers
Music: Paul Field

All you have to do is to ask the Lord

to for-give the wrong things you have done.

Tell Him that you're sor-ry you have hurt____ Him, and

then be-lieve that Je-sus is God's Son. He died on the cross to be your

All you have to do is to ask the Lord
to forgive the wrong things you have done.
Tell Him that you're sorry you have hurt Him,
and then believe that Jesus is God's Son.
He died on the cross to be your Saviour,
rose from the dead to be your special friend.
Ask Him in your heart, make a brand new start.
Love and serve Him till your life shall end.

308 Alleluia

Words and music: Anon
Music arranged Christopher Norton

1 Alleluia. (*8 times*)

2 How I love Him . . .

3 Blessèd Jesus . . .

4 My Redeemer . . .

5 Jesus, Master . . .

6 Alleluia . . .

309 Are you humbly grateful

Words and music: Kathie Hill
and Janet McMahan

Calypso feel

Are you hum-bl-y grate-ful or grum-bl-y hate-ful? What's your at-ti-tude?

Do you grum-ble and groan, or let it be known you're

*Are you humbly grateful
or grumbly hateful?
What's your attitude?
Do you grumble and groan,
or let it be known
you're grateful for all
God's done for you?*

1 When Jonah found himself
  in the belly of a whale,
  did he cause a riot inside?
  No!
  He headed for shore
  with his message from God
  and thanked the Lord
  for his free ride.
  Phew!
    Are you humbly grateful . . .

2 When Noah found himself
  in the floating zoo,
  did he ever try to jump ship?
  No!
  For forty long days
  and for forty long nights
  he cleared the deck
  on that long trip!
  Phew!
    Are you humbly grateful . . .

Which one are you?
Spoken Which one are you?

310 And we know that all things

Words and music: Peter and Hanneke Jacobs
Music arranged Phil Burt

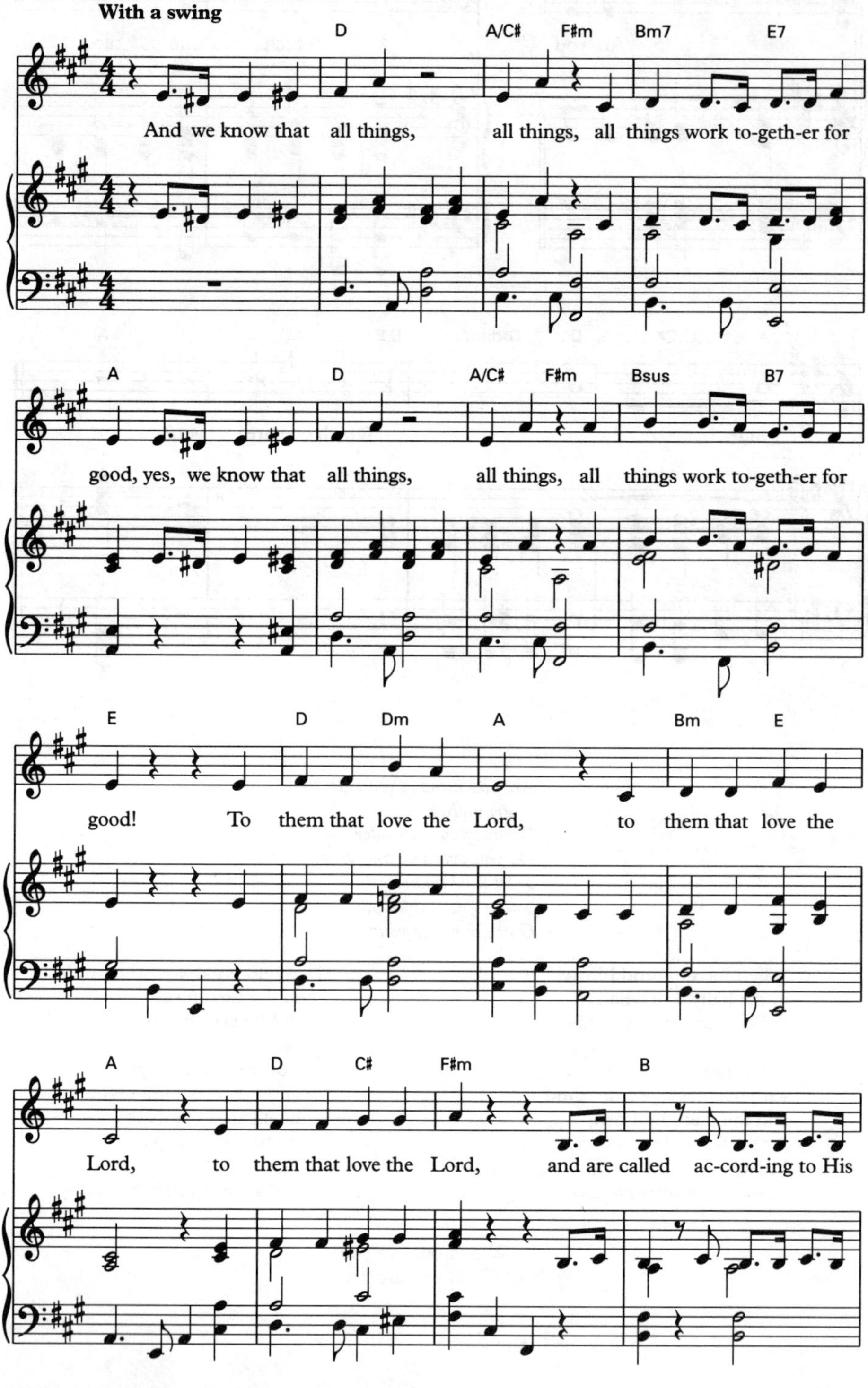

With a swing
D A/C# F#m Bm7 E7
And we know that all things, all things, all things work to-geth-er for
A D A/C# F#m Bsus B7
good, yes, we know that all things, all things, all things work to-geth-er for
E D Dm A Bm E
good! To them that love the Lord, to them that love the
A D C# F#m B
Lord, to them that love the Lord, and are called ac-cord-ing to His

And we know that all things,
all things, all things work together for good,
yes, we know that all things,
all things, all things work together for good!
To them that love the Lord,
to them that love the Lord,
to them that love the Lord,
and are called according to His purpose.
And we know that all things,
all things, all things work together for good,
yes, we know that all things,
all things, all things work together for good.
Romans eight, verse twenty-eight.

311

At harvest time
(Celebrate the harvest)

Words and music: S Lesley Scarr

At har - vest time we ce - le - brate God's gift to us of food and drink. We thank Him for the care He's shown for farm - ers and the seeds they've sown. Praise the Lord! Praise the Lord! Praise the Lord! Praise the Lord!

Sing chorus twice at end

Praise the Lord!   Praise the Lord!   Thank   Him   for   har - vest.

1 At harvest time we celebrate
  God's gift to us of food and drink.
  We thank Him for the care He's shown
  for farmers and the seeds they've sown.
   Praise the Lord! Praise the Lord!
   Praise the Lord! Praise the Lord!
   Praise the Lord! Praise the Lord!
   Thank Him for harvest.

2 God's watched the fields through day and night,
  He's given the seeds both dark and light.
  He's watered them with fresh cool rain
  and now there's fields and fields of grain.
   Praise the Lord . . .

3 God helps the farmers cut the corn,
  He keeps the weather dry and warm,
  until it's baled and brought inside,
  before the start of wintertide.
   Praise the Lord . . .

4 Now once the crops are in their barns
  there's work to do still on the farms.
  It's time to put the crops to use
  to make the different kinds of foods.
   Praise the Lord . . .

5 At harvest time we celebrate
  God's gifts to us of food and drink.
  Let's sing and clap to show our thanks
  for all the care God takes of us.
   Praise the Lord . . .
   Praise the Lord . . .

312   Be careful, little hands

Words and music: Anon
Music arranged Phil Burt

Be careful, little hands, what you do,
be careful, little hands, what you do.
There's a Father up above who is looking down in love,
so be careful, little hands, what you do.

313 Born in the night

MARY'S CHILD

Words and music: Geoffrey Ainger

Gently

Born____ in the night, Ma - ry's child, a
long way from Your home:____ com - ing in need,
Ma-ry's child, born__ in a bor-rowed room.____ room.

1 Born in the night,
    Mary's child,
  a long way from Your home:
  coming in need,
    Mary's child,
  born in a borrowed room.

2 Clear shining light,
    Mary's child,
  Your face lights up our way:
  light of the world,
    Mary's child,
  dawn on our darkened day.

3 Truth of our life,
    Mary's child,
  You tell us God is good:
  prove it is true,
    Mary's child,
  go to Your cross of wood.

4 Hope of the world,
    Mary's child,
  You're coming soon to reign:
  King of the earth,
    Mary's child,
  walk in our streets again.

314

Be holy

Words and music: Alan Brown
Music arranged Christopher Hayward

With movement

Be ho-ly in all that you do,_____ be ho-ly in all that you do,_____ be ho-ly in all that you do to-day,_ be ho-ly in all that you do, you are a cho - sen_

1 Be holy in all that you do,
be holy in all that you do,
be holy in all that you do today,
be holy in all that you do,
you are a chosen people,
be holy in all that you do,
you are a chosen people,
be holy in all that you do.

2 Be holy in all that you say . . .

3 Be holy in all that you think . . .

4 Be holy in all that you are . . .

315
Bring your Christingle

Words: Valerie Ruddle and William Horton
Music: Valerie Ruddle

Joyfully

Bring your Christ - in - gle with glad - ness and joy! Sing
praise to God who gave us His Son; so give Him, ____
give Him your love. Here is an or - ange = ____

LEADER

Fine

Repeat as necessary

D.C. al Fine

An or - ange as round as the world that God made.

Bring your Christingle with gladness and joy!
Sing praise to God who gave us His Son;
so give Him, give Him your love.

LEADER
1 Here is an orange –
ALL
An orange as round as the world that God made.
   Bring your Christingle . . .

LEADER
2 Here is a candle –
ALL
A candle for Jesus, the Light of the world,
an orange as round as the world that God made;
   Bring your Christingle . . .

LEADER
3 Here is red ribbon –
ALL
Red ribbon reminds us Christ died for us all;
a candle for Jesus, the Light of the world;
an orange as round as the world that God made;
   Bring your Christingle . . .

LEADER
4 Here are the fruits –
ALL
The fruits of the earth God has given us to share;
red ribbon reminds us Christ died for us all;
a candle for Jesus, the Light of the world;
an orange as round as the world that God made;
   Bring your Christingle . . .

316

Can you be sure

Words: Geoffrey Marshall-Taylor
Music: Roger Hurrell

With assurance

Can_ you be sure that the rain will fall? Can you be sure that_ birds will fly? Can_ you be sure that rivers will flow? Or that the sun will light___ the sky? *God has pro - mised. God ne-ver breaks a pro - mise He makes. His word is al-ways true.*

317

1 Can you be sure that the rain will fall?
Can you be sure that birds will fly?
Can you be sure that rivers will flow?
Or that the sun will light the sky?
God has promised.
God never breaks a promise He makes.
His word is always true.

2 Can you be sure that the tide will turn?
Can you be sure that grass will grow?
Can you be sure that night will come,
or that the sun will melt the snow?
God has promised . . .

3 You can be sure that God is near;
you can be sure He won't let you down;
you can be sure He'll always hear;
and that He's given Jesus, His Son.
God has promised . . .

317 Can you count the stars

Words and music: Paul Field

Happily

Can you count the stars shin - ing in the sky?

Can you hold the moon-light in your hand?

Can you stop the waves rol - ling on the shore? Or

find the place where rain-bows meet the land? _ I've

got a friend, who knows how all these things are done,

Je - sus, Lord of all, God's on - ly Son.

1 Can you count the stars shining in the sky?
  Can you hold the moonlight in your hand?
  Can you stop the waves rolling on the shore?
  Or find the place where rainbows meet the land?
    I've got a friend, who knows how all these things are done,
    Jesus, Lord of all, God's only Son.

2 Up in outer space, planets spinning round,
  millions more than we can ever see.
  It's hard to understand how God, who made it all,
  still cares about someone like you and me.
    I've got a friend . . .

318

Can you imagine

Words and music: Jeanette Smart

Can you i-ma-gine how it feels to know the God who made the earth and sky and sea?

When He cre-at-ed all the u-ni-verse, His migh-ty plan in-clud-ed you and me.

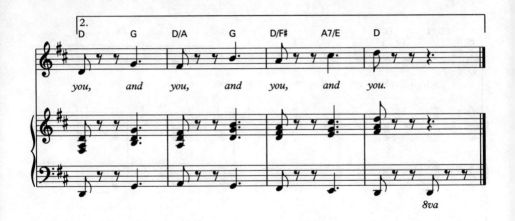

you,   and   you,   and   you,   and   you.

8va

1 Can you imagine how it feels to know
   the God who made the earth and sky and sea?
   When He created all the universe,
   His mighty plan included you and me.
   Well, this experience is not imagination;
   it's a fact, oh yes, it's true.
   And I just can't keep it to myself;
   I'll pass it on to you.

2 Can you imagine how it feels to have
   a Friend who never slumbers, never sleeps?
   Can you believe that when He comes into
   your heart and says He'll live there, it's for keeps?
   Well, this experience is not imagination;
   it's a fact, oh yes, it's true.
   And I just can't keep it to myself;
   I'll pass it on to you,
   and you, and you, and you.

319 Christy be my leader

SLANE

Words: Timothy Dudley-Smith
Music: Irish traditional melody
arranged Christopher Hayward

1 Christ be my leader by night as by day;
  safe through the darkness,
    for He is the way.
  Gladly I follow, my future His care;
  darkness is daylight when Jesus is there.

2 Christ be my teacher in age as in youth,
  drifting or doubting, for He is the truth.
  Grant me to trust Him,
    though shifting as sand;
  doubt cannot daunt me, in Jesus I stand.

3 Christ be my Saviour in calm as in strife;
  death cannot hold me, for He is the life.
  Not darkness nor doubting
    nor sin and its stain
  can touch my salvation: with Jesus I reign.

320 Children, join the celebration

Words and music: Joe E Parks

Children, join the celebration on this happy Easter day; Christ the Lord is risen as He said! Mary on that early morning heard the angel gladly say:

1 Children, join the celebration
   on this happy Easter day;
   Christ the Lord is risen as He said!
   Mary on that early morning
   heard the angel gladly say:
   'Jesus lives – He is no longer dead!'

2 Praise Him now with songs of gladness,
   sing triumphant hymns of praise:
   Christ the Lord is risen as He said!
   Children, join the celebration,
   with the hosts of heaven say:
   'Jesus Christ, our Saviour, lives today!'

321   Christmas is a time to love

Words and music: Ernie and Debbie Rettino
Music arranged Christopher Hayward

Words and music: © Maranatha! Music, administered by CopyCare Ltd,
PO Box 77, Hailsham, East Sussex BN27 3EF, UK. Used by permission

Christmas is a time, Christmas is a time,
Christmas is a time to love.
Christmas is a time, Christmas is a time,
Christmas is a time to love.

We often start to worry, and people get upset
if things don't all go right on Christmas day.
What we should remember in all the push and shove,
is Christmas is a time of love.

Christmas is a time, Christmas is a time,
Christmas is a time to love.
Christmas is a time, Christmas is a time,
Christmas is a time to love.

322 Christmas isn't Christmas

Words and music: Jimmy and Carol Owens

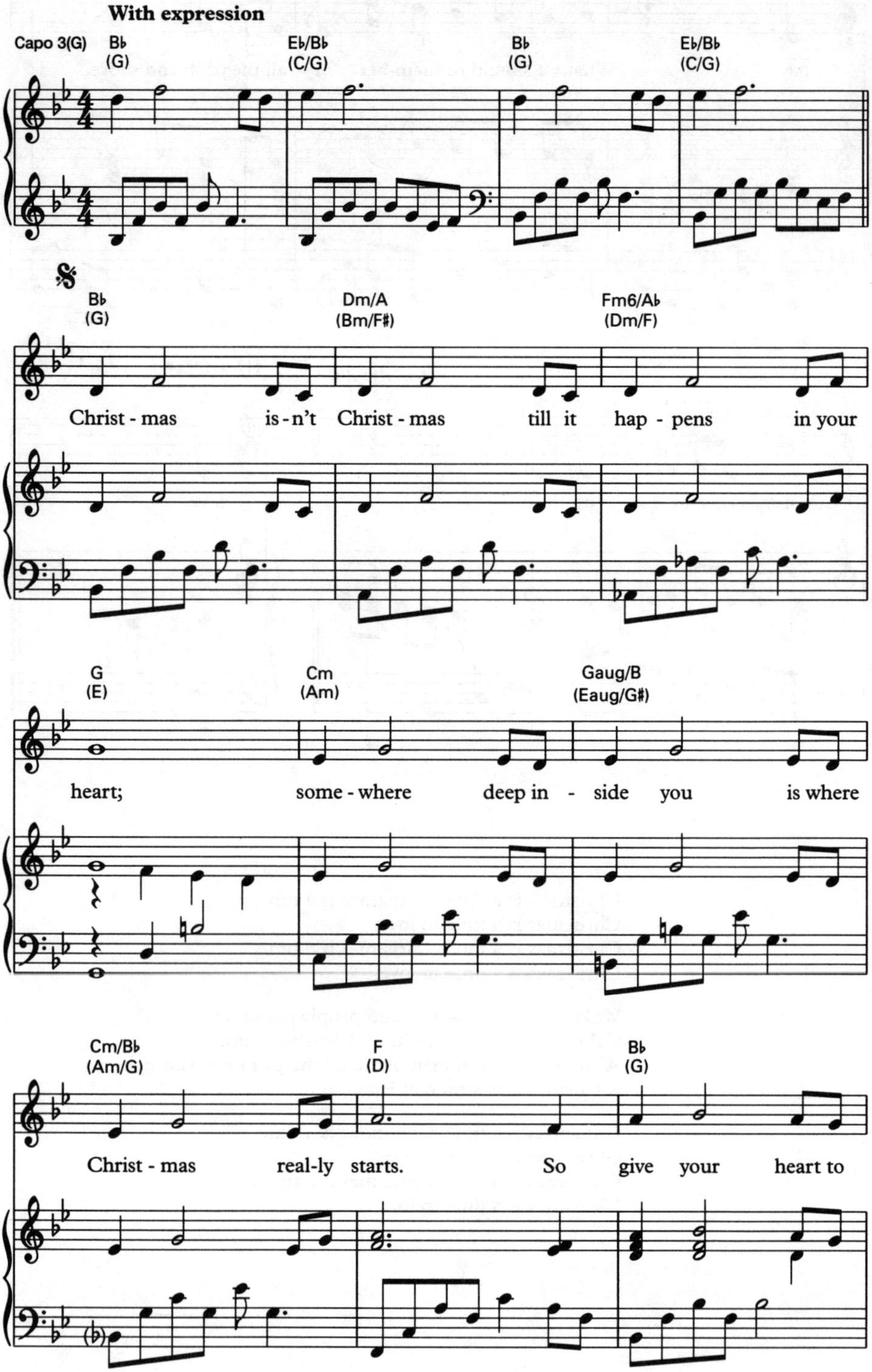

With expression

Christ-mas is-n't Christ-mas till it hap-pens in your heart; some-where deep in-side you is where Christ-mas real-ly starts. So give your heart to

Je - sus; you'll dis - cov - er when you do that it's

Christ-mas, real-ly Christ-mas for you.

Je-sus brings warmth like a win - ter fire, a light like a can - dle's

glow. He's wait - ing now to come in - side as He

Christmas isn't Christmas till it happens in your heart;
somewhere deep inside you is where Christmas really starts.
So give your heart to Jesus; you'll discover when you do
that it's Christmas, really Christmas for you.

Jesus brings warmth like a winter fire,
a light like a candle's glow.
He's waiting now to come inside
as He did so long ago.
Jesus brings gifts of truth and life,
and makes them bloom and grow.
So welcome Him with a song of joy,
and when He comes, you'll know,

that Christmas isn't Christmas till it happens in your heart;
somewhere deep inside you is where Christmas really starts.
So give your heart to Jesus; you'll discover when you do
that it's Christmas, really Christmas;
Christmas, really Christmas for you.

323 Come and join the celebration

CELEBRATIONS 11 14 with refrain

Words and music: Valerie Collison

Come and join the ce - le - bra - tion, it's a ve - ry spe - cial day; come and share our ju - bi - la - tion, there's a new King born__ to - day!__

See the shep - herds hur - ry down to Beth - le -

Come and join the celebration,
it's a very special day;
come and share our jubilation,
there's a new King born today!

1 See the shepherds
   hurry down to Bethlehem;
   gaze in wonder
   at the Son of God who lay before them.
   Come and join . . .

2 Wise men journey,
   led to worship by a star;
   kneel in homage,
   bringing precious gifts from lands afar, so
   Come and join . . .

3 'God is with us,'
   round the world the message bring;
   He is with us,
   'Welcome!' all the bells on earth are pealing.
   Come and join . . .

324   Come, let us sing for joy

From Psalm 95
Words and music: Ruth Hooke

BOYS	Come, let us sing for joy to the Lord.
GIRLS	Come, let us sing for joy to the Lord.
BOYS	We will sing, we will sing, we will sing.
GIRLS	We will sing, we will sing, we will sing.
BOYS	Let us shout aloud to the rock of our salvation.
GIRLS	Let us shout aloud to the rock of our salvation.
BOYS	We will shout! We will shout! We will shout!
GIRLS	We will shout! We will shout! We will shout!
ALL	For the Lord is the great God, the great King above all gods.
BOYS	Splendour and majesty,
GIRLS	splendour and majesty,
BOYS	are before Him,
GIRLS	are before Him.
BOYS	Strength and glory,
GIRLS	strength and glory,
ALL	are in His sanctuary.

325 Come on and celebrate

Words and music: Patricia Morgan
and Dave Bankhead
Music arranged David Peacock

ce - le - brate and sing to the King!

Come on and celebrate!
His gift of love we will celebrate –
the Son of God, who loved us
and gave us life.

We'll shout Your praise, O King:
You give us joy nothing else can bring;
we'll give to You our offering
in celebration praise.

Come on and celebrate, celebrate,
celebrate and sing,
celebrate and sing to the King.
Come on and celebrate, celebrate,
celebrate and sing,
celebrate and sing to the King!

326 Counting, counting one, two, three

Words: Carolyn Keats
Music: Greg Leavers
Music arranged Christopher Hayward

Counting, counting, one, two, three,
clap my hands and
sing for joy, for
God made ME!
Three, four, five, six, and number seven too;
shout it loud, make
sure you're heard, for
God made YOU!

1 I have ten toes, ten fingers,
   two legs on which I stand,
   an arm on either side of me,
   at the end of each a hand;
   a right ear and a left ear,
   a head to shake and nod,
   two eyes, one nose, a mouth, a voice
   to whisper or to SHOUT!
     Counting, counting . . .

2 God made me very different
   from everyone I see,
   my size and shape and colour,
   He chose it carefully.
   God is so very clever
   He made the whole world too;
   He put the life in everything
   including me and you.
     Counting, counting . . .

327 Crackers and turkeys

Words and music: Ian White
Music arranged Christopher Hayward

Happy waltz

Crack-ers and tur-keys and pud-ding and cream, toys in the win-dows that I've ne - ver seen. This is the Christ-mas that ev-ery-one sees, but Christ-mas means more to me. It's some-bo-dy's birth - day I won't for - get, as I o-pen the

things that I get. I'll re - mem - ber the inn and the sta - ble so bare, and Je - sus who once lay there.

1 Crackers and turkeys and pudding and cream,
   toys in the windows that I've never seen.
   This is the Christmas that everyone sees,
   but Christmas means more to me.
   It's somebody's birthday I won't forget,
   as I open the things that I get.
   I'll remember the inn and the stable so bare,
   and Jesus who once lay there.

2 Everyone's out shopping late every night,
   for candles and presents and Christmas tree lights.
   This is the Christmas that everyone sees,
   but Christmas means more to me.
   It's somebody's birthday . . .

3 Christmas morning, the start of the day,
   there's presents to open and new games to play.
   This is the Christmas that everyone sees,
   but Christmas means more to me.
   It's somebody's birthday . . .

328

Don't know much
(This is God's world)

Words: Ralph Chambers
Music: Paul Field

Don't know much a-bout the o - zone lay - er, rain for-ests seem

miles a - way. But each of us can be a play - er,

fight to save the world God has made. This is___ God's

world. This is___ God's world,

Don't know much about the ozone layer,
rain forests seem miles away.
But each of us can be a player,
fight to save the world God has made.
This is God's world.
This is God's world,
and you're a member of the human race.
This is God's world.
This is God's world.
Let's try to make it a better place.

329   Did you ever talk to God above

Words and music: Frances Towle Rath
Music arrangement Christopher Hayward

1 Did you ev - er talk to God a - bove? Tell Him that you need a
(2) cares and woes? Ev - ery ti - ny lit - tle
(5) word; it's true. You'll be strong be-cause He

friend to love? Pray in Je - sus' name be - liev - ing that God ans-wers
fear He knows. You can know He'll al - ways hear and He will ans-wer
walks with you. By His faith - ful - ness He'll change you too. God ans-wers

prayer?   2 Have you told Him all your prayer.

1 Did you ever talk to God above?
  Tell Him that you need a friend to love?
  Pray in Jesus' name believing
  that God answers prayer?

2 Have you told Him all your cares and woes?
  Every tiny little fear He knows.
  You can know He'll always hear
  and He will answer prayer.

3 You can whisper in a crowd to Him.
  You can cry when you're alone to Him.
  You don't have to pray out loud to Him;
  He knows your thoughts.

4 On a lofty mountain peak, He's there.
  In a meadow by a stream, He's there.
  Anywhere on earth you go
  He's been there from the start.

5 Find the answer in His word; it's true.
  You'll be strong because He walks with you.
  By His faithfulness He'll change you too.
  God answers prayer.

330 Even if I don't
(In spirit and in truth)

Words and music: Sam Horner

With expression

Ev-en if I don't_ like the way things went to-day,_ ev-en if I'm feel-ing down, I'll praise You a - ny - way._ If I'm feel-ing lone - ly, if I'm feel-ing bad,

1 Even if I don't like the way things went today,
  even if I'm feeling down, I'll praise You anyway.
  If I'm feeling lonely, if I'm feeling bad,
  I'll think about the things You've done, and even when I'm sad:
    I will worship You in spirit and in truth,
    I will worship You in spirit and in truth,
    I will worship You in spirit and in truth,
    I will worship You in spirit and in truth.

2 When my life is going great, when everything is right,
  help me not to forget You, Lord, or keep You out of sight.
  I don't want to leave You out, not even for a day,
  I want to see Your hand at work and hear the words You say.
    I will worship You . . .

331 Every day, if you go astray

Words and music: Greg Leavers
Music arranged Christopher Hayward

Ev-ery day, if you go a-stray, stop! and turn a-round. Then don't wor-ry if you've said sor-ry, stop! and turn a-round. When we come to Je-sus He says He'll for-give us, for He cares a-bout us, this is what He

pro-mi - ses. _ When we come to Je - sus He says

He'll for-give us for He cares a-bout us all. _____

1 Every day, if you go astray,
   stop! and turn around.
   Then don't worry if you've said sorry,
   stop! and turn around.
   When we come to Jesus
   He says He'll forgive us,
   for He cares about us.
   This is what He promises.
   When we come to Jesus
   He says He'll forgive us
   for He cares about us all.

2 Every day as we walk God's way
   stop! and praise the Lord.
   He will change us for He's living in us,
   stop! and praise the Lord.
   Jesus, You forgive us,
   then bring Your life to us
   through Your Holy Spirit.
   This is what You promise us.
   Jesus, You forgive us,
   then bring Your life to us
   through Your Spirit in our lives.

3 Jesus, Saviour, Redeemer and King,
   let's go! and live for Him.
   Son of God, our helper and friend,
   go! and live for Him.
   Jesus, how we thank You,
   Jesus, how we love You,
   Jesus, help us trust You
   till the day You come again.
   Jesus, how we thank You,
   Jesus, how we love You,
   Jesus, help us trust You more.

332 Everybody join in singing

Words and music: Greg Leavers
Music arranged Christopher Hayward

Lively

Ev - ery - bo-dy join in sing-ing this song, thank-ing God for all the

good things He's done: show - ing love for us through Je-sus His Son,

good and bad and the____ weak and strong. Young and old all can____

____ sing a - long; come on, ev-ery-bo-dy sing this song. ____ *Fine*

Everybody join in singing this song,
thanking God for all the good things He's done:
showing love for us through Jesus His Son,
good and bad and the weak and strong.
Young and old all can sing along;
come on, everybody sing this song.

1 Thank God for the gift of life.
   Thank Him for His care.
   When our lives then get messed up,
   He'll clear out the bad things there.
      Everybody join in singing . . .

2 In our lives God wants to live,
   make His presence known.
   If we're sorry He'll forgive,
   then our hearts can be His home.
      Everybody join in singing . . .

333 Everyone in the whole wide world
(Everyone matters to Jesus)

Words and music: Derek and Jackie Llewellyn

Happily

Ev - ery-one in the whole wide world mat-ters to our friend Je - sus.

Ev - ery-one, ev-ery boy or girl, we all mat-ter to Him.

Jump up if you're wear-ing red. (*Jump up*)

Wave your arms if you're wear-ing blue. (*Wave*)

D.C.

Clap your hands if you're wear-ing green.   (*Clap*)

Stamp your feet if you're wear-ing shoes.   (*Stamp*)

Everyone in the whole wide world
matters to our friend Jesus.
Everyone, every boy or girl,
we all matter to Him.

1 Jump up if you're wearing red.   (*Jump up*)
   Wave your arms if you're wearing blue.   (*Wave*)
   Clap your hands if you're wearing green.   (*Clap*)
   Stamp your feet if you're wearing shoes.   (*Stamp*)
   Everyone in the whole wide world . . .

2 Jump up if you've ridden a bike.   (*Jump*)
   Wave your arms if you've flown in a plane.   (*Wave*)
   Clap your hands if you've been in a car.   (*Clap*)
   Stamp your feet if you've been on a train.   (*Stamp*)
   Everyone in the whole wide world . . .

334   Everywhere He walks with me

Words and music: Ian White

With expression

Ev - ery - where   He walks with me, ___ and through prayer   He talks with me. ___ He has cared e - nough for me, ___ to die to set me free.

Since then you have been raised with Christ,

set your hearts on things a-bove. Where Christ is seat-ed at God's right

hand, set your minds on things a-bove. Ev-ery-

Everywhere He walks with me,
and through prayer He talks with me.
He has cared enough for me,
to die to set me free.

1 Since then you have been raised with Christ,
set your hearts on things above.
Where Christ is seated at God's right hand,
set your minds on things above.
Everywhere He walks with me . . .

2 Put to death whatever is sin,
rid yourselves of all these things.
You have been renewed in the Lord,
and He is all, and is in all.
Everywhere He walks with me . . .

3 Let His peace now rule in your hearts.
Let His word be rich in you.
Sing psalms and hymns with thanks to God,
praise Him in all that you do.
Everywhere He walks with me . . .

335   Father, be with her family

Words and music: Greg Leavers
Music arranged Phil Burt

1 Father, be with *her/his/their family,
   as they cry with sadness today.
   Aching hearts feeling such a loss:
   may they know Your love.

2 Comfort them with Your love, O Lord,
   as they try to understand
   why You called *her/him/them to be with You;
   may they know Your peace.

* (Use the relevant word or use the child's name)

336   Father, for our friends we pray

Words and music: Greg Leavers
Music arranged Phil Burt

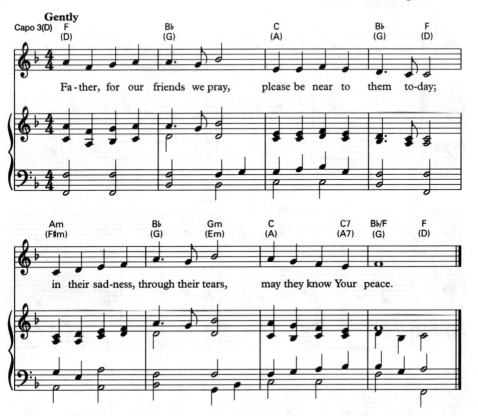

1 Father, for our friends we pray,
   please be near to them today;
   in their sadness, through their tears,
   may they know Your peace.

2 Now that he/she is by Your side
   comfort friends when they ask why
   their dear loved one had to die;
   may they know Your love.

3 Though part of their lives has gone,
   give them strength to carry on.
   As they face the days to come,
   may they know Your care.

337 Father God, I wonder

Words and music: Ian Smale
Music arranged David Peacock

Lively Spanish style

Fa-ther God, I won-der how I man-aged to ex-ist with-out the know-ledge of Your par-ent-hood and Your lov-ing care. But now I am Your son, I am a-dopt-ed in Your fa-mi-ly, and I can ne-ver be a-lone 'cause, Fa-ther God, You're there be-side me.

I will sing Your prais-es, I will sing Your prais-es, I will sing Your prais-es for ev-er - more. for ev-er - more.

Father God, I wonder
how I managed to exist
without the knowledge
of Your parenthood
and Your loving care.
But now I am Your son,
I am adopted in Your family,
and I can never be alone
'cause, Father God,
You're there beside me.

I will sing Your praises,
I will sing Your praises,
I will sing Your praises for evermore.
I will sing Your praises,
I will sing Your praises,
I will sing Your praises for evermore.

338 Father, Your word

Words and music: Paul Crouch
and David Mudie

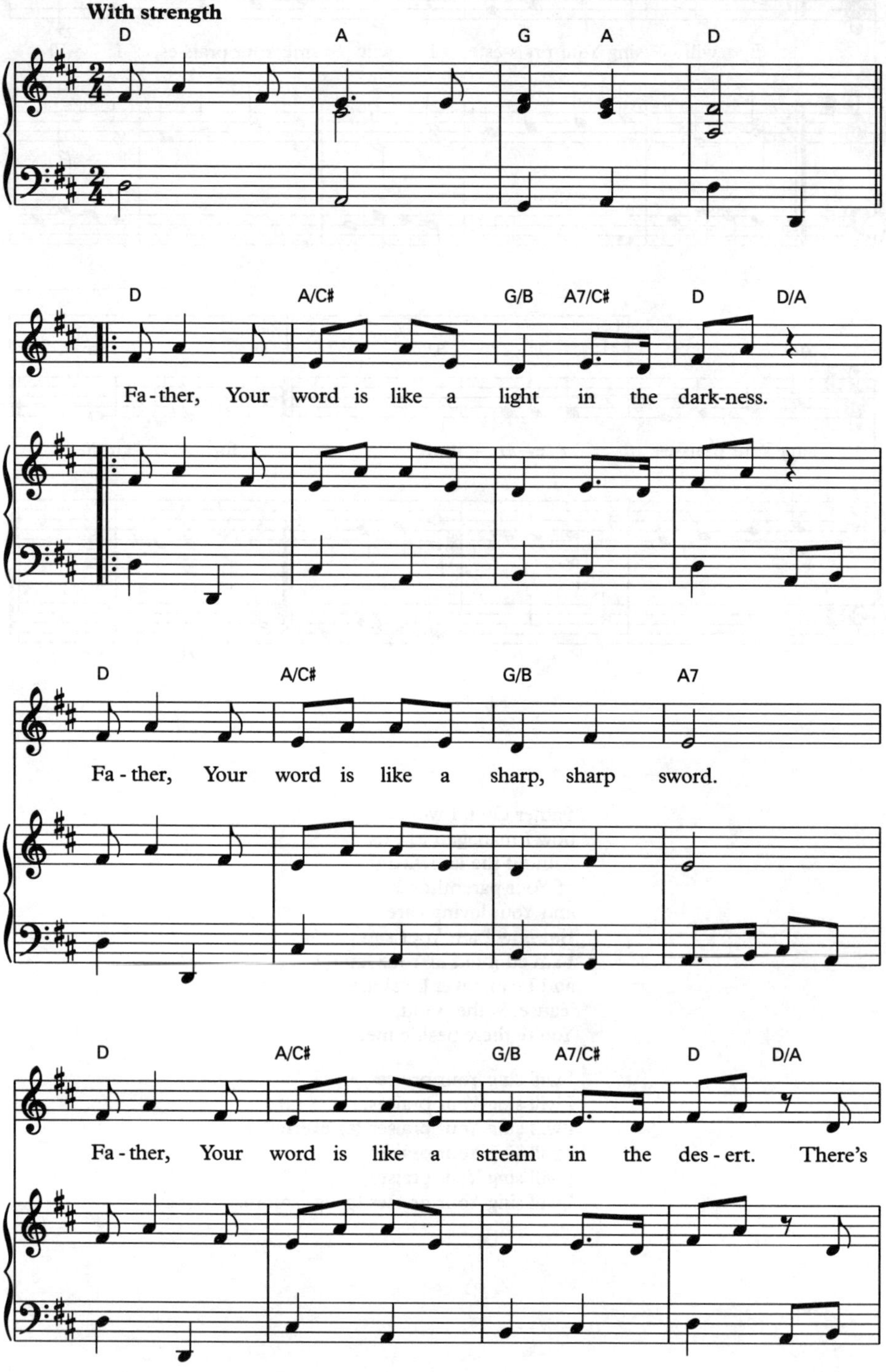

With strength
D A G A D
D A/C# G/B A7/C# D D/A
Fa-ther, Your word is like a light in the dark-ness.
D A/C# G/B A7
Fa - ther, Your word is like a sharp, sharp sword.
D A/C# G/B A7/C# D D/A
Fa - ther, Your word is like a stream in the des - ert. There's

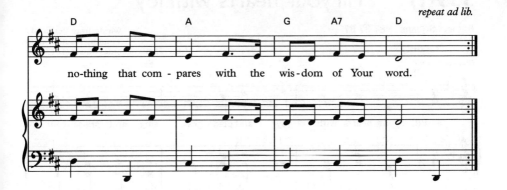

repeat ad lib.

no-thing that com - pares with the wis-dom of Your word.

Father, Your word is like a light in the darkness.
Father, Your word is like a sharp, sharp sword.
Father, Your word is like a stream in the desert.
There's nothing that compares with the wisdom of Your word.

339(i)   Fill your hearts with joy

REGENT SQUARE   87 87 87

Words: from Psalm 147
Timothy Dudley-Smith
Music: Henry Thomas Smart (1813–79)

Joyfully

Capo 3(G)

Fill your hearts with joy and glad - ness, sing and praise your
God and mine! Great the Lord in love and wis - dom,
might and ma - jes - ty di - vine! He who framed the
star - ry hea - vens knows and names them as they shine.

1 Fill your hearts with joy and gladness,
sing and praise your God and mine!
Great the Lord in love and wisdom,
might and majesty divine!
He who framed the starry heavens
knows and names them as they shine.

2 Praise the Lord, His people, praise Him!
wounded souls His comfort know;
those who fear Him find His mercies,
peace for pain and joy for woe;
humble hearts are high exalted,
human pride and power laid low.

3 Praise the Lord for times and seasons,
cloud and sunshine, wind and rain;
spring to melt the snows of winter
till the waters flow again;
grass upon the mountain pastures,
golden valleys thick with grain.

4 Fill your hearts with joy and gladness,
peace and plenty crown your days;
love His laws, declare His judgements,
walk in all His words and ways;
He the Lord and we His children –
praise the Lord, all people, praise!

339(ii) Fill your hearts with joy

LAUS ET HONOR

Words: from Psalm 147
Timothy Dudley-Smith
Music: Gordon Hartless
Music arranged Douglas Coombes

Fill your hearts with joy and glad-ness, sing and praise your God and mine! Great the Lord in love and wis-dom, might and ma-jes-ty di-vine! He who framed the

star - ry hea-vens knows and names them as they shine,

knows and names them as they shine.

1 Fill your hearts with joy and gladness,
   sing and praise your God and mine!
   Great the Lord in love and wisdom,
   might and majesty divine!
   He who framed the starry heavens
   knows and names them as they shine,
   knows and names them as they shine.

2 Praise the Lord, His people, praise Him!
   wounded souls His comfort know;
   those who fear Him find His mercies,
   peace for pain and joy for woe;
   humble hearts are high exalted,
   human pride and power laid low,
   human pride and power laid low.

3 Praise the Lord for times and seasons,
   cloud and sunshine, wind and rain;
   spring to melt the snows of winter
   till the waters flow again;
   grass upon the mountain pastures,
   golden valleys thick with grain,
   golden valleys thick with grain.

4 Fill your hearts with joy and gladness,
   peace and plenty crown your days;
   love His laws, declare His judgements,
   walk in all His words and ways;
   He the Lord and we His children –
   praise the Lord, all people, praise!
   praise the Lord, all people, praise!

340 For the foolishness of God
(God's wisdom)

Words and music: Paul Crouch
and David Mudie

Laid back
Capo 3(D)

For the fool - ish - ness of God is wis - er than man's wis-dom, and the weak-ness of God is strong-er than man's strength. For the fool - ish - ness of God is wis - er than man's wis-dom, and the weak-ness of God is

D.S.

For the foolishness of God is wiser than man's wisdom,
and the weakness of God is stronger than man's strength.
For the foolishness of God is wiser than man's wisdom,
and the weakness of God is stronger than man's strength.
For the foolishness of God is wiser than man's wisdom,
and the weakness of God is stronger than man's strength.
For the foolishness of God is wiser than man's wisdom,
and the weakness of God is stronger than man's strength.

God knows all about the world, the things we cannot see,
the things that we don't understand that baffle you and me.
His strength is never-ending and we are weak and small.
His hand supports the universe and He is in control.

For the foolishness of God . . .

341

From heaven You came
(The Servant King)

Words and music: Graham Kendrick
Music arranged David Peacock

From heaven You came, help-less babe, en-tered our world, Your glo - ry veiled, not to be served but to serve, and give Your life that we might live. *This is our*

1 From heaven You came, helpless babe,
  entered our world, Your glory veiled,
  not to be served but to serve,
  and give Your life that we might live.
    This is our God, the Servant King,
    He calls us now to follow Him,
    to bring our lives as a daily offering
    of worship to the Servant King.

2 There in the garden of tears
  my heavy load He chose to bear;
  His heart with sorrow was torn,
  'Yet not my will but yours,' He said.
    This is our God . . .

3 Come see His hands and His feet,
  the scars that speak of sacrifice,
  hands that flung stars into space
  to cruel nails surrendered.
    This is our God . . .

4 So let us learn how to serve
  and in our lives enthrone Him,
  each other's needs to prefer,
  for it is Christ we're serving.
    This is our God . . .

342   From my knees to my nose

Words and music: Greg Leavers
Music arranged Christopher Hayward

From my knees to my nose, from my head to my toes, does God___ know all a - bout me? If I'm hap - py or sad, if I'm good or I'm bad, does God___ know all a - bout me? The ans - wer is yes___ and He

From my knees to my nose,
from my head to my toes,
does God know all about me?
If I'm happy or sad,
if I'm good or I'm bad,
does God know all about me?
The answer is yes
and He loves me the best,
though He knows everything about me.
The answer is yes
and He loves me the best,
and He knows that my name is . . . (*shout name*)

343 Get up out of bed

Words and music: C Powell and K Wood

CODA

'Thank you,_____ it's a brand new, thank you,_____ it's a brand new,

thank you,_____ it's a brand new day!'_____

Get up out of bed,
have a yawn and scratch your head
and say, 'Thank you, it's a brand new day.'

Stretch out, touch your toes,
blink your eyes and blow your nose
and say, 'Thank you, it's a brand new day.'

Actions for the chorus:
Crouch down and jump up.
Hand over mouth, scratch head.
Lift right palm upwards on the word 'Thank',
    lift left palm on the word 'you'.
Arms out, bend over, touch your toes.
Clench fists and eyes, then open, hand to nose.
As before.

1 Jesus taught us all to go His way.
  Get out of bed and go with Him today.
      Get up out of bed . . .

2 Jesus showed us that He can make us new.
  Get out of bed and ask Him what to do.
      Get up out of bed . . .

3 Jesus loves us all just like He said.
  Get out of bed and shake your sleepy head.
      Get up out of bed . . .

344   Girls and boys, leave your toys

ZITHER CAROL

Words: Malcolm Sargent (1895–1967)
in this version Word & Music
Music: Czech traditional melody
Music arranged David Peacock

Al - le - lu - ia, the church bells ring. 'Al - le - lu - ia!' the an - gels sing,

al - le - lu - ia from ev - ery - thing – all must draw near!

1 Girls and boys, leave your toys, make no noise,
kneel at His crib and worship Him.
For this shrine, Child divine, is the sign
our Saviour's here.
   Alleluia, the church bells ring.
   'Alleluia!' the angels sing,
   alleluia from everything –
   all must draw near!

2 On that day, far away, Jesus lay –
angels were watching round His head.
Holy Child, mother mild, undefiled,
we sing Your praise.
   Alleluia . . .
   our hearts we raise.

3 Shepherds came at the fame of Your name,
angels their guide to Bethlehem;
in that place, saw Your face filled with grace,
stood at Your door.
   Alleluia . . .
   love evermore.

345 Give thanks to the Lord

Words and music: Janet Morgan
Music arranged Christopher Hayward

Give thanks to the Lord for He is good.
Give thanks to the Lord for ever.
Give thanks to the Lord for He is good.

1 When you jump out of bed
   and you touch your toes,
   when you brush your teeth
   and put on your clothes,
       Give thanks . . .

2 When you eat your dinner
   and you're all full up,
   when your Mum says (*Name*)
   and you help wash up,
       Give thanks . . .

3 When you stretch up high
   and you touch the ground,
   when you stretch out wide
   and you turn around,
       Give thanks . . .

4 When you click your fingers
   and you stamp your feet,
   when you clap your hands
   and you slap your knees,
       Give thanks . . .
       Give thanks to the Lord. Amen.

346

God has made me

Words and music: Gillian E Hutchinson
Music arranged Phil Burt

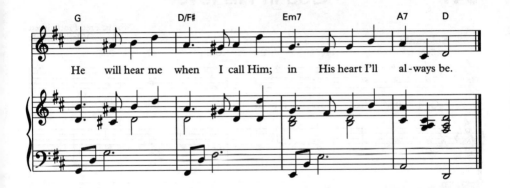

He will hear me when I call Him; in His heart I'll al-ways be.

1 God has made me, and He knows me,
   He will listen to my prayer.
   Understanding, ever-loving,
   He's the God who's always there.
   Even though He made the world, He
   knows my name and cares for me.
   He will hear me when I call Him;
   in His heart I'll always be.

2 Help me, Lord, to understand
   that I'm a child who's loved by You.
   You'll protect me, and be with me
   in the things I have to do.
   Thank You, Lord, that I can trust You,
   thank You for the love You bring.
   Thank You that You'll never leave me;
   Father God, Your praise I sing.

347 God in His love

Words: Fred Pratt Green
Music: Valerie Ruddle

God in His love for us lent us this pla - net,
gave it a pur - pose in time and in space:
small as a spark from the fire of cre - a - tion, cra - dle of
life and the home of our race. world with - out end!

1 God in His love for us lent us this planet,
   gave it a purpose in time and in space:
   small as a spark from the fire of creation,
   cradle of life and the home of our race.

2 Thanks be to God for its bounty and beauty,
   life that sustains us in body and mind:
   plenty for all, if we learn how to share it,
   riches undreamed of to fathom and find.

3 Long have the wars of man ruined its harvest;
   long has earth bowed to the terror of force;
   long have we wasted what others have need of,
   poisoned the fountain of life at its source.

4 Earth is the Lord's: it is ours to enjoy it;
   ours, as His stewards, to farm and defend.
   From its pollution, misuse and destruction,
   good Lord deliver us, world without end!

348

God loves you

Words and music: Anon
Music arranged Christopher Hayward

God loves you, and I love you,
and that's the way it should be.
God loves you, and I love you,
and that's the way it should be.

1 You can be happy, and I can be happy,
and that's the way it should be.
You can be happy, and I can be happy,
and that's the way it should be.
    God loves you . . .

2 You can be very sad, I can be very sad;
and that's the way it can be.
You can be very sad, I can be very sad;
and that's the way it can be.
    God loves you . . .

3 We can love others like sisters and brothers,
and that's the way it should be.
We can love others like sisters and brothers,
and that's the way it should be.
    God loves you . . .

349   God loves you so much

Words and music: Derek Llewellyn

Happily

God loves you so much,
God wants you so much, God wants to tell you
so much that He put it in a book for you. *And it's the* Bi-
-ble, yes, it's the Bi-ble, oh, it's the Bi-

1 God loves you so much,
  God wants you so much,
  God wants to tell you so much
  that He put it in a book for you.
    And it's the Bible,
    yes, it's the Bible,
    oh, it's the Bible.
    Yes, He put it in a letter
    so we could know Him better.

2 He wants to know you so much,
  He wants to show you so much,
  God wants to tell you so much
  that He put it in a book for you.
    And it's the Bible . . .

3 God loves you so much,
  God wants you so much,
  God wants to tell you so much
  that He put it in a book,
  put it in a book for,
  put it in a book for you.

350

God of all mercy

Words and music: Fiona Inkpen

A two-part round

Gently

God of all mer-cy, Your for-give-ness and com-pas-sion

call forth songs from with-in that fill our hearts with glad-ness.

God of all mercy,
Your forgiveness and compassion
call forth songs from within
that fill our hearts with gladness.

351 God told Joshua

Words and music: Greg Leavers
Music arranged Christopher Hayward

With a swing

God told Josh-ua__ to take Je-ri-cho.__
God told Josh-ua__ to take Je-ri-cho.__
He said, 'Do it My way.' Josh-ua said,__ 'O K.'__
So through faith the ci-ty walls came__ down!

Fine

God told Joshua to take Jericho.
God told Joshua to take Jericho.
He said, 'Do it My way.'
Joshua said, 'OK.'
So through faith the city walls came down!

1 Marching round the city,
   priests are at the front,
   blowing on their trumpets,
   going round just once.
   This they did for six days,
   just as God had said;
   the priests were making all the noise, the rest were saying,
      God told Joshua . . .

2 God said on day seven,
   'Here is what you do:
   march around for six times,
   then do something new.
   When you're on lap seven,
   Jericho look out!
   All their walls will crumble when you give a great big SHOUT!!'
      God told Joshua . . .

352

God was there
(Yesterday, today, forever)

Words and music: Peter Lewis
Music arranged Christopher Hayward

God was there be-fore the world was made.

God is here, He's with us ev-ery day.

God is love and that will ne-ver change.

Yes-ter-day, to-day, for-ev-er He's the same.

Yes - ter - day, to - day, for - ev - er He's the same.

1 God was there before the world was made.
God is here, He's with us every day.
God is love and that will never change.
Yesterday, today, forever
He's the same.
Yesterday, today, forever
He's the same.

2 God is good, the Bible tells us so.
God is wise, He knows what we don't know.
God is true, no matter what we do.
Yesterday, today, forever
our life through.
Yesterday, today, forever
our life through.

3 God is like a Father to us all.
God will always listen when we call.
God's the one we worship and adore.
Yesterday, today, forever
He is Lord.
Yesterday, today, forever
He is Lord.

353 God whose love is everywhere

FALLING FIFTHS 7 7 7 5 7 7 5

Words: Timothy Dudley-Smith
Music: Noël Tredinnick

God whose love is ev-ery - where_ made our earth and all things fair, __ ev - er keeps them in His care; praise the God of love! He who hung the stars in space holds the spin - ning world in place;

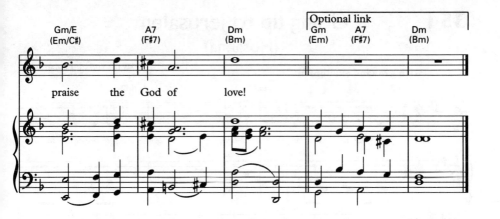

The orange
representing
all the world

The sticks,
fruit and nuts,
representing
the four
seasons and
the fruit of
the earth

The red
ribbon,
representing
the blood of
Christ shed
for us

The lighted
candle,
representing
Christ
the Light of
the world

1 God whose love is everywhere
made our earth and all things fair,
ever keeps them in His care;
    praise the God of love!
He who hung the stars in space
holds the spinning world in place;
    praise the God of love!

2 Come with thankful songs to sing
of the gifts the seasons bring,
summer, winter, autumn, spring;
    praise the God of love!
He who gave us breath and birth
gives us all the fruitful earth;
    praise the God of love!

3 Mark what love the Lord displayed,
all our sins upon Him laid,
by His blood our ransom paid;
    praise the God of love!
Circled by that scarlet band
all the world is in His hand;
    praise the God of love!

4 See the sign of love appear,
flame of glory, bright and clear,
light for all the world is here;
    praise the God of love!
Gloom and darkness, get you gone!
Christ the Light of life has shone;
    praise the God of love!

354

Going up to Jerusalem
(Hosanna)

Words and music: Ian White

With growing excitement

Go-ing up to Je - ru - sa-lem, go-ing up to Je-

- ru - sa-lem, go-ing up to Je - ru - sa-lem, (Je-sus go-ing

up), go-ing up to Je - ru - sa-lem, (Je-sus go-ing up). Going up to Je-

- ru - sa-lem. 1 Ho - san - na,— ho - san - na,— we

Going up to Jerusalem,
going up to Jerusalem,
going up to Jerusalem, (Jesus going up),
going up to Jerusalem, (Jesus going up).
Going up to Jerusalem,
going up to Jerusalem,
going up to Jerusalem, (Jesus going up),
going up to Jerusalem.

1 Hosanna, hosanna,
  we lay our branches down.
  Hosanna, hosanna,
  the King is coming to our town.
  Hosanna, hosanna today.

2 He's the Saviour, He's the Saviour,
  we lay our branches down.
  He's the Saviour, He's the Saviour,
  the King is coming to our town.
  Hosanna, hosanna today.

355   Grace is

Words and music: Paul Crouch and David Mudie
Music arranged Christopher Hayward

Grace is when God gives us the things we don't de-serve. Grace is when God gives us the things we don't de-serve. He does it be-cause He loves us. He does it be-cause He loves us.

Grace is when God gives us the things we don't de - serve.

1 Grace is when God gives us
  the things we don't deserve.
  Grace is when God gives us
  the things we don't deserve.
  He does it because He loves us.
  He does it because He loves us.
  Grace is when God gives us
  the things we don't deserve.

2 Mercy is when God gives us
  the things we don't deserve.
  Mercy is when God gives us
  the things we don't deserve.
  He does it because He loves us.
  He does it because He loves us.
  Mercy is when God gives us
  the things we don't deserve.

356

Hang on

Words and music: Richard Hubbard
Music arranged Christopher Hayward

Hang on, stand still, stay put, hold tight; wait for the Spi-rit of God. — Don't push, don't shove, don't move, that's right; just wait for the Spi-rit of God. — Hang on, stand still, stay put, hold tight; wait for the Spi-rit of God. — Don't

1 Hang on, stand still,
  stay put, hold tight;
  wait for the Spirit of God.
  Don't push, don't shove,
  don't move, that's right;
  just wait for the Spirit of God.
  Hang on . . .

  For you will receive the power of God.
  You will receive the power of God.
  You will receive the power of God
  when the Holy Spirit is upon you.

2 Let go, launch out,
  press on, don't fight;
  be filled with the Spirit of God.
  Move on, make way,
  step out, that's right;
  be filled with the Spirit of God.
  Let go . . .

  For you have received the power of God.
  You have received the power of God.
  You have received the power of God
  now the Holy Spirit lives within you.

357 Have you got an appetite

Words and music: Mick Gisbey
Music arranged Christopher Hayward

Have you got an ap-pet - ite? Do you eat what is right? Are you feed-ing on the word of God? Are you fat or are you thin? Are you real - ly full with - in? Do you find your strength in Him, or are you starv - ing?

1 Have you got an appetite?
  Do you eat what is right?
  Are you feeding on the word of God?
  Are you fat or are you thin?
  Are you really full within?
  Do you find your strength in Him, or are you starving?
    You and me all should be exercising regularly,
    standing strong, all day long, giving God the glory.
    Feeding on the living bread, not eating crumbs but loaves instead;
    standing stronger, living longer, giving God the glory.
    You and me all should be exercising regularly,
    standing strong, all day long, giving God the glory.
    Feeding on the living bread, not eating crumbs but loaves instead;
    standing stronger, living longer, giving God the glory.

2 If it's milk or meat you need,
  why not have a slap-up feed,
  and stop looking like a weed and start to grow?
  Take the full-of-fitness food,
  taste and see that God is good,
  come on, feed on what you should and be healthy.
    You and me all should be exercising regularly,
    standing strong, all day long, giving God the glory.
    Feeding on the living bread, not eating crumbs but loaves instead;
    standing stronger, living longer, giving God the glory.
    You and me all should be exercising regularly,
    standing strong, all day long, giving God the glory.
    Feeding on the living bread, not eating crumbs but loaves instead;
    standing stronger, living longer, giving God the,
    giving God the, giving God the glory.

358 Heavenly Father
(Children of God's family)

Words and music: Ian Smale
Music arranged Christopher Norton

Hea - ven-ly Fa-ther, we would sing out Your praise, You're ev-ery-thing a Fa-ther

should be. Made us Your sons and daught-ers, made us Your own,

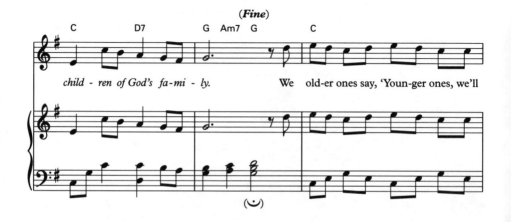

(Fine)

child - ren of God's fa-mi - ly. We old-er ones say, 'Youn-ger ones, we'll

Heavenly Father, we would sing out Your praise,
You're everything a Father should be.
Made us Your sons and daughters,
made us Your own, children of God's family.

1 We older ones say, 'Younger ones,
  we'll love and care for you.'
  We young ones say to older ones,
  'Our love respects you too.'
  We love you.
    Heavenly Father ...

2 Father, as a family
  we will live forever.
  Your Church is made of all ages
  who love to be together.
  We love you.
    Heavenly Father ...

359 He made the water wet
(That's good)

Words and music: Dennis and Nan Allen
Music arranged Christopher Hayward

He made the wa-ter wet, He made the land stay dry. He put twin-kle in the stars and blue in the sky. And when He was sure it worked as it should, God looked at His world and said, 'That's good!' Good, good, good! He said, 'That's good!'

Good, good, good! God looked at His world and said, 'That's

good!' 2 He good, that's good, that's good!
2nd time (That's)

1 He made the water wet,
He made the land stay dry.
He put twinkle in the stars
and blue in the sky.
And when He was sure
it worked as it should,
God looked at His world and said,
'That's good!'
Good, good, good! He said, 'That's good!'
Good, good, good! God looked at His world and said,
'That's good!'

2 He put a touch of wag
in a puppy dog's tail,
then put a little slow
in a silly old snail.
And when He was sure
it worked as it should,
God looked at His world and said,
'That's good!'
Good, good, good . . .

That's good, that's good,
(shouted) that's good!

360 He gives me strength

Words and music: Peter and Hanneke Jacobs
Music arranged Christopher Hayward

He gives me strength, yes, He gives me strength.
I can do all things through Christ who gives me strength.
Yes, He gives me strength, He gives me strength.
I can do all things through Christ who gives me strength.

361   Hey, you, do you love Jesus

Refrain: F Whitfield
Music arranged Christopher Norton

The first part of this song is a dialogue. It can work as follows:
One person starts it and the one who is named sings the answers,
and in turn asks the questions the second time round.
A good concluding verse is 'Hey, saints' (or 'family' or 'kids') . . .
some term which includes all of those present.

Music arrangement: © 1992 HarperCollins*Religious*, administered by
CopyCare Ltd, PO Box 77, Hailsham, East Sussex BN27 3EF, UK. Used by permission

QUESTION	Hey, you, (*name*) do you love Jesus?
ANSWER	oh, yes, I love Jesus.
QUESTION	Are you sure you love Jesus?
ANSWER	Yes, I'm sure I love Jesus.
QUESTION	Tell me, why do you love Jesus?
ANSWER	This is why I love Jesus,
ALL	because He first loved me.
	Yes, I love Him, this is why I love Him.

Oh, how I love Jesus.
Oh, how I love Jesus.
Oh, how I love Jesus,
because He first loved me.
Yes, I love Him, this is why I love Him.

362   Hey! Hey! Anybody listening

Words and music: Richard K Avery
and Donald S Marsh
Music arranged Christopher Hayward

D.C. al Fine

ev - ery-where,   ev - ery-where,   ev - ery-where,   ev - ery-where.

Hey! Hey! Anybody listening?
Hey! Hey! Anybody there?
Hey! Hey! Anybody listening?
Anybody care?

1 We've got good news, good news, good news, good news:
   Christ the Lord will soon be found here!
   Good news, good news, good news, good news:
   let's help spread the news around here!
   If I had a drum I'd drum it,
   a mandolin I'd strum it,
   a humming-bird hum I'd hum it,
   everywhere, everywhere, everywhere, everywhere.
      Hey! Hey! . . .

2 People come on, come on, come on, come on:
   let's sing out for Mary's Son here!
   Come on, come on, come on, come on:
   He'll bring joy for everyone here!
   If I had a harp I'd twang it,
   a tambourine I'd bang it,
   a fireman's bell I'd clang it,
   everywhere, everywhere, everywhere, everywhere.
      Hey! Hey! . . .

3 Come on, sing out, sing out, sing out, sing out!
   Tell the world about His birth now!
   Sing out, sing out, sing out, sing out
   loud and clear to all the earth now!
   If I had a chime I'd ring it,
   a finger cymbal ching it,
   we've got this song let's sing it,
   everywhere, everywhere, everywhere, everywhere.
      Hey! Hey! . . .

363

His name was Saul

Words and music: Andy Silver

His name was Saul of Tar-sus, a clever Pha-ri-see; he stud-ied Greek and La-tin and he spoke them flu-ent-ly. The on-ly thing he want-ed was to wipe out those who said, 'We are fol-low-ers of Je-sus and His

set all peo-ple free.

last time

1 His name was Saul of Tarsus,
   a clever Pharisee;
   he studied Greek and Latin
   and he spoke them fluently.
   The only thing he wanted
   was to wipe out those who said,
   'We are followers of Jesus
   and His truth we want to spread!'
   Saul, Saul, Saul, Saul, you're persecuting Me;
   the Christians that you're killing are true followers of Me.
   Saul, Saul, Saul, Saul, you really need to see
   I came to bring forgiveness and to set all people free.

2 Determined to pursue them
   on his way he quickly strode,
   heading for Damascus
   along the well-worn road.
   The followers of Jesus
   he wanted locked away,
   but little did he know
   that God would speak to him that day.
   Saul, Saul . . .

3 When God had finished speaking
   Saul stood and tried to find
   the men who had been with him,
   but the light had made him blind.
   They led him to a little house,
   he stayed for just three days.
   When he realised what had happened
   he was simply quite amazed.
   Saul, Saul . . .

4 This brought about a change in Saul,
   he'd never be the same;
   not only had his life been changed
   he'd got a different name.
   The Lord had given to Paul the task
   to go to everyone,
   and tell them that the way to God
   is only through His Son.
   Saul, Saul . . .

364 His ways are not our ways

Words and music: Iain Craig

Happily

His ways are not our___ ways but His ways are the best. ___

If we fol-low Je-sus we know that we'll be blessed.

If we trust Him He will help us, lis-ten when we pray.

last time **to Coda** ⊕

His ways are not our ways but His ways are the best. ___

His ways are not our ways
but His ways are the best.
If we follow Jesus
we know that we'll be blessed.
If we trust Him He will help us,
listen when we pray.
His ways are not our ways
but His ways are the best.

1 When I call He listens, when I fall He's near.
  He has promised He will help me,
  I will never fear.
  His ways . . .

2 If I ever wander, if I turn from Him,
  He has promised He will help me,
  I will never fear.
  His ways . . .

3 He will always love me, He will always care.
  He has promised He will help me,
  I will never fear.
  His ways . . .

365

Hosanna, hosanna

Words and music: Carl Tuttle

Ho - san - na, ho - san - na, ho - san-na in the high - est; ho - san - na, ho - san - na, ho - san-na in the high - est. Lord, we lift up Your name, with hearts full of praise.

Be ex-alt-ed, O__ Lord my God – ho-san-na, in the high - est.

1 Hosanna, hosanna, hosanna in the highest;
   hosanna, hosanna, hosanna in the highest.
   Lord, we lift up Your name,
   with hearts full of praise.
   Be exalted, O Lord my God –
   hosanna, in the highest.

2 Glory, glory, glory to the King of kings;
   glory, glory, glory to the King of kings.
   Lord, we lift up Your name,
   with hearts full of praise.
   Be exalted, O Lord my God –
   glory to the King of kings.

366

I am like a house

Words and music: Greg Leavers
Music arranged Phil Burt and Christopher Hayward

I am like a house with two win-dows and a door,___ but
un-der-neath I have two legs that reach down to the floor;___ two
ears to hear what's hap-pen-ing and a thatched roof up a-bove,___ but
right in-side God's giv-en me___ a heart that's full of love. So

I am like a house with two windows and a door,
but underneath I have two legs that reach down to the floor;
two ears to hear what's happening and a thatched roof up above,
but right inside God's given me a heart that's full of love.
So jump up and turn around
and thank the Lord with joyful sound.
So jump up and turn around
and thank the Lord, and now sit down!

367

I am the Church
(We are the Church)

Words and music: Richard K Avery
and Donald S Marsh

Church is not a rest-ing-place, the Church is a peo-ple!

I am the Church! – (With your thumb, point to yourself)
You are the Church! – (Point to your partner)
We are the Church together! – (Shake hands)
All who follow Jesus, – (Reach out with both hands)
all around the world, – (Circle arms over head)
yes, we're the Church together. – (Link arms)

1 The Church is not a building, the Church is not a steeple.
The Church is not a resting-place, the Church is a people!
I am the Church . . .

2 We're many kinds of people with many kinds of faces:
all colours and all ages, too, from all times and places.
I am the Church . . .

3 Sometimes the Church is marching, sometimes it's bravely burning,
sometimes it's riding, sometimes hiding. Always it's learning!
I am the Church . . .

4 And when the people gather there's singing and there's praying,
there's laughing and there's crying sometimes, all of it saying:
I am the Church . . .

5 At Pentecost some people received the Holy Spirit
and told the good news through the world to all who would hear it.
I am the Church . . .

6 I count if I am ninety, or nine, or just a baby;
there's one thing I am sure about and I don't mean maybe:
I am the Church . . .

368 I am the resurrection

Words and music: Peter and Hanneke Jacobs
Music arranged Christopher Hayward

Joyfully

I am the re - sur - rec - tion and the life. I am the re - sur - rec - tion and the life. He that be - lieves in Me_ though he may die yet shall he live a - gain. And who - ev - er lives and be - lieves in___ Me, and who - ev - er lives and be -

I am the resurrection and the life.
I am the resurrection and the life.
He that believes in Me though he may die
yet shall he live again.
And whoever lives and believes in Me,
and whoever lives and believes in Me,
the Bible says in John eleven twenty-five and twenty-six
that we shall never die.

369   I cast all my cares upon You

Words and music: Kelly Willard

1 I cast all my cares upon You.
  I lay all of my burdens down at Your feet.
  And any time that I don't know what to do,
  I will cast all my cares upon You.

2 I cast all my cares upon You.
  I lay all of my burdens down at Your feet.
  And any time that I don't know what to do,
  I will cast all of my cares upon You.
  I will cast all my cares upon You.

370 I have a friend

Words and music: Susan Sayers
Music arranged Gerald Fitzpatrick

With a swing

I have a friend who is deep - er than the o - cean;

I have a friend who is wid - er than the sky.

I have a friend who al - ways un - der-stands me,

wheth - er I'm   hap - py, or   rea - dy to   cry.

1 I have a friend who is deeper than the ocean;
  I have a friend who is wider than the sky.
  I have a friend who always understands me,
  whether I'm happy, or ready to cry.

2 If I am lost He will search until He finds me;
  if I am scared He will help me to be brave.
  All I've to do is to turn to Him and ask Him.
  I know He'll keep the promise He gave:

3 'Don't be afraid,' said Jesus, 'I am with you.'
  'Don't be afraid,' said Jesus, 'I am here.
  Now and forever, anywhere you travel,
  I shall be with you, I'll always be near.'

371   I look out through the doorway

Words and music: Greg Leavers
Music arranged Christopher Hayward

With a swing

I look out through the door - way, who's that I see be-fore me? My young son com - ing__ home.__ I must run to meet him, hug him when I greet him, and say, 'Son, wel - come home.' We will have a par - ty__ and

I look out through the doorway,
who's that I see before me?
My young son coming home.
I must run to meet him,
hug him when I greet him,
and say, 'Son, welcome home.'
We will have a party
and I can't wait to start.
He must have the very finest food,
the best robe, ring and sandals.
He was lost, but now is found.
Welcome home, son, welcome home.

372 I love You, Lord Jesus

Words and music: Paul Crouch and David Mudie

I love You, Lord Jesus,
the King of all things.
You love me, Lord Jesus,
Your love never ends.
To You I am special,
Your promises are true.
You love me, Lord Jesus,
and Lord, I love You.

373

I am a sheep

Words and music: Anon
Music arranged Christopher Hayward

I am a sheep, baa, baa, and I like to be well fed; but like a sheep, baa, baa, I'm a lit-tle stu-pid in the head. I go a-stray most ev-ery day. Oh, what a trou-ble I must be! I'm glad I've got the good shep-herd look-ing af-ter me, ha, ha, ha, ha, baa, baa.

I am a sheep, baa, baa,
and I like to be well fed;
but like a sheep, baa, baa,
I'm a little stupid in the head.

I go astray most every day.
Oh, what a trouble I must be!
I'm glad I've got the good shepherd (*spoken*)
looking after me, ha, ha, ha, ha, baa, baa.

374 I want to love You, Lord
(This is my prayer)

Words and music: Doug Holck

1 I want to love You, Lord;
I want to serve You, Lord;
I want to please You, Lord;
this is my prayer.

2 I want to love You, Lord;
I want to serve You, Lord;
I want to please You, Lord;
this is my prayer.

375
I want to tell you

Words and music: Greg Leavers
Music arranged Christopher Hayward

In the verse the leader sings a phrase and then everybody else repeats it.

Words and music: © 1990 Greg Leavers

ve-ry, ve-ry, ve-ry ve-ry spe-cial, you see. __ There's no-one, not one, __ in the world like me, __ for God made me just the way He want-ed me to be. __

1 I want to tell you (I want to tell you)
   my eyes are blue (my eyes are blue),
   I want to show you (I want to show you)
   what I can do *(clap! clap!)* (what I can do) *(clap! clap!)*.
      There's no-one, not one, in the world like me.
      I'm so very, very, very, very special, you see.
      There's no-one, not one, in the world like me,
      for God made me just the way He wanted me to be.

2 There are so many (there are so many)
   things I can do (things I can do).
   I don't feel useless (I don't feel useless),
   these words are true (these words are true).
      There's no-one . . .

3 Jesus is special (Jesus is special),
   I'm special too (I'm special too).
   He says He loves me (He says He loves me)
   and He loves you (and He loves you).
      There's no-one . . .

376 I will wave my hands

Words and music: Ian Smale
Music arranged Christopher Hayward

Happily

I will wave my hands in praise and a-do-ra-tion; I will wave my hands in praise and a-do-ra-tion; I will wave my hands in praise and a-do-ra-tion, praise and a-do-ra-tion to the liv-ing God. For He's gi-ven me hands that just love clap-ping— one, two,

377   I'm a footstep follower

Words and music: Greg Leavers
Music arranged Phil Burt and Christopher Hayward

I'm a foot-step follow-er for Jesus leads the way. He knows the life that's best for me: a plan for ev-ery day. As I walk and talk with Him, He'll never let me stray.

I'm a footstep follower
for Jesus leads the way.
He knows the life that's best for me:
a plan for every day.
As I walk and talk with Him,
He'll never let me stray.
I'm a footstep follower
for Jesus leads the way.

378 I'm going to hide God's word inside my heart

Words and music: Peter and Hanneke Jacobs

Lyrics:

I'm going to hide God's word inside my heart and learn each verse from me - mo -

I'm going to hide God's word inside my heart
and learn each verse from memory.
I'm going to hide God's word inside my heart
until His word is part of me.

God's word will help me each and every day
to know what is right from what is wrong.
The more that I read it, the more I learn of Him,
and His word will make me strong.

That's why I'm going to hide God's word inside my heart
and learn each verse from memory.
I'm going to hide God's word inside my heart
until His word is part of me,
until His word is part of me.

379 I'm going to say my prayers

Words and music: Ian Smale
Music arranged David Peacock

I'm going to say my prayers, read my Bi - ble ev - ery morn-ing; going to

get some fel-low-ship, wit-ness ev-ery day. I'm going to wit-ness ev-ery day.

I am going to pray ev-ery morn-ing, I am going to

pray ev-ery day.   I   am going to   pray ev-ery day. *I'm going to*

I'm going to say my prayers,
read my Bible every morning;
going to get some fellowship,
witness every day.
I'm going to say my prayers,
read my Bible every morning;
going to get some fellowship,
witness every day.

1   I am going to pray every morning,
    I am going to pray every day.
    I am going to pray every morning,
    I am going to pray every day.
    I'm going to say . . .

2   I am going to read my Bible every morning,
    I am going to read my Bible every day.
    I am going to read my Bible every morning,
    I am going to read my Bible every day.
    I'm going to say . . .

3   I am going to fellowship every morning,
    I am going to fellowship every day.
    I am going to fellowship every morning,
    I am going to fellowship every day.
    I'm going to say . . .

4   I am going to witness every morning,
    I am going to witness every day.
    I am going to witness every morning,
    I am going to witness every day.
    I'm going to say . . .

380

I'm going to stand up

Words and music: Ernie and Debbie Rettino

With strength

I'm going to stand___ up,___ I'm going to stand ___ up,___

I'm going to stand___ up,

stand up and live_ for Je - sus. Oo___ I, I'm going to stand

1st time repeat
2nd time continue
3rd time repeat
4th time to Bridge
5th time repeat
6th time to Coda

CODA

I'm going to stand____ up,____ I'm going to stand ____ up. ____ Stand up!

I'm going to stand up, I'm going to stand up,
I'm going to stand up, I'm going to stand up.

I'm going to stand up, stand up and live for Jesus.
Oo I, I'm going to stand up, stand up and live for Him.
I'm going to give up, give up my life for Jesus.
Oo I, I'm going to give up, give up my life for Him.

Lord, we will live our lives for You,
serve You faithfully, like You want us to.
Lord, You give us the power to live for You,
live for You.

I'm going to stand up . . .

Let's take a stand for Jesus,
let's live our lives for Jesus.
Let's give it all for Jesus.
Stand up for Jesus! Stand up for Jesus!
Stand up, stand up, stand up, stand up, stand up!

I'm going to stand up . . .

I'm going to stand up, I'm going to stand up,
I'm going to stand up, I'm going to stand up.
Stand up!

381   I'm going to take a step of faith

Words and music: Greg Leavers
Music arranged Christopher Hayward

I'm going to take_____ a step of___ faith, I'm going to
(clap clap)

put my trust in the Lord.___

He has___ the po - wer___ to car - ry me through. If I

lis - ten care - ful - ly,_____ He'll tell me what to do. I'm going to

1 I'm going to take (*clap clap*) a step of faith,
I'm going to put my trust in the Lord.
He has the power to carry me through.
If I listen carefully, He'll tell me what to do.
I'm going to take (*clap clap*) a step of faith,
and put my trust in the Lord.

2 I'm going to take (*clap clap*) a step of faith,
I'm going to put my trust in the Lord.
He made a promise He loves me so,
wherever He might lead me, He'll never let me go.
I'm going to take (*clap clap*) a step of faith,
and put my trust in the Lord.

382   I'm going to set my heart

Words and music: Greg Leavers
Music arranged Christopher Hayward

I'm going to set my heart
on the precious word of God;
I'm going to feed my heart
on His many promises.

His word helps me in trouble,
it teaches me to praise.
I don't want to live with a hungry heart;
I'm going to feed on the word of God.

383   I've come to a time

Words and music: Gillian E Hutchinson
Music arranged Phil Burt

I've come to a time when I must change, a time when I have to choose,___ to or-der my own life, or fol - low Christ, and gain what I can - not lose.___ My

1 I've come to a time when I must change,
   a time when I have to choose,
   to order my own life, or follow Christ,
   and gain what I cannot lose.
   My Lord, I come,
   I'm giving my life to You.
   Fill me with Your Spirit,
   and make over my heart anew.

2 The ways of the past, I leave, I leave,
   my life in His hands I place.
   His strength will uphold me through anything,
   sufficient for me His grace.
   My Lord . . .

3 The wrong that I've done, I now confess,
   I know that He will forgive.
   His love is far greater than all my sin,
   He'll teach me the way to live.
   My Lord . . .

4 From love of myself, I turn, I turn,
   to serving the King of kings.
   My life will be filled with the love of Christ,
   whatever the future brings.
   My Lord . . .

5 I've come to a time when I must change,
   a time when I have to choose,
   to order my own life, or follow Christ,
   and gain what I cannot lose.

384   If any man come after Me

Words and music: Terrye Coelho

If any man come after Me, let him deny himself,
pick up his cross and follow Me into life eternally.
Deny yourself, pick up your cross, and follow Jesus.
He is the way, truth, and life.

Optional 2nd part

Alleluia! Praise the Lord, worship Him in one accord.
Alleluia! He is King, Master, Lord of everything.
Jesus Christ, Lord of all, loving great and small;
He is the way, truth, and life.

385 If it pleases the King

Words and music: Gillian E Hutchinson
Music arranged Phil Burt

If it pleas-es the King, I want to live my life for Him. If it of-fers Him praise, I will fol-low His ways. Sin - ful I may be, but He will wel-come me. My life

to Him I'll bring, if it pleas-es the King.

1 If it pleases the King,
 I want to live my life for Him.
 If it offers Him praise,
 I will follow His ways.
 Sinful I may be,
 but He will welcome me.
 My life to Him I'll bring,
 if it pleases the King.

2 If it pleases the King,
 I want to give my love to Him.
 If it honours the Lord,
 I will trust in His word.
 I need never fear,
 for He'll be ever near.
 My love to Him I'll sing,
 if it pleases the King.

386   If Jesus is de vine

Words and music: Sam Horner

1 If Jesus is de vine, we must be de branches.
  If Jesus is de vine, we must be de branches.
  If Jesus is de vine, we must be de branches,
  and bear fruit in the kingdom of God.

2 If Jesus is de rock, we should be a little boulder.
  If Jesus is de rock, we should be a little boulder.
  If Jesus is de rock, we should be a little boulder,
  to bear fruit in the kingdom of God.

3 If Jesus is de bread, is your name on the roll now?
  If Jesus is de bread, is your name on the roll now?
  If Jesus is de bread, is your name on the roll now?
  Let's bear fruit in the kingdom of God.

387 If you love Me

Words and music: Andy Hughes
Music arranged Christopher Hayward

If you love Me___ you will o-bey My com-mand-ments. If you love Me___ you will do what I say;___ and if you love Me___ then ev-ery day you will seek Me say-ing, 'Lord, what shall I do to-day?'___ Just like Josh-u-a___ stand-ing at the Jor-dan's side;

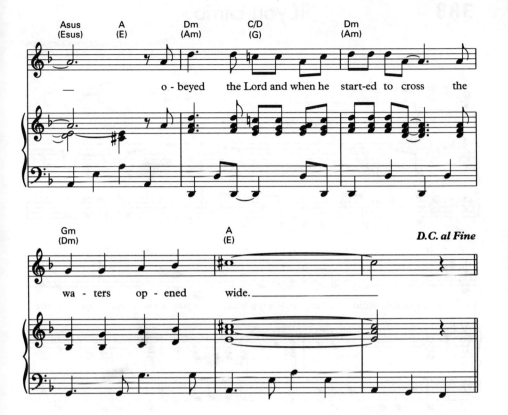

o - beyed the Lord and when he start-ed to cross the
wa - ters op - ened wide.

D.C. al Fine

If you love Me you will obey My commandments.
If you love Me you will do what I say;
and if you love Me then every day you will seek Me
saying, 'Lord, what shall I do today?'

1 Just like Joshua
   standing at the Jordan's side;
   obeyed the Lord and when he started to cross
   the waters opened wide.
      If you love Me . . .

2 As the disciples
   obeyed and brought Him fish and bread.
   So Jesus blessed it and they handed it round
   and five thousand men were fed.
      If you love Me . . .

388 If you climb

Words and music: Derek Llewellyn
Music arranged Phil Burt and Christopher Hayward

1 If you climb (*stamp stamp*) to the top of a moun-tain, if you swim (*splish splish*) in the o-cean blue, if you're lost (*sniff sniff*) in the deep-est for-est,— Je-sus will al-ways find you.—

2 If you fall (*scream*) in-to the dark-est cave,— if you

1 If you climb (*stamp stamp*) to the top of a mountain,
 if you swim (*splish splish*) in the ocean blue,
 if you're lost (*sniff sniff*) in the deepest forest,
 Jesus will always find you.

2 If you fall (*scream*) into the darkest cave,
 if you fly (*zoom*) right up into the air,
 if you run (*run on the spot*) all around the world,
 Jesus will always be there.

3 So if you're feeling lonely,
 if you're feeling sad,
 Jesus will always be close to you,
 so you can always feel glad.

4 If you climb (*stamp stamp*) to the top of a mountain,
 if you swim (*splish splish*) in the ocean blue,
 if you're lost (*sniff sniff*) in the deepest forest,
 Jesus will always find you.

389

If you want to be great
(Servant of all)

Words and music: Michael Ryan
Music arranged Lyndell Leatherman

With a shuffle

If you want to be great_____ in God's king-dom,_____ learn to be the ser - vant of all. If you want to be great_____ in God's king - dom,_____

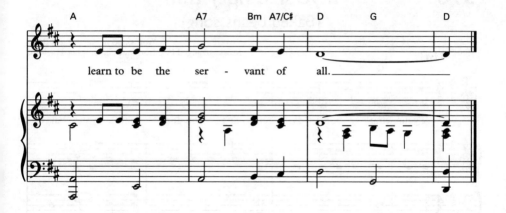

If you want to be great in God's kingdom,
learn to be the servant of all.
If you want to be great in God's kingdom,
learn to be the servant of all.
Learn to be the servant of all,
learn to be the servant of all.
If you want to be great in God's kingdom,
learn to be the servant of all.

390 If your empty tum
(Baked beans song)

Words and music: Angela Reith
Music arranged Phil Burt and Christopher Hayward

If your emp-ty tum‿ is rumb-ling‿ you don't leave‿ your baked beans (*munch munch*). If it's light-ning and‿ it's thunder-ing‿ you don't stand be-neath the trees.‿ And if you climb a high steep hill you don't re-fuse a Coke (*pshhh*). And if your best friend's feel-ing ill‿

put your Bi - ble out of sight if you want to do what's right._____ You don't

put your Bi - ble out of sight if you want to do what's right. _

If your empty tum is rumbling
you don't leave your baked beans (*munch munch*).
If it's lightning and it's thundering
you don't stand beneath the trees.
And if you climb a high steep hill
you don't refuse a Coke (*pshhh*).
And if your best friend's feeling ill
you don't treat it like a joke (*ha ha*).
You don't run across the high street
if you want to grow old.
You don't look down at your feet
if you want to score a goal (*clap clap*).
So don't forget to pray
if you want to follow God today.
You don't put your Bible out of sight
if you want to do what's right.
You don't put your Bible out of sight
if you want to do what's right.

391

In everything that I do
(Show me)

Words and music: Ian White

In everything that I do, show me what Jesus would do.
In everything that I do, show me what Jesus would do.
I will not be afraid, for I can always pray,
show me what Jesus would do.

392   I'm going to shine, shine, shine

Words and music: Alan J Price

be the per - son God has made me,

last time **D.S. al Fine**

let - ting His love flow through! I'm going to

I'm going to shine, shine, shine,
a light in the world I'll be;
I want to shine, shine, shine,
let people see Jesus in me!

1 I want to glorify the Father
by the things I do;
be the person God has made me,
letting His love flow through!
I'm going to . . .

2 And when it's hard and it's not so easy
to know and do what's right;
I'll trust the Holy Spirit in me,
to help me win each fight!
I'm going to . . .

3 Even if I fail Him often
and my light is dim;
He has promised to forgive me,
I can come back to Him!
I'm going to . . .

393 In the morning
(God is near)

Words: Marjorie Allen Anderson
Music: Phil Burt

1 In the morning when I rise,
   when I open up my eyes,
   rain or shine or cold and ice,
   God is near, God is near.

2 When I help and when I play,
   He is there to show the way,
   close behind me all the day,
   God is near, God is near.

3 Then when I turn off the light,
   when I go to sleep at night,
   I am always in His sight,
   God is near, God is near.

394 Into my heart

Words and music: Harry D Clarke

With a gentle lilt

1 Into my heart, into my heart,
  come into my heart, Lord Jesus.
  Come in today, come in to stay;
  come into my heart, Lord Jesus.

2 Rule in my heart, rule in my heart,
  O King of my heart, Lord Jesus.
  Make this Your throne, rule there alone;
  O King of my heart, Lord Jesus.

395   It takes an almighty hand

Words and music: Ian White

Joyfully

It takes an al - migh - ty hand, to make your har - vest grow. It takes an al - migh - ty hand, how - ev - er you may sow. It takes an al - migh - ty hand, the world a - round me shows. It takes the al - migh - ty hand of God.

It takes an almighty hand, to make your harvest grow.
It takes an almighty hand, however you may sow.
It takes an almighty hand, the world around me shows.
It takes the almighty hand of God.

1 It takes His hand to grow your garden,
　all from a secret in a seed;
　part of a plan He spoke and started,
　and said is 'very good indeed!'
　　It takes . . .

2 It takes His hand to turn the seasons,
　to give the sun and snow their hour;
　and in this plan we learn His reason,
　His nature and eternal power.
　　It takes . . .

3 It took His hands to carry sorrow,
　for every sin that we have done;
　and on a cross He bought tomorrow,
　a world of good, like He'd begun.
　　It takes . . .

4 And in His hands there is perfection,
　that in this land we only taste;
　for now we see a poor reflection,
　then we shall see Him face to face.
　　It takes . . .

396

It was on a starry night

Words and music: Joy Webb

Moderately

Capo 1(D)

It was on a star-ry night_____ when the hills were bright,_____ earth lay sleep-ing, sleep-ing calm and still;_____ then in a cat-tle shed,_____ in a

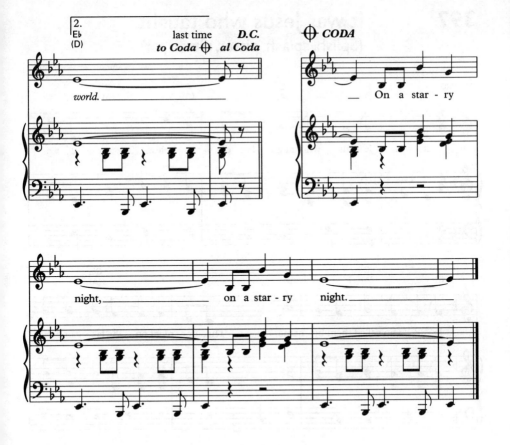

1 It was on a starry night when the hills were bright,
earth lay sleeping, sleeping calm and still;
then in a cattle shed, in a manger bed
a boy was born, King of all the world.
And all the angels sang for Him,
the bells of heaven rang for Him;
for a boy was born, King of all the world.
And all the angels sang for Him,
the bells of heaven rang for Him;
for a boy was born, King of all the world.

2 Soon the shepherds came that way, where the baby lay,
and were kneeling, kneeling by His side.
And their hearts believed again, for the peace of men;
for a boy was born, King of all the world.
And all the angels . . .

On a starry night, on a starry night.

397

It was Jesus who taught
(Splish, splash, pitter, pitter pat)

Words and music: Andy Silver

It was Je - sus who taught His dis - ci - ples,_ it was Je-sus who called them by name. Then one night on the lake came the wind and the rain, and the waves splashed right o - ver the boat._ Splish, splash, pit - ter pit - ter pat, down came the storm with a

bang and a crash. Splish, splash, pit-ter pit-ter pat, down came the storm with a bang and a crash.

1 It was Jesus who taught His disciples,
   it was Jesus who called them by name.
   Then one night on the lake came the wind and the rain,
   and the waves splashed right over the boat.
     Splish, splash, pitter pitter pat,
     down came the storm with a bang and a crash.
     Splish, splash, pitter pitter pat,
     down came the storm with a bang and a crash.

2 It was Jesus asleep in the trawler,
   it was Jesus who woke to their cries.
   'Don't you care that we drown, we're afraid we'll go down!'
   and the waves splashed right over the boat.
     Splish splash . . .

3 It was Jesus who stood to attention,
   it was Jesus who spoke to the waves.
   'You, be quiet, do no harm'; right away there was calm.
   'Who's this man?' asked the men in the boat.
     Splish splash . . .

398   It's a song of praise

Words and music: Greg Leavers
Music arrangement Christopher Hayward

With a swing

It's a song of___ praise,___ it's a song of___

thank-ful-ness; it's a song of___ joy,___

for ev-ery girl___ and boy.___

God gave me my hands,___

God gave me my voice;_ God gave me a

thank-ful heart, so now I can re-joice._

D.C.

It's a song of praise,
it's a song of thankfulness;
it's a song of joy,
for every girl and boy.

1 God gave me my hands,
   God gave me my voice;
   God gave me a thankful heart,
   so now I can rejoice.
     It's a song of praise ...

2 God gave me my feet,
   God gave me my arms;
   the life and love He gives to me
   makes me want to dance.
     It's a song of praise ...

399

It's an adventure

Words and music: Alan J Price

It's an ad-ven-ture fol-low-ing Je-sus, it's an ad-ven-ture learn-ing of Him. It's an ad-ven-ture liv-ing for Je-sus, it's an ad-ven-ture fol-low-ing Him. Let's go where He leads us, turn a-way from wrong; for we know we can

trust Him to help us as we go a - long.

It's an adventure following Jesus,
it's an adventure learning of Him.
It's an adventure living for Jesus,
it's an adventure following Him.
Let's go where He leads us,
turn away from wrong;
for we know we can trust Him
to help us as we go along.

It's an adventure following Jesus,
it's an adventure learning of Him.
It's an adventure living for Jesus,
it's an adventure following Him.

400   It's easy to be a believer

Words and music: Paul Crouch
and David Mudie

Joyfully

It's ea-sy to be a be-liev-er, be-cause it's plain as plain can be that Je-sus came from God and went to die at Cal-va- -ry. But three days la-ter He rose___ up and was

It's easy to be a believer,
because it's plain as plain can be
that Jesus came from God and went
to die at Calvary.
But three days later He rose up
and was seen by at least five hundred people,
and then went back to heaven
to sit at God's right hand.

401 It's not very nice saying

Words and music: Greg Leavers
Music arranged Christopher Hayward

It's not ve-ry nice say - ing, 'Na na na na na na'; it's not ve-ry good say - ing, 'It's not_ fair.' It's not ve-ry kind_ to fight your sis - ter or your bro - ther, or to sneer at oth-ers say-ing, 'I don't care.' God does-n't_

It's not very nice saying, 'Na na na na na na';
it's not very good saying, 'It's not fair.'
It's not very kind to fight your sister or your brother,
or to sneer at others saying, 'I don't care.'

God doesn't like these things –
He tells us in the Bible they're called sins;
God doesn't like these things.
We do it (*Uh huh*), we know it (*That's right*),
and we need help to stop it.

402   It's rounded like an orange

CHRISTINGLE CAROL

Words: Basil Bridge

It's round-ed like an or - ange, this earth on which we stand; and we praise the God who holds it in the hol-low of His hand. So Fa-ther, we would thank You for all that You have done, and for all that You have gi-ven us through the com-ing of Your Son.

1 It's rounded like an orange,
   this earth on which we stand;
and we praise the God who holds it
   in the hollow of His hand.
So Father, we would thank You
   for all that You have done,
and for all that You have given us
   through the coming of Your Son.

2 A candle, burning brightly,
   can cheer the darkest night
and these candles tell how Jesus
   came to bring a dark world light.
So Father . . .

3 The ribbon round the orange
   reminds us of the cost;
how the shepherd, strong and gentle,
   gave His life to save the lost.
So Father . . .

4 Four seasons with their harvest
   supply the food we need,
and the Spirit gives a harvest
   that can make us rich indeed.
So Father . . .

5 We come with our Christingles
   to tell of Jesus' birth
and we praise the God who blessed us
   by His coming to this earth.
So Father . . .

403   It's the little things

Words and music: Bacon Boyd
Music arranged Joseph Linn

1 It's the little things that show our love for Jesus.
It's the little things that show our love for Him.
It's in little things that we can truly serve Him.
It's with little things that we begin.
Give a little more love and a little more hope
to others as you serve Him.
Give a little more love and a little more hope
to others you may meet.
Give a little more love each day to those around you.
Then a little more love and a little more faith,
and a little more love and a little more faith
will make you more like Him.

2 It's the little things we do each day for others.
It's the little things that show we really care.
It's in little things our faith becomes much stronger.
It's with little things that we begin.
Give a little more love and a little more hope
to others as you serve Him.
Give a little more love and a little more hope
to others you may meet.
Give a little more love each day to those around you.
Then a little more love and a little more faith,
and a little more love and a little more faith,
and a little more love and a little more faith,
and a little more love and a little more faith
will make you more like Him.
I want to be more like Him, more like Him.

404

Jehovah Jireh
(Hebrew names for God)

Words and music: Ian Smale
Music arranged Christopher Hayward

Hebrew style

Je-ho-vah Ji - reh, God will pro-vide. _ Je-ho-vah
Ro - phe, God heals. Je-ho-vah Ma - ked - desh, God who
sanc-ti-fies. Je-ho-vah Nis-si, God is my ban-ner. Je-ho-vah
Ro - hi, God my shep-herd. Je-ho-vah Sha - lom, God is

peace. Je - ho-vah Tsid - ke - nu, God our

right-eous-ness. Je - ho-vah Sham-mah, God who is there.

Jehovah Jireh, God will provide.
Jehovah Rophe, God heals.
Jehovah Makeddesh, God who sanctifies.
Jehovah Nissi, God is my banner.
Jehovah Rohi, God my shepherd.
Jehovah Shalom, God is peace.
Jehovah Tsidkenu, God our righteousness.
Jehovah Shammah, God who is there.

405 Jerusalem man

Words and music: Andy Silver

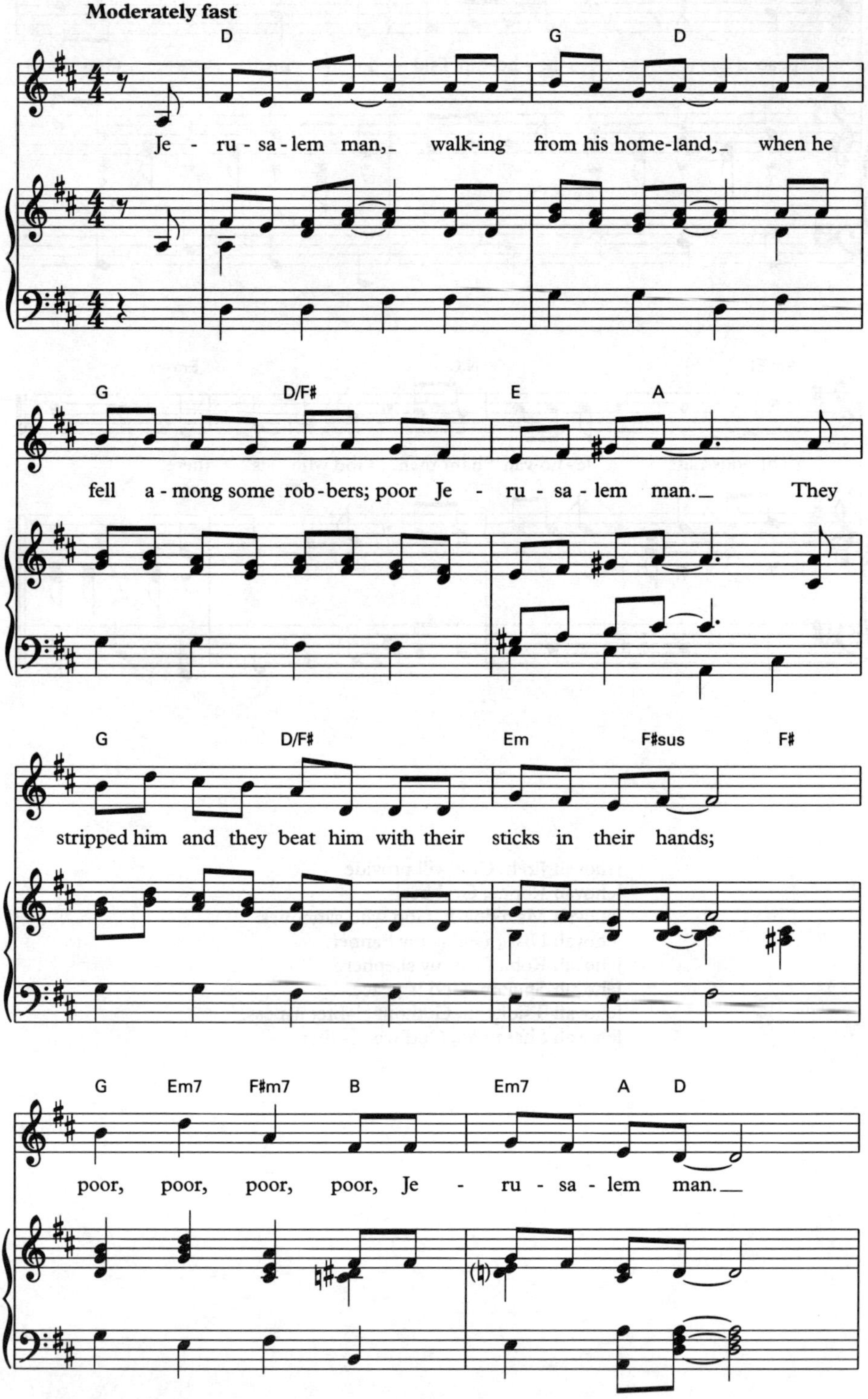

Moderately fast
D G D
Je - ru - sa - lem man, walk-ing from his home-land, when he
G D/F# E A
fell a - mong some rob-bers; poor Je - ru - sa - lem man. They
G D/F# Em F#sus F#
stripped him and they beat him with their sticks in their hands;
G Em7 F#m7 B Em7 A D
poor, poor, poor, poor, Je - ru - sa - lem man.

1 Jerusalem man, walking from his homeland,
when he fell among some robbers, poor Jerusalem man.
They stripped him and they beat him with their sticks in their hands;
poor, poor, poor, poor Jerusalem man.

2 They hastily fled as he fell down and bled,
but a man who was a preacher saw the victim ahead.
He passed him and ignored him – not a word had been said;
poor, poor, poor, poor Jerusalem man.

3 Along came a man who was very well read,
now he must have seen the victim who by now was half dead.
He passed him and ignored him not a word had been said;
poor, poor, poor, poor Jerusalem man.

4 The next man to pass, a Samaritan man,
though he always had been taught to hate a true Jewish man,
he helped him and he took him to an inn near his land;
good, good, good, good Samaritan man.

Jesus has promised

Words and music: Scott Lawrence
Music arranged Christopher Hayward

Gentle waltz

Je - sus has pro - mised my shep - herd to be, that's why I love Him so;_____ and to the child - ren He said, 'Come to Me', that's why I love Him so._____ That's why I love Him, that's why I love Him, be - cause He

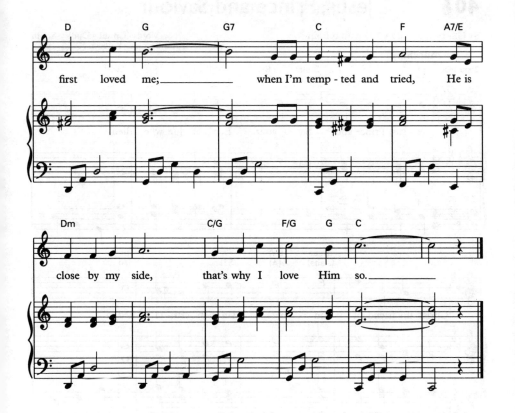

first loved me;_____ when I'm temp-ted and tried, He is close by my side, that's why I love Him so._____

Jesus has promised my shepherd to be,
that's why I love Him so;
and to the children He said, 'Come to Me',
that's why I love Him so.

That's why I love Him, that's why I love Him,
because He first loved me;
when I'm tempted and tried, He is close by my side,
that's why I love Him so.

407 Jesus, Prince and Saviour

St Gertrude   65 65 D with refrain

Words: Timothy Dudley-Smith
Music: Arthur Seymour Sullivan (1842–1900)

Je - sus, Prince and Sav - iour, Lord of life who died:

Christ, the friend of sin - ners, sin - ners cru - ci - fied.

For a lost world's ran - som, all Him - self He gave,

lay at last death's vic - tim,___ life - less in the grave.

Lord of life triumphant, ris - en now to reign!
King of end - less a - ges, Je - sus lives a - gain!

1 Jesus, Prince and Saviour,
   Lord of life who died:
   Christ, the friend of sinners,
   sinners crucified.
   For a lost world's ransom,
   all Himself He gave,
   lay at last death's victim,
   lifeless in the grave.
     Lord of life triumphant,
     risen now to reign!
     King of endless ages,
     Jesus lives again!

2 In His power and Godhead
   every victory won,
   pain and passion ended,
   all His purpose done:
   Christ the Lord is risen!
   sighs and sorrows past,
   death's dark night is over,
   morning comes at last!
     Lord of life . . .

3 Resurrection morning!
   sinners' bondage freed.
   Christ the Lord is risen –
   He is risen indeed!
   Jesus, Prince and Saviour,
   Lord of life who died,
   Christ the King of glory
   now is glorified!
     Lord of life . . .

408 Jesus put this song into our hearts

Words and music: Graham Kendrick
Music arranged David Peacock

hearts. _____   —   (*Hey!*)

1   Jesus put this song into our hearts,
    Jesus put this song into our hearts;
    it's a song of joy no-one can take away.
    Jesus put this song into our hearts.

2   Jesus taught us how to live in harmony,
    Jesus taught us how to live in harmony;
    different faces, different races,
      He made us one –
    Jesus taught us how to live in harmony.

3   Jesus taught us how to be a family,
    Jesus taught us how to be a family;
    loving one another
      with the love that He gives –
    Jesus taught us how to be a family.

4   Jesus turned our sorrow into dancing,
    Jesus turned our sorrow into dancing;
    changed our tears of sadness
      into rivers of joy –
    Jesus turned our sorrow into a dance. (*Hey!*)

409 Jesus, send me the helper

Words and music: Derek Llewellyn

Lively

Je - sus, send me the help - er, send me the help - er to __ help me. __ Je - sus, send me the Ho - ly Spi - rit, send the Ho - ly Spi - rit to me. __

Fine

He gives us love __ to keep on lov - ing. He makes us brave

to do what is right.___ He gives us faith___ to keep on go -

D.C. al Fine

- ing. He gives us power___ to keep us shin - ing so bright.

Jesus, send me the helper, send me the helper to help me.
Jesus, send me the Holy Spirit, send the Holy Spirit to me.
Jesus, send me the helper, send me the helper to help me.
Jesus, send me the Holy Spirit, send the Holy Spirit to me.

He gives us love to keep on loving.
He makes us brave to do what is right.
He gives us faith to keep on going.
He gives us power to keep us shining so bright.

Jesus, send me the helper, send me the helper to help me.
Jesus, send me the Holy Spirit, send the Holy Spirit to me.

410

Jesus, I love You

Words and music: Otis Skillings
Music arranged Phil Burt

1 Jesus, I love You, love You, love You.
Jesus, I love You; Jesus, my Lord.

2 Jesus, I serve You, serve You, serve You.
Jesus, I serve You; Jesus, my Lord.

3 Jesus, I praise You, praise You, praise You.
Jesus, I praise You; Jesus, my Lord;
Jesus, my Lord.

411   Jesus was the Son of God

Words: J Watson
Music: J Mackenzie

1 Jesus was the Son of God,
   He became a man.
   He was strong and good and kind,
   followed all God's plan,
   followed all God's plan.

2 When He was a strong young man
   Jesus had to die.
   All his friends were very sad,
   and they wondered why,
   and they wondered why.

3 It's so hard to understand
   why this had to be;
   but I know it was because
   He cared for you and me,
   He cared for you and me.

412

Jesus will never, ever

Words and music: Greg Leavers
Music arranged Phil Burt and Christopher Hayward

Je - sus will ne - ver, ev - er, no not ev - er,
ne - ver, ev - er change. He will al - ways, al - ways,
that's for all days, al - ways be the same. So as
Son of God and King of kings He will for - ev - er reign.

Yes - ter - day, to - day, for - ev - er, Je - sus is the same.

Yes - ter - day, to - day, for - ev - er, Je - sus is the same.

8va

Jesus will never, ever,
no not ever, never, ever change.
He will always, always,
that's for all days,
always be the same.
So as Son of God and
King of kings
He will forever reign.
Yesterday, today, forever,
Jesus is the same.
Yesterday, today, forever,
Jesus is the same.

413 Joseph was sold as a slave

Words and music: S and J Doddridge

Jo - seph was sold as a slave,___ and la - ter was thrown in - to pri - son;___ but God helped him be ve - ry brave,___ be - cause he had done no - thing wrong.___ For God knows, yes, God knows, God

knows the truth;_____ for God knows, yes, God

knows, God knows the truth._____

(2.)

Joseph was sold as a slave,
and later was thrown into prison;
but God helped him be very brave,
because he had done nothing wrong.
For God knows, yes, God knows, God knows the truth;
for God knows, yes, God knows, God knows the truth.

414 Kids under construction

Words: Gloria Gaither and Gary S Paxton
Music: William J Gaither and Gary S Paxton
Music arranged Christopher Hayward

Kids un-der con-struc - tion; may-be the paint is still wet.___ Kids un-der con-struc - tion; the Lord might not be fin-ished yet.___ We're ___ more than just ac-ci-dents with-out the cause; we're more than just

D.C. al Fine

Kids under construction;
maybe the paint is still wet.
Kids under construction;
the Lord might not be finished yet.

1 We're more than just accidents without the cause;
we're more than just bodies and brains.
God made us on purpose, we're part of a plan;
He cares and He knows us by name. Oh!
    Kids under construction . . .

2 Now, mister, I know that I get in your way;
I'm noisy and just bug you so.
But there's lots of questions I just have to ask
if I'm ever going to know. Oh!
    Kids under construction . . .

3 Dear Jesus, please make us more patient and kind;
and help us to be more like You.
And make room for all other children of Yours,
for they are still growing up, too. Oh!
    Kids under construction . . .

415

Large creatures
(Creature praise)

Words and music: David Matthews
Music arranged Roger Mayor

Large crea-tures, small crea-tures, short__ and tall crea-tures,

come now and praise the Lord.__

1 Large creatures, small creatures,
   short and tall creatures,
   come now and praise the Lord.
   Young creatures, old creatures,
   hot and cold creatures,
   come now and praise the Lord.
   Sing praise to the Father, sing praise to the Son,
   sing praise to the Spirit who makes all creatures one.
   Sing praise for the goodness of what the Lord has done.
   Let all creatures praise the Lord.

2 Low creatures, high creatures,
   flying in the sky creatures,
   come now and praise the Lord.
   White creatures, brown creatures,
   all the world around creatures,
   come now and praise the Lord.
   Sing praise . . .

3 Day creatures, night creatures,
   left and right creatures,
   come now and praise the Lord.
   Near creatures, far creatures,
   anywhere you are creatures,
   come now and praise the Lord.
   Sing praise . . .

416 Let's go and tell our friends

Words and music: Greg Leavers
Music arranged Christopher Hayward

With a swing

Let's go and tell our friends that Je - sus cares;

— let's go and tell our friends that Je - sus cares.

— We've got to go out and tell how Je - sus

died for them; to tell___ them how He loves

Let's go and tell our friends that Jesus cares;
let's go and tell our friends that Jesus cares.
We've got to go out and tell how Jesus died for them;
to tell them how He loves them; (*that's right!*)
to tell them He'll forgive them; (*that's true!*)
to tell them He'll be with them; (*Amen!*)
to tell them that He wants to be their friend.

417 Let's praise God together

Words and music: Alison Moon

Lively

Let's praise God to-geth - er, let us clap and praise the Lord; for He loves to hear_ us—He is King for ev - er-more._

Je - sus, ho - ly is Your name; high a -

-bove   all   oth - ers,   power   and

glo - ry be - long_____ to You.___

Let's praise God together,
let us clap and praise the Lord;
for He loves to hear us –
He is King for evermore.

1 Jesus, holy is Your name;
   high above all others,
   power and glory belong to You.
   Let's all dance together,
   let us dance and praise the Lord;
   for he loves to see us –
   He is King for evermore.

2 Jesus, mighty is Your name;
   high above all others,
   power and glory belong to You.
   Let's praise God together,
   let us clap and praise the Lord;
   for He loves to hear us –
   He is King for evermore.

   Let's all dance together,
   let us dance and praise the Lord;
   for he loves to see us –
   He is King for evermore.

418 Long ago there was born

Words: Anon
Music: adapted from Johannes Brahms (1833–97)
arranged Christopher Hayward

Long a-go there was born, in the ci-ty of Da-vid, a sweet, ho-ly babe who was Je-sus, our King. An-gels sang at His birth, 'Lul-la-by, peace on earth.' An-gels

1 Long ago there was born, in the city of David,
a sweet, holy babe who was Jesus, our King.
Angels sang at His birth, 'Lullaby, peace on earth.'
Angels sang at His birth, 'Lullaby, peace on earth.'

2 Jesus came as a child from His Father in heaven,
and has shown us the way to be loving and kind.
While the stars sang above, 'Lullaby, God is love.'
While the stars sang above, 'Lullaby, God is love.'

419

Long, long ago

Words and music: Andy Silver

Long, long a-go be-fore our time be-gan
ev - ery-thing was out of shape and no - thing filled the land.
God, who saw the emp - ti-ness, made a plan to clear the mess,
God spoke____ and it was done.

1 Long, long ago before our time began
  everything was out of shape and nothing filled the land.
  God, who saw the emptiness, made a plan to clear the mess,
  God spoke and it was done.
  Day one, came the light and the day and night;
  day two, came the clouds and the sea and sky;
  day three, came the land and the plants and trees;
  day four, came the sun and the moon and the stars.

2 God took a look and He was happy and was pleased.
  Now the world was taking shape and all because God breathed;
  but He thought the sky and sea needed some activity –
  God spoke and it was done.
  Day five, came the fish and the birds that fly;
  day six, came the beasts and the animals;
  and then came the people called Adam and Eve;
  day seven, all was done and God rested at ease.

3 God was very glad to see the different forms of life,
  but the part most wonderful was Adam and his wife.
  All He wanted them to do was love and serve Him through and through;
  God spoke and it was done.

420

Lord Jesus, You are faithful

Words and music: Bev Gammon
Music arranged Christopher Hayward

Lord Je-sus, You are faith-ful, al-ways with us, ne-ver leav-ing us; Lord Je - sus. Lord

1 Lord Jesus,
   You are faithful,
   always with us,
   never leaving us;
   Lord Jesus.

2 Lord Jesus,
   You are blameless,
   You are perfect,
   You are sinless;
   Lord Jesus.

3 Lord Jesus,
   You are so pure,
   pure and lovely,
   pure and holy;
   Lord Jesus.

421 Lord, make me a mountain

Words and music: Paul Field

Strong 4

Lord, make me a moun - tain stand-ing tall for You;___ strong and free and ho - ly, in ev-ery-thing I do.___ Lord, make me a ri - ver of wa-ter pure and sweet.___

1 Lord, make me a mountain standing tall for You;
  strong and free and holy, in everything I do.
  Lord, make me a river of water pure and sweet.
  Lord, make me the servant of everyone I meet.

2 Lord, make me a candle shining with Your light;
  steadfastly unflickering, standing for the right.
  Lord, make me a fire burning strong for You.
  Lord, make me be humble in everything I do.

3 Lord, make me a mountain, strong and tall for You;
  Lord, make me a fountain of water clear and new.
  Lord, make me a shepherd that I may feed Your sheep;
  Lord, make me the servant of everyone I meet.

422 Lord, we've come to worship You

Words and music: Ian Smale
Music arranged Christopher Hayward

Lord, we've come to wor - ship You; Lord, we've come to praise. Lord, we've come to wor - ship You in oh, so ma-ny ways. Some of us shout and some of us sing, and some of us whis - per the praise we bring;

but Lord, we_ all are gather-ing_ to give to You our praise.

Lord, we've come to worship You;
Lord, we've come to praise.
Lord, we've come to worship You
in oh, so many ways.
Some of us shout and some of us sing,
and some of us whisper the praise we bring;
but Lord, we all are gathering
to give to You our praise.

423 Lord, You are brilliant

Words and music: Greg Leavers
Music arranged Christopher Hayward

Lord, You are bril-liant, cham-pion of cham-pions;

to You our thanks and praise we bring.

You made all the world, no-one's as great__ as You;

You know ev-ery-thing and all Your words__ are true.

1 Lord, You are brilliant, champion of champions;
  to You our thanks and praise we bring.
  You made all the world, no-one's as great as You;
  You know everything and all Your words are true.
  Lord, You are brilliant, champion of champions;
  so we proclaim You are the King.

2 Lord, You are brilliant, champion of champions;
  to You our thanks and praise we bring.
  You see everything, all that we say and do;
  You're incredible, no-one loves us like You.
  Lord, You are brilliant, champion of champions;
  so we proclaim You are the King.

424 Lord, You are the Light

Words and music: Fiona Inkpen
Music arranged Christopher Norton

Lord, You are the Light of the world, shine in our hearts.
Let that light shine across the earth, Light of the world, our God.

Lord, You are the Light of the world, shine in our hearts.
Let that light shine across the earth, Light of the world, our God.

1 In the warmth of Your love we would walk in Your light.
   Lord, You are . . .

2 Midst the sorrow of man may Your love fill our hearts.
   Lord, You are . . .

3 Lord, the truth and the life, revealing Your way!
   Lord, You are . . .

425 Love, joy, peace

Words and music: Peter and Hanneke Jacobs

Love, joy,— peace,— pa-tience, kind-ness, good-ness, faith, gen-tle-ness, and self-con-trol;— this is the fruit of the Spi-rit. Love, joy,— peace,

Love, joy, peace,
patience, kindness, goodness, faith,
gentleness, and self-control;
this is the fruit of the Spirit.
Love, joy, peace,
patience, kindness, goodness, faith,
gentleness and self-control;
the fruit of the Spirit of God.

You'll find it in Galatians, chapter five,
verse twenty-two.
And if you're walking close to God,
this fruit will grow in you.

And you'll have love, joy, peace,
patience, kindness, goodness, faith,
gentleness, and self-control;
this is the fruit of the Spirit.
Love, joy, peace,
patience, kindness, goodness, faith,
gentleness and self-control;
the fruit of the Spirit of God,
the fruit of the Spirit of God.

426 M-m-m-m-must I really go

Words and music: Gillian E Hutchinson
Music arranged Phil Burt and Christopher Hayward

Me._____ Through him, the good news will spread to ma-ny na-tions,

bring-ing life and li - ber - ty._____ You.

1 M-m-m-m-must I really go and visit him?
I'd n-not be very good at it, you know.
Surely there's s-someone else who's w-w-willing to;
I'm a-f-f-fraid to go!

2 He's been p-p-persecuting Your followers,
some have been k-killed, and some were thrown in jail.
Please d-d-don't make me go and v-v-visit him;
I'll be sh-sh-sure to fail.

Listen, Ananias, I've chosen this man
to be a witness for Me.
Through him, the good news will spread to many nations,
bringing life and liberty.

3 If I really must, Lord, I'll be o-b-bedient;
I know You'll go with me, You'll s-see me through.
Even when the task is hard or d-d-dangerous,
help me to t-trust in You.

427
Make way, make way

Words and music: Graham Kendrick
Music arranged David Peacock

Joyfully

Make way, make way, for Christ the King in splen - dour ar -

- rives; fling wide the gates and wel - come Him in - to your

lives. *Make way, (make way,) make way, (make way,) for the*

King of kings; (for the King of kings;) make way, (make way,) make

way, (make way,) and__ let His king - dom in!

1 Make way, make way,
   for Christ the King in splendour arrives;
   fling wide the gates
   and welcome Him into your lives.
     Make way, make way,
     for the King of kings;
     make way, make way,
     and let His kingdom in!

2 He comes the broken hearts to heal,
   the prisoners to free;
   the deaf shall hear, the lame shall dance,
   the blind shall see.
     Make way . . .

3 And those who mourn with heavy hearts,
   who weep and sigh,
   with laughter, joy and royal crown
   He'll beautify.
     Make way . . .

4 We call you now to worship Him
   as Lord of all;
   to have no gods before Him,
   their thrones must fall!
     Make way . . .

428 Matthew had been sitting
(Let's have a party)

Words and music: Andy Silver

Mat - thew had been sit - ting in his

lit - tle___ hut,___ col - lect - ing lots of mo - ney from the

Jews. He had a rep - u - ta - tion,___

par - ty.   Come, let's have   a   P. A. R. T. Y.

1   Matthew had been sitting in his little hut,
   collecting lots of money from the Jews.
   He had a reputation, dealing in deception,
   working for the Inland Revenue.
   Jesus had been walking on the shore that day,
   and called out, 'Matthew, come and follow Me!'
   There was no hesitation, he didn't even question,
   he left his hut and followed straight away.
   Come, let's have a party,
   come and meet the Lord who called and found me;
   bring your friends and neighbours to the party.
   Come, let's have a P.A.R.T.Y.

2   Jesus heard the whispers from the Pharisees,
   'See Him eating with these wicked men.'
   They didn't stop complaining, gossiping and jeering,
   thinking they were holy, righteous men.
   Jesus spoke directly to the Pharisees:
   'What sort of people need a doctor's help?
   The healthy do not need him, but people sick and ailing;
   I've come to call all sinners to repent!'
   Come, let's have . . .

429　Maybe you can't draw or sing

Words and music: Carol Gaddy
Music arranged Joseph Linn

Simply

May-be you can't draw or sing or be a foot-ball star; but just re-mem-ber, be your-self,___ He made you___ like you are. It-'ll be a big thing when Je-sus takes con-trol, ev-en though it seems like some-thing ve-ry

1 Maybe you can't draw or sing or be a football star;
   but just remember, be yourself,
   He made you like you are.
      It'll be a big thing when Jesus takes control,
      even though it seems like something very slim.
      From a tiny lunch He blessed the bread and fed the multitudes;
      and He'll use us, too, when we give ourselves to Him.

2 You may not have the brightest smile or make the highest score;
   but if you give Him what you have,
   He'll make it something more.
      It'll be a big . . .

3 If you love our blessèd Lord and want to do your part,
   don't worry if you've nothing else –
   the best gift is your heart.
      It'll be a big . . .

430

Mighty in victory

Words and music: Mavis Ford

Migh-ty in vic-tory, glo-rious in ma-jes-ty: ev-ery eye shall see Him when He ap-pears, com-ing in the clouds with pow-er and glo-ry. Hail to the King! We must be rea-dy,

Mighty in victory, glorious in majesty:
every eye shall see Him when He appears,
coming in the clouds with power and glory.
    Hail to the King!
We must be ready, watching and praying,
serving each other, building His kingdom;
then every knee shall bow, then every tongue confess,
    Jesus is Lord!

431 Mighty is our God

Words and music: Eugene Greco,
Don Moen and Gerrit Gustafson

Energetic

Migh-ty is our God, migh-ty is our King. Migh-ty is our Lord, rul-er of ev-ery-thing. His name is high-er, high-er than a-ny oth-

D.C. al Fine

Mighty is our God,
mighty is our King.
Mighty is our Lord,
ruler of everything.
Glory to our God,
glory to our King.
Glory to our Lord,
ruler of everything.

His name is higher,
higher than any other name.
His power is greater,
for He has created *everything.

Mighty is our God . . .

* throw arm up in the air

432   Noah was the only good man

Words and music: Peter Lewis

Words and music: © Peter Lewis,
22 Marlborough Rise, Aston, Sheffield S31 0ET, UK

Noah was the only good man,
Noah was the only good man,
Noah was the only good man,
and everyone else was bad.

1 The Lord looked at the world He made
and He was very sad,
as almost everyone He saw
was wicked and was bad.
So God said He would send a flood
to wash them all away,
and He said, 'Noah, build an ark
to float upon the waves!'
Noah was . . .

2 So Noah built a wooden ark
the way God told him to,
and took his family safe inside
with animals two by two.
So God saved Noah from the flood
and promised then and there
that He would never send again
a flood upon the earth.
Noah was . . .

3 God made a rainbow in the sky
of yellow, blue and red,
so no-one ever would forget
the flood and what He said.
And when we see the rainbow now
remember God's own words:
that He would never send again
a flood upon the earth.
Noah was . . .

433 Now Saul was rejected

Words and music: Gillian E Hutchinson
Music arranged Phil Burt

Now Saul was re - ject - ed as king of the
land, so God spoke to Sam - uel, 'Now hear my com -
- mand. Go straight down to Beth - le - hem, there wor - ship
Me; a - noint one of Jes - se's sons as king to

be!' _____

1 Now Saul was rejected as king of the land,
   so God spoke to Samuel, 'Now hear my command.
   Go straight down to Bethlehem, there worship Me;
   anoint one of Jesse's sons as king to be!'

2 Now all Jesse's family were handsome and strong,
   and when Samuel asked them, they all came along;
   and Samuel was wondering as in they all trod,
   which one of the brothers was chosen by God.

3 He looked on Eliab, and he was impressed
   with the curls of his hair and the breadth of his chest;
   but God said to Samuel, 'That's not where I start –
   you look on his body, but I see his heart!'

4 So six more fine offspring of Jesse's passed by
   but each was rejected by God the Most High;
   then Samuel asked Jesse, 'Are those all you've got?'
   He answered, 'There's David – the babe of the lot!'

5 Now David, the shepherd, the youngest of eight,
   was out with the sheep on the hills until late.
   He had to be sent for; and when he came in,
   the Lord said, 'Rise up and anoint him as king!'

6 You may be dressed smartly, your face may be fair,
   but God's not concerned with your clothes or your hair;
   your outward appearance is only a part –
   when God looks upon you, He looks on your heart.

434 O give thanks to the Lord

Words and music: Joanne Pond
Music arranged David Peacock

With pace

O give thanks to the Lord, all you His peo-ple; O give thanks to the Lord, for He is good._____ Let us praise, let us thank, let us ce-le-brate and dance; O give

O give thanks to the Lord,
all you His people;
O give thanks to the Lord,
  for He is good.
Let us praise, let us thank,
let us celebrate and dance;
O give thanks to the Lord,
  for He is good.

435 O Lord, You're great

Words and music: Ian Smale
Music arranged Phil Burt

Slowly, as a twist

O Lord, You're great, You are fa-bu-lous. We love You more than a-ny words can sing, sing, sing. O Lord, You're great, You are so ge-ner-ous;_ You lav-ish us with gifts when we don't de-serve a thing. *Al — le — lu,*

1 O Lord, You're great, You are fabulous.
  We love You more than any words can sing, sing, sing.
  O Lord, You're great, You are so generous;
  You lavish us with gifts when we don't deserve a thing.
    Allelu, alleluia, praise You, Lord.
    Alleluia, praise You, Lord, alleluia, praise You, Lord.
    Allelu, alleluia, praise You, Lord.
    Alleluia, praise You, Lord, alleluia, praise You, Lord.

2 O Lord, You're great, You are so powerful;
  You hold the mighty universe in Your hand, hand, hand.
  O Lord, You're great, You are so wonderful,
  You've poured out Your love on this undeserving land.
    Allelu, alleluia . . .

436   Oh, how He loves you and me

Words and music: Kurt Kaiser

Oh, how He loves you and me;
oh, how He loves you and me.
He gave His life – what more could He give?
Oh, how He loves you; oh, how He loves me;

oh, how He loves you and me.

1 Oh, how He loves you and me;
  oh, how He loves you and me.
  He gave His life –
  what more could He give?
    Oh, how He loves you;
    oh, how He loves me;
    oh, how He loves you and me.

2 Jesus to Calvary did go,
  His love for sinners to show.
  What He did there
  brought hope from despair.
    Oh, how He . . .

437 Oh no! The wine's all gone

Words and music: Greg Leavers

Oh no! The wine's all gone! How can the wed - ding feast

now go on?_ Oh dear! What can be_ done? Just

lis - ten to Je - sus, Ma - ry's Son._ Oh yes! We'll

Oh no! The wine's all gone!
How can the wedding feast now go on?
Oh dear! What can be done?
Just listen to Jesus, Mary's Son.
Oh yes! We'll do what He says –
fill the stone jars with water that's fresh.
Oh my! They're pouring it out!
What, wine? That's a miracle! without a doubt!

438

Oh, oh, oh, oh

Words and music: Angela Flynn
Music arranged Christopher Hayward

A four-part round

1 Oh, oh, oh, oh, oh, oh, oh, oh.
   Oh, oh, oh, oh, oh, oh, oh, oh.

2 Hallelujah, hallelujah.
   Hallelujah, hallelujah.

3 Christ died and rose. He will come again.
   Christ died and rose. He will come again.

4 Praise the Lord.
   Praise the Lord.

439   Oh, yes I am

Words and music: Sam Horner

Oh, yes I am, oh, yes I am,
I am saved and kept secure in Jesus' hand.
Oh, yes I am, oh, yes I am,
I am saved and kept secure in Jesus' hand.

1 I'm redeemed, the price was paid by Him;
justified, just as if I'd never sinned;
sanctified, holy, set apart;
and it's all because of Jesus' loving heart.
    Oh, yes I am . . .

2 I am saved, from death and sin and hell.
I'm empowered, by the Spirit of God as well.
I'm born again, I've got a brand new start;
and it's all because of Jesus' loving heart.
    Oh, yes I am . . .

3 I belong to my Father who's above.
I am kept by His never-ending love.
I will survive the devil's fiery darts;
and it's all because of Jesus' loving heart.
    Oh, yes I am . . .

440 Old man Noah

Words: Anon
Music: Traditional
Music arranged Phil Burt

Happily

Old man No-ah built an ark – ham-mer, ham-mer, bang, bang, ow! And that old ark was built of wood – ham-mer, ham-mer, bang, bang, ow!

repeat as needed for verses 2–4

With a saw, saw, here and a nail, nail, there; here a nail, there a saw, ev-ery-where a nail, nail; Old man No-ah

built an ark – ham-mer, ham-mer, bang, bang, ow! The ow!

1 Old man Noah built an ark –
   hammer, hammer, bang, bang, ow!
   And that old ark was built of wood –
   hammer, hammer, bang, bang, ow!
   With a saw, saw, here and a nail, nail, there;
   here a nail, there a saw,
   everywhere a nail, nail;
   Old man Noah built an ark –
   hammer, hammer, bang, bang, ow!

2 The ark had a door without a knocker –
   hammer, hammer, bang, bang, ow!
   Everyone said, 'Noah's off his rocker' –
   hammer, hammer, bang, bang, ow!
   With a 'ha ha' here, and a 'ho ho' there,
   here a 'ha', there a 'ho',
   everywhere a 'ha ha';
   saw, saw here . . .

3 God shut the door and sent the rain –
   pitter patter, pitter patter, splosh!
   But all the people cried in vain –
   pitter patter, pitter patter, splosh!
   With a wail, wail here, and a shout, shout there,
   here a shout, there a wail,
   everywhere a shout, shout;
   flush, flush here . . .
   'ha ha' here . . .
   saw, saw here . . .

4 For forty days they were afloat –
   pitter patter, pitter patter, splosh!
   But they were safe inside God's boat –
   pitter patter, pitter patter, splosh!
   So trust God here, believe God there,
   here believe, there trust,
   everywhere believe God;
   wail, wail here . . .
   flush, flush here . . .
   'ha ha' here . . .
   saw, saw here . . .

441   On Christmas night

SUSSEX CAROL   88 88 88

Words: Traditional
Music: English traditional melody
Music arranged Ralph Vaughan Williams (1872–1958)

1 On Christmas night all Christians sing
to hear the news the angels bring:
on Christmas night all Christians sing
to hear the news the angels bring:
news of great joy, news of great mirth,
news of our merciful King's birth.

2 Then why should we on earth be so sad,
since our Redeemer made us glad?
Then why should we on earth be so sad,
since our Redeemer made us glad;
when from our sin He set us free,
all for to gain our liberty?

3 When sin departs before His grace,
then life and health come in its place;
When sin departs before His grace,
then life and health come in its place;
angels and men with joy may sing,
all for to see the new-born King.

4 All out of darkness we have light,
which made the angels sing this night:
all out of darkness we have light,
which made the angels sing this night:
'Glory to God and peace to men,
now and for evermore. Amen.'

442   On the road to Damascus

Words and music: Anthony Welsh
Music arranged Gerald Fitzpatrick

Saul!   Saul!   Do not per - se - cute Me!'

1 On the road to Damascus
   the Lord appeared as a man was riding by:
   his name was Saul.
   I saw him fall
   at a blinding flash from the sky.
   'Saul! Saul! Do not persecute Me!
   Saul! Saul! Do not persecute Me!'

2 On the road to Damascus
   the Lord cried out to the man who could not see.
   I heard Him call,
   'Now tell Me, Saul,
   just why do you persecute Me?
   Saul! Saul! Do not persecute Me!
   Saul! Saul! Do not persecute Me!'

3 On the road to Damascus
   the Lord's voice came to the man whose eyes were blind.
   I heard Him call
   'Now hear Me, Saul,
   I will change your name and your mind.
   Saul! Saul! Do not persecute Me!
   Saul! Saul! Do not persecute Me!'

4 On the road to Damascus
   I saw him fall to his knees before the Lord.
   I heard Him call,
   'Your name is Paul,
   you must go out and spread My word!
   Paul! Paul! Teach the world of Jesus!
   Paul! Paul! Teach the world of Jesus!'

5 On the road to Damascus
   yes, I was there when the Lord's great power He showed.
   I watched as Paul
   received God's call
   and then on my back he rode!
   'Paul! Paul! Teach the world of Jesus!
   Paul! Paul! Teach the world of Jesus!'

443 Once upon a time

Words and music: Andy Silver

Happily

Once up-on a time – it was ma-ny years a-go – Je-sus told a sto-ry of a

man that you should know. He grew up on a farm and he

had a hun-dred sheep; the sheep would eat and eat and eat and eat.

'You're the sheep,' Je-sus said, 'far from home, all a-lone. I have come,

God's own Son, to find you and to bring you back to Him.'

1 Once upon a time – it was many years ago –
  Jesus told a story of a man that you should know.
  He grew up on a farm and he had a hundred sheep;
  the sheep would eat and eat and eat and eat.
    'You're the sheep,' Jesus said,
    'far from home, all alone.
    I have come, God's own Son,
    to find you and to bring you back to Him.'

2 When the sun went down he would lead them safely home;
  one and two and three and four, he'd count them on his own.
  Then one night he had a fright – he counted ninety-nine;
  ninety, ninety, ninety, ninety-nine.
    'You're the sheep . . .

3 Out he went to find where the missing sheep had strayed;
  searching high and low, he was feeling quite dismayed.
  Then he thought he heard a noise, it sounded like a bleat –
  he'd found the silly, sad and sorry sheep.
    'You're the sheep . . .

444

Once there was a house
(Busy little house)

Words and music: Ian White

1 Once there was a house, a busy little house;
and this is all about the busy little house.

2 Jesus Christ had come, teaching everyone;
so everyone had to run to the busy little house.

3 Everyone was there, you couldn't find a chair;
in fact you had to fight for air, in the busy little house.

4 A man who couldn't walk, was carried to the spot;
but the place was chock-a-block, in the busy little house.

5 Whatever shall we do, whatever shall we do?
We'll never get him through into the busy little house.

6 We'll open up the roof, we'll open up the roof;
and then we'll put him through into the busy little house.

7 Then Jesus turned His eyes, and saw to His surprise,
the man coming from the skies into the busy little house.

8 Then Jesus turned and said, 'Get up and take your bed,
and run along instead!' from the busy little house.

445 One and two and three and four

Words and music: Greg Leavers
Music arranged Christopher Hayward

One and two and three and four, — count-ing sheep in through the door; — fif - ty - one and fif-ty-two — one is lost, what shall I do? —

One and two and three and four,
counting sheep in through the door;
fifty-one and fifty-two –
one is lost, what shall I do?
Ninety-eight and ninety-nine,
I will search until I find.
I will keep on looking just because I care.
There he is, caught in some thorns way over there,
he was lost but now is found.
So it's ninety-eight, ninety-nine, (*click fingers*) one hundred;
yes, it's ninety-eight, ninety-nine, (*click fingers*) one hundred!

446 Praise Him
(All God's faithful children)

Words and music: Ian Smale
Music arranged Phil Burt

Joyfully

Praise Him, praise Him, bring prai-ses to the Lord our God.

All God's faith-ful child-ren must learn to praise Him.

learn to praise Him. *Sing hal-le-lu,__ hal-le-lu,__ sing*

hal-le-lu-jah to our God. All God's faith-ful child-ren sing

1 Praise Him, praise Him,
   bring praises to the Lord our God.
   All God's faithful children
   must learn to praise Him.
   Praise Him, praise Him,
   bring praises to the Lord our God.
   All God's faithful children
   must learn to praise Him.
   Sing hallelu, hallelu,
   sing hallelujah to our God.
   All God's faithful children
   sing hallelujah God.
   Sing hallelu, hallelu,
   sing hallelujah to our God.
   All God's faithful children
   sing hallelujah God.

2 Worship Him, worship Him,
   bring worship to the Lord our God.
   All God's faithful children
   must learn to worship Him.
   Worship Him, worship Him,
   bring worship to the Lord our God.
   All God's faithful children
   must learn to worship Him.
   Sing hallelu . . .

447   Praise and thanksgiving

Words and music: Anon
Music arranged Greg Leavers

A three-part round

Praise and thanksgiving let everyone bring,
unto our Father for every good thing!
All together, joyfully sing!

448 Prayer is like a telephone
(Prayer phone)

Words and music: Paul Crouch
and David Mudie

Prayer is like a telephone
for us to talk to Jesus.
Prayer is like a telephone
for us to talk to God.
Prayer is like a telephone
for us to talk to Jesus.
Pick it up and use it every day.

We can shout out loud,
we can whisper softly,
we can make no noise at all;
but He'll always hear our call.

. . . . . . is like a telephone
for us to talk to Jesus.
. . . . . . is like a telephone
for us to talk to God.
. . . . . . is like a telephone
for us to talk to Jesus.
Pick it up and use it every day.

We can . . .

. . . . . . is like a . . . .
for us to talk to Jesus.
. . . . . . is like a . . . .
for us to talk to God.
. . . . . . is like a . . . .
for us to talk to Jesus.
Pick it up and use it every day.

We can . . .

. . . . . . is like a . . . .
for us to talk to . . . . .
. . . . . . is like a . . . .
for us to talk to . . .
. . . . . . is like a . . . .
for us to talk to . . . . .
Pick it up and use it every day.
Pick it up and use it every day.
Pick it up and use it every day.

449 Roll the stone

Words and music: Ian White

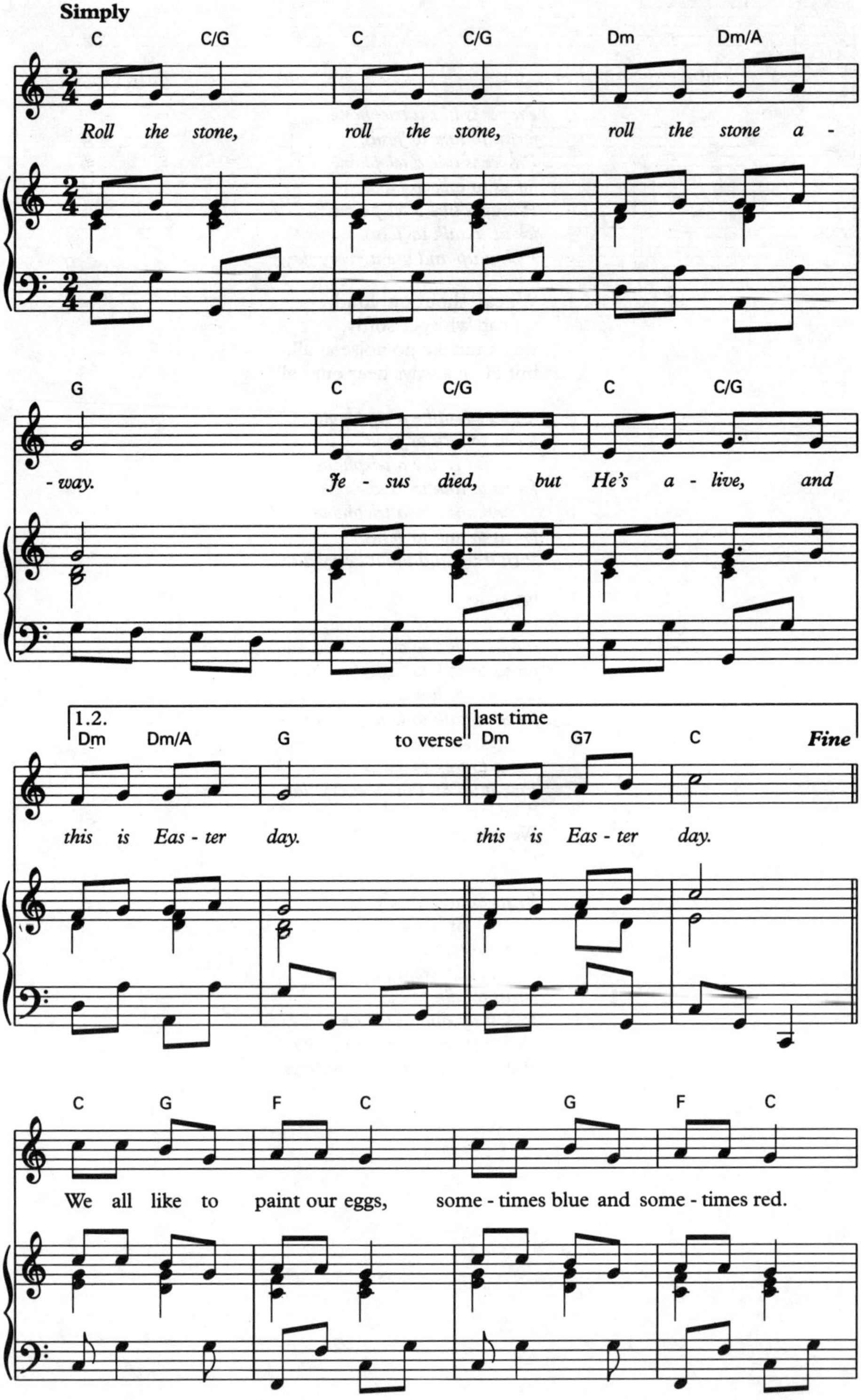

Simply
C C/G C C/G Dm Dm/A
Roll the stone, roll the stone, roll the stone a -
G C C/G C C/G
- way. Je - sus died, but He's a - live, and
1.2.
Dm Dm/A G to verse
this is Eas - ter day.
last time
Dm G7 C Fine
this is Eas - ter day.
C G F C G F C
We all like to paint our eggs, some - times blue and some - times red.

First we roll them till they crunch, then we eat them, munch, munch, munch!

Roll the stone, roll the stone,
roll the stone away.
Jesus died, but He's alive,
and this is Easter day.

1 We all like to paint our eggs,
   sometimes blue and sometimes red.
   First we roll them till they crunch,
   then we eat them,
   (*spoken*) munch, munch, munch!
   Roll the stone . . .

2 We have chocolate eggs to eat,
   and inside there's lots of sweets.
   First they open with a crunch,
   then we eat them,
   (*spoken*) munch, munch, munch!
   Roll the stone . . .

450 Saul had made himself

Words and music: Gillian E Hutchinson
Music arranged Phil Burt

With feeling

Saul had made him-self a num - ber of e - ne-mies,
who were bu-sy plot-ting his death. But his friends had no de -
- sire to dis-co-ver him suf-fer-ing from short-age of breath.
To a - void a tra - ge-dy, they re-moved him sec - ret - ly,

1 Saul had made himself a number of enemies,
who were busy plotting his death.
But his friends had no desire to discover him
suffering from shortage of breath.
To avoid a tragedy, they removed him secretly,
demonstrating brotherly love.
From enforced captivity, carefully they set him free,
demonstrating brotherly love.

2 Following the Lord can sometimes be difficult
if we try to do it alone.
We all need each other's help and encouragement
as we learn to live as He's shown;
serving others joyfully, showing generosity,
demonstrating brotherly love;
living in humility, bearing burdens patiently,
demonstrating brotherly love.

3 All of us have different gifts and abilities,
which we need to learn how to share.
We can all take part in building the fellowship,
showing the world we care.
Always speaking truthfully, harbouring no enmity,
demonstrating brotherly love;
working for Him faithfully, joined in perfect unity,
demonstrating brotherly love.

451 See the man walking
(This is a miracle)

Words and music: Ian White

Simply

See the man walk-ing, see the man walk-ing, see the man walk-ing on the wa - - ter.

This is a mi-ra-cle, His name is *Je-sus.* *How does He do it?* He is the Son of God. Can I be-

BOYS
GIRLS
BOYS
GIRLS
BOYS

1 See the man walking, see the man walking,
see the man walking on the water.
BOYS   *This is a miracle,*
GIRLS *His name is Jesus.*
BOYS   *How does He do it?*
GIRLS *He is the Son of God.*
BOYS   *Can I believe Him?*
GIRLS *You can believe Him.*
BOYS   *Really believe Him?*
GIRLS *Really believe Him.*

2 Hear the man talking, hear the man talking,
hear the man talking words of wisdom.
        This is a miracle . . .

3 See the man healing, see the man healing,
see the man healing people blind and lame.
        This is a miracle . . .

4 See the man dying, see the man dying,
see the man dying and come back to life.
        This is a miracle . . .

5 Hear the man promise, hear the man promise,
hear the man promise to be with me.
        This is a miracle . . .

452 See, to us a Child is born

INNOCENTS 7 7 7 7

Words: Timothy Dudley-Smith
Music: *The Parish Choir*, 1850

Joyfully

See, to us a Child is born – glo-ry breaks on Christ-mas morn! Now to us a Son is given – praise to God in high-est heaven.

1 See, to us a Child is born –
   glory breaks on Christmas morn!
   Now to us a Son is given –
   praise to God in highest heaven.

2 On His shoulder rule shall rest –
   in Him all the earth be blest!
   Wise and wonderful His name –
   heaven's Lord in human frame!

3 Mighty God, who mercy brings –
   Lord of lords and King of kings!
   Father of eternal days –
   every creature sing His praise!

4 Everlasting Prince of peace –
   truth and righteousness increase!
   He shall reign from shore to shore –
   Christ is King for evermore!

453 Shine bright

Words: Steve Kersys
Music: Greg Leavers
Music arranged Christopher Hayward

With a swing

Shine bright, daz-zle, daz-zle, shine bright, daz-zle, daz-zle._ The light of Je-sus is shin-ing bright; shine bright, daz-zle, daz-zle, shine bright, daz-zle, daz-zle. The light of Je-sus is shin-ing bright. His life of love; His life of light;

shines   clear and bright   in the dark-est   night.

Shine bright, dazzle, dazzle, shine bright, dazzle, dazzle.
The light of Jesus is shining bright;
shine bright, dazzle, dazzle, shine bright, dazzle, dazzle.
The light of Jesus is shining bright.
His life of love;
His life of light;
shines clear and bright in the darkest night.

454   Sing a new song to the Lord

ONSLOW SQUARE   7 7 11 8

From Psalm 98
Words: Timothy Dudley-Smith
Music: David Wilson

Sing a new song to the Lord, He to whom won-ders be-long! Re-joice in His tri-umph and tell of His power O sing to the Lord a new song!

1 Sing a new song to the Lord,
   He to whom wonders belong!
   Rejoice in His triumph and tell of His power –
   O sing to the Lord a new song!

2 Now to the ends of the earth
   see His salvation is shown;
   and still He remembers His mercy and truth,
   unchanging in love to His own.

3 Sing a new song and rejoice,
   publish His praises abroad!
   Let voices in chorus, with trumpet and horn,
   resound for the joy of the Lord!

4 Join with the hills and the sea
   thunders of praise to prolong!
   In judgement and justice He comes to the earth –
   O sing to the Lord a new song!

455

Sing praise

Words and music: Derek Llewellyn

Lively

Sing praise to God the Fa - ther,

Repeat as necessary in verses 3 and 4

God the Spi-rit, God the Son.__ Sing praise to

God who loves us. Praise Him, ev-ery-one!__ Sing __

1 Sing praise to God the Father,
God the Spirit, God the Son.
Sing praise to God who loves us.
Praise Him, everyone!

2 Sing praise to God the Father,
clap your hands and jump for joy.
He made the world around us
and He loves us all.

3 Sing praise to God's Son Jesus,
clap your hands and jump for joy.
Wave your arms and turn around.
He teaches us about the Father
and He loves us all.

4 Sing praise to the Holy Spirit,
clap your hands and jump for joy.
Wave your arms and turn around.
Stamp your feet and shout hooray.
He helps us to live like Jesus
and He loves us all.

5 Sing praise to God the Father,
God the Spirit, God the Son:
Sing praise to God who loves us.
Praise Him everyone!

456 Sing and celebrate
(Christmas)

Words and music: Greg Leavers

Sing and celebrate (sing and celebrate);
God gave Jesus (God gave Jesus);
Light for all the world (Light for all the world);
born at Christmas (born at Christmas time).

1 Jesus, our light,
shines bright,
what delight;
came to reach us,
teach us,
lead us;
  Sing and celebrate . . .

2 God so loved us,
gave us
Jesus;
Lord, we thank You,
love You,
serve You;
  Sing and celebrate . . .

*Jesus, Light of the world,
God's great gift of love.*

457

Sing and celebrate
(Easter)

Words: Greg Leavers

Music as for 456

Sing and celebrate (sing and celebrate);
Christ is risen (Christ is risen);
Champion of the world (Champion of the world);
lives for ever (lives for evermore).

1 God so loved us,
  gave us
  Jesus;
  died on Calvary,
  set free
  you and me;
    Sing and celebrate . . .

2 Jesus our friend,
  died, then
  rose again;
  Lord, we love You,
  thank You,
  praise You;
    Sing and celebrate . . .

Jesus died for the world,
God's great gift of love.

458 Six hundred years old
(He's got everything under control)

Words and music: Eddie Smith

Six hun-dred years old was the preach-er No - ah when the
Lord said to build a boat;___ said a flood would come and
co - ver the earth,___ and on - ly No - ah would stay a - float.
___ Though the peo-ple laughed and called him names, he

part of His plan; He's got ev-ery-thing un-der con-trol.

1 Six hundred years old was the preacher Noah
   when the Lord said to build a boat;
   said a flood would come and cover the earth,
   and only Noah would stay afloat.
   Though the people laughed and called him names,
   he stayed right with his job.
   When he felt those drops, he knew his God
   had everything under control.
   He's got everything under control,
   He's got everything under control.
   The stars and the planets are in His hand,
   the wind and the rain at His command.
   You and I, we're a part of His plan;
   He's got everything under control.

2 Now Jonah had a whale of a problem
   when he turned that revival down.
   God tracked him down and boxed him in
   'cause he wouldn't go to that town.
   When He tells you to do what He wants you to do,
   don't think you can let it roll,
   'cause the God who made this universe
   has everything under control.
   He's got everything . . .

3 King Nebuchadnezzar lost his religion
   when the Hebrews wouldn't bow down.
   He lost his cool, fired up the furnace,
   called a holiday in the town.
   When he opened the door and threw them in,
   they smiled at the burning coals,
   'cause the God that allowed that fire to burn
   had everything under control.
   He's got everything . . .

4 Daniel was invited to be on the menu
   at the meeting of the lions' club,
   'cause he continued to pray three times a day
   to the Lord he had learned to love.
   When they threw him in he began to grin,
   'cause he knew what we all know;
   that the God who made those lions growl
   had everything under control.
   He's got everything . . .

459 So we're marching along

Words and music: Ian Smale
Music arranged Christopher Hayward

So we're march-ing a-long, sing-ing a song, we're in the Lord's ar - my. We're fight-ing for right as we're learn-ing what's wrong, 'cause — we're in the Lord's ar - my. He's got the vic - tory, so let's real-ly shout, we're in the Lord's ar -

So we're marching along, singing a song,
we're in the Lord's army.
We're fighting for right as we're learning what's wrong,
'cause – we're in the Lord's army.
He's got the victory, so let's really shout,
we're in the Lord's army.
We're in the Lord's (*yeah*), we're in the Lord's (*right*),
we're in the Lord's army.
So we're marching along . . .

460 Sometimes I'm naughty

Words and music: Greg Leavers
Music arranged Phil Burt

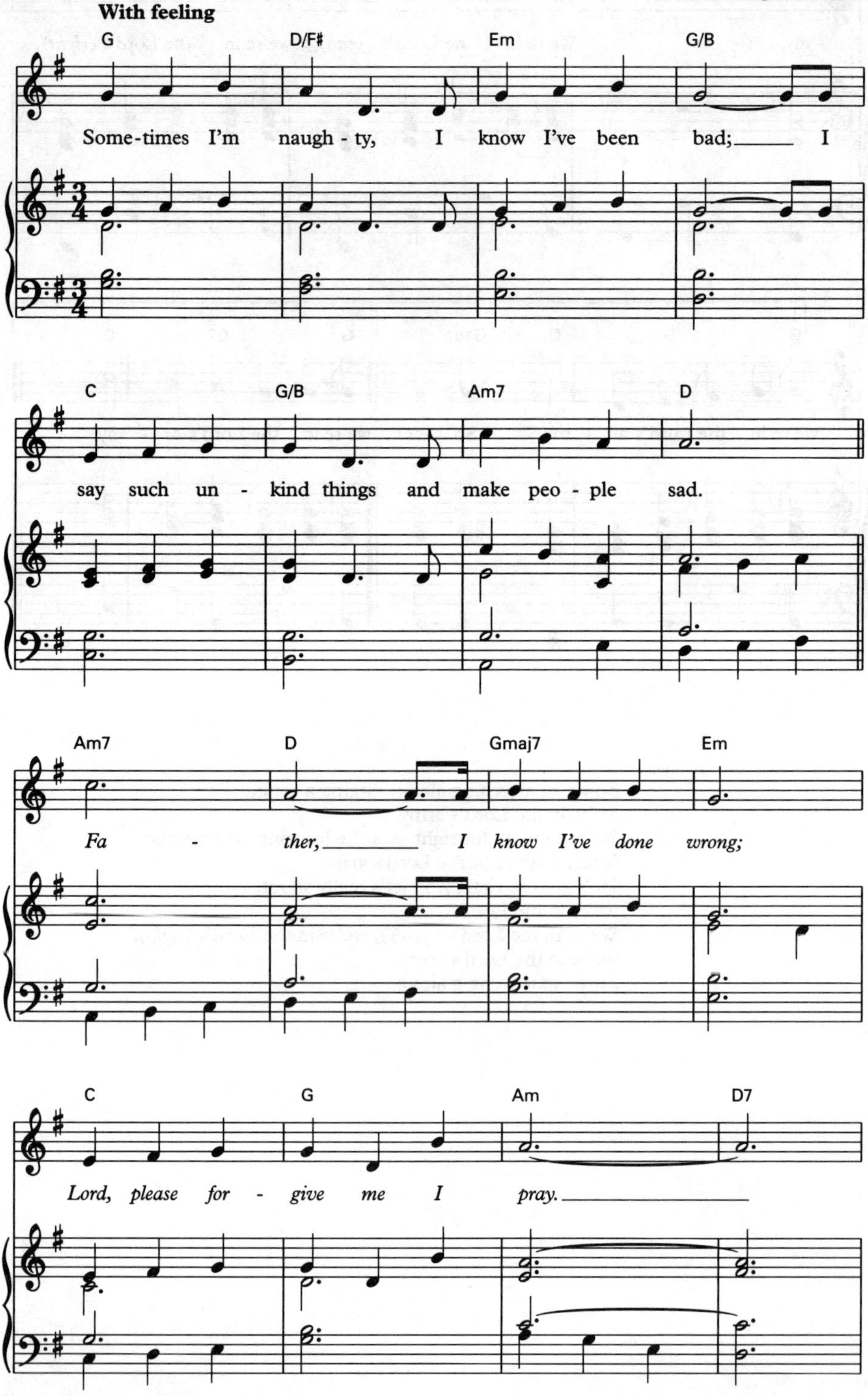

With feeling
G
D/F#
Em
G/B
Some-times I'm naugh - ty, I know I've been bad; I
C
G/B
Am7
D
say such un - kind things and make peo - ple sad.
Am7
D
Gmaj7
Em
Fa - ther, I know I've done wrong;
C
G
Am
D7
Lord, please for - give me I pray.

I want to say,___ I want to say___
that I'm so sor - ry, ___ Lord. _____

1 Sometimes I'm naughty,
  I know I've been bad;
  I say such unkind things
  and make people sad.
    Father, I know I've done wrong;
    Lord, please forgive me I pray.
    I want to say,
    I want to say
    that I'm so sorry, Lord.

2 I'm rude to my family,
  I want my own way.
  I don't show them kindness
  or do what they say.
    Father, I know . . .

3 In love You forgive me,
  I'm glad I'm Your child.
  Your Spirit lives in me
  to change me inside.
    Father, help me today;
    help me to please You, I pray.
    I want to say,
    I want to say
    how much I love You, Lord.

461 Sometimes problems

Words and music: Greg Leavers
Music arranged Phil Burt

Some-times prob-lems can be BIG, some-times prob-lems can be *small*; but it does-n't real-ly mat-ter for what-ev-er the size, Je-sus wants to help us with them all—so we can tell Him all a-bout_ it.

Trust His word, don't doubt it. Don't be a - fraid;

DON'T BE A - FRAID, just (1, 2, 3, 4) be - lieve.

1 Sometimes problems can be BIG,
  sometimes problems can be *small*;
  but it doesn't really matter
  for whatever the size,
  Jesus wants to help us with them all –
  so we can tell Him all about it.
  Trust His word, don't doubt it.
  Don't be afraid;
  DON'T BE AFRAID,
  just (1, 2, 3, 4) believe.

2 Some days I wake up feeling GLAD,
  some days I wake up feeling *sad*;
  but it doesn't really matter
  for whatever the day
  Jesus wants to help us through them all.
  He's promised He will never leave us;
  He will not forsake us;
  don't be dismayed,
  DON'T BE AFRAID,
  just (1, 2, 3, 4) believe.

Words in Capitals spoken with a loud voice
Words in Italics spoken quietly

462 Some people laugh
(What do you do)

Words and music: Sam Horner

1 Some people laugh, some people sing,
 some people clap; and so they bring
 their worship to the King of kings.
 What do you do? What do you do?

2 Some people dance, some bring a word,
 some people cry before the Lord;
 and so they bring their worship to
 the King of kings, the King of kings.

3 Some people march and raise their hands
 and some are quiet but understand.
 There are many ways of worshipping
 the King of kings, the King of kings.

463   Sorry, Lord

Words and music: Greg Leavers
Music arranged Christopher Hayward

1 Sorry, Lord, for all the things
  that I've done wrong; please
  make me clean, forgive my sin –
  I want to follow You.

2 Thank You, Lord, for dying on
  the cross to save me;
  fill my heart for my new start –
  please come and live in me.

3 I love You, please help me Lord
  to follow closely;
  from today, in every way
  please make me more like You.

464 Spies were sent out

Words and music: S and J Doddridge
Music arranged Christopher Hayward

Spies were sent out to view the prom-ised land.

Ten said, 'There are gi - ants there: we can't do as we planned.'

Josh - u - a and Ca - leb said, 'We must make a stand.' The

Lord said, 'Fol - low Me, I'll place them in your hand.' *We've got to*

hear, be-lieve and o-bey, _____ what - ev-er the Fa - ther might say; _____ for

He is a good God and He on - ly wants the best for us.

1 Spies were sent out to
view the promised land.
Ten said, 'There are giants there:
we can't do as we planned.'
Joshua and Caleb said,
'We must make a stand.'
The Lord said, 'Follow Me,
I'll place them in your hand.'
We've got to hear, believe and obey,
whatever the Father might say;
for He is a good God and He only wants
the best for us.

2 When Joshua saw the size of
Jericho's great wall –
towering high above him,
many metres tall –
though it looked impossible
to take the town at all,
the Lord said, 'Obey Me
and down the walls will fall.'
We've got to . . .

3 So when you're feeling scared or
things are looking blue –
you've a job that seems so
difficult to do –
don't forget His promises
He's made to help you through:
the Lord says, 'Don't be afraid,
I'll always be with you.'
We've got to . . .

465   Spirit of God

Words and music: Ian Smale
Music arranged Phil Burt

Spirit of God, please fill me now to overflowing.
Spirit of God, give me the words You want me to say.
Spirit of God, release my tongue to praise the Holy Son;
Spirit of God, free this spirit of mine.

466 Standing in Your presence, Lord

Words and music: Gillian E Hutchinson
Music arranged Phil Burt

Stand-ing in Your pres-ence, Lord,

we are here to praise Your name.

Stand-ing in Your pres-ence, Lord, Your great good-ness we pro-

-claim. You a-lone are God the Lord,____

Standing in Your presence, Lord,
we are here to praise Your name.
Standing in Your presence, Lord,
Your great goodness we proclaim.

1 You alone are God the Lord,
Master of the earth and sky.
All the stars in heaven worship, and yet,
when we call You Lord, You hear our cry.
    Standing in Your presence, Lord,
    we will lift our hands to You.
    Standing in Your presence, Lord,
    giving thanks for all You do.

2 You have brought us here today,
kept and guided for so long.
There's no need for tears or sadness,
the joy that You give us, Lord, will make us strong.
    Standing in Your presence, Lord,
    listening to Your holy law.
    Standing in Your presence, Lord,
    we will praise You evermore.

467 Thank You for the love

Words and music: Andy Silver

Thank You for the love that our mums give to us each day;

thank You for the help and the care that they bring our way.

Lord, we thank You for ev - ery - thing they do,

show us how to help them too. Show us how to live, teach-ing

Thank You for the love that our mums give to us each day;
thank You for the help and the care that they bring our way.
Lord, we thank You for everything they do,
show us how to help them too.
Show us how to live, teaching us to appreciate;
show us how to live so that we don't infuriate.
Lord, we ask that in everything they do,
may our mums be blessed by You.

468 The journey of life

Words and music: Valerie Collison

The jour-ney of life may be ea-sy, may be hard, there'll be dan-gers on the way; with Christ at my side I'll do bat-tle as I ride 'gainst the foe that would lead me a-stray. *Will you ride, ride, ride with the King of kings, will you*

1 The journey of life may be easy, may be hard,
  there'll be dangers on the way;
  with Christ at my side I'll do battle as I ride
  'gainst the foe that would lead me astray.
  Will you ride, ride, ride with the King of kings,
  will you follow my Leader true;
  will you shout 'Hosanna!' to the holy Son of God,
  who died for me and you?

2 My burden is light and a song is in my heart,
  as I travel on life's way;
  for Christ is my Lord and He's given me His word,
  that by my side He'll stay.
  Will you ride . . .

3 When doubts arise and when tears are in my eyes,
  when all seems lost to me;
  with Christ as my guide I can smile whate'er betide,
  for He my strength will be.
  Will you ride . . .

4 I'll follow my Leader wherever he may go,
  for Jesus is my friend;
  He'll lead me on to the place where He has gone,
  when I come to my journey's end.
  Will you ride . . .

469 The Lord is risen today

A two-part round

Words and music: Paul Kenchington

1 The Lord is risen today!
  The Lord is risen today!
  The Lord is risen today!
  The Lord is risen today!
  Alleluia! Alleluia! Alleluia!
  The Lord is risen today!

2 And we will sing His praise,
  and we will sing His praise,
  and we will sing His praise;
  the Lord is risen today!
  Alleluia! Alleluia! Alleluia!
  The Lord is risen today!

3 O, Jesus died for me!
  Yes, Jesus died for me!
  Yes, Jesus died for me,
  but the Lord is risen indeed!
  Alleluia! Alleluia! Alleluia!
  The Lord is risen today!

All sing 1 in unison, followed by 2 in unison.
One group begins 1 again and as they reach 2,
the other group begins at 1.
The accompaniment is common in both 1 and 2.

470 The most important thing

Words and music: Ian Smale
Music arranged Phil Burt

The most important thing for us as Christians
is not what we eat or drink,
but stirring up goodness, peace and joy
from the Holy Spirit.

471 The shepherds found
(In the stable)

Words: Hilda Rostron
Music: Colin Peters

Like a prayer

1 The shepherds found the stable
   and saw the Baby there;
   they quietly knelt beside Him
   and said a 'thank you' prayer.

2 The wise men found the Baby
   and gave gifts, one, two, three;
   today it is His birthday:
   My gift is – LOVE from me.

472 The Spirit lives

WALK IN THE LIGHT

Words and music: Damien Lundy

Happily

The Spi-rit lives to set us free, walk, walk in the light; He
binds us all in u-ni-ty, walk, walk in the light.
Walk in the light, __ walk in the light, __
walk in the light, __ walk in the light of the Lord.

1 The Spirit lives to set us free,
   walk, walk in the light;
   He binds us all in unity,
   walk, walk in the light.
      Walk in the light,
      walk in the light,
      walk in the light,
      walk in the light of the Lord.

2 Jesus promised life to all,
   walk, walk in the light;
   the dead were wakened by His call,
   walk, walk in the light.
      Walk in the light . . .

3 He died in pain on Calvary,
   walk, walk in the light;
   to save the lost like you and me,
   walk, walk in the light.
      Walk in the light . . .

4 We know His death was not the end,
   walk, walk in the light;
   He gave His Spirit to be our friend,
   walk, walk in the light.
      Walk in the light . . .

5 By Jesus' life our wounds are healed,
   walk, walk in the light;
   the Father's kindness is revealed,
   walk, walk in the light.
      Walk in the light . . .

6 The Spirit lives in you and me,
   walk, walk in the light;
   His light will shine for all to see,
   walk, walk in the light.
      Walk in the light . . .

473 The word of the Lord is planted
(The sower song)

Words and music: Alan J Price

The word of the Lord is plan-ted in my heart and I want to see it grow. The word of the Lord is plan-ted in my heart and I want you to know. I won't let the e-ne-my take it, or let bad times

The word of the Lord is planted in my heart
and I want to see it grow.
The word of the Lord is planted in my heart
and I want you to know.
I won't let the enemy take it,
or let bad times shake it;
I won't let other things choke it out, (*choke choke choke choke*)
'cause I want to let it grow, grow, grow,
'cause I want to let it grow! (*last time*) (*Yeah!*)

474 The word of God

Words and music: Mick Gisbey
Music arranged Christopher Hayward

Hebrew style

The word of God is liv - ing and act - ive,__ sharp-er than a-ny dou - ble-edged sword.___ The word of God is liv - ing and act-ive,_ sharp-er than a-ny dou-ble-edged sword.

The word of God is living and active,
sharper than any double-edged sword.
The word of God is living and active,
sharper than any double-edged sword.

475   There he stood – Goliath

Words and music: Gillian E Hutchinson
Music arranged Christopher Hayward

There he stood – Go - li - ath – migh - ty man in arm - our bright; com -
'Do you think I am a dog, to fight me with a stick? I'll

- pared to him you'd not say Da - vid was pre - pared to fight.
throw your flesh to a - ni - mals, your bones for birds to pick!'

When Go - li - ath saw him, he could not be - lieve his eyes: be -
Shout-ing mur-derous cur - ses, he cried out, 'Pre-pare to die!' But

-vide;_____ I'm fight-ing on the Lord al-migh-ty's side!'

1 There he stood – Goliath – mighty man in armour bright;
   compared to him you'd not say David was prepared to fight.
   When Goliath saw him, he could not believe his eyes:
   before him stood a boy he did despise.
   'Do you think I am a dog, to fight me with a stick?
   I'll throw your flesh to animals, your bones for birds to pick!'
   Shouting murderous curses, he cried out, 'Prepare to die!'
   But David spoke up boldly in reply.
      'Not with spear, not with sword
      but in the name of the Lord;
      in the name of the One you have defied.
      He's victorious in battle,
      He will save us by His power;
      strength and deliverance He'll provide;
      I'm fighting on the Lord almighty's side!'

2 Moving closer in, Goliath started his attack
   but David ran to meet him – he did not turn and run back.
   With his sling he threw a stone which to Goliath sped;
   it broke his skull and sank into his head!
   The giant had been conquered – he fell down upon the floor –
   then David chopped his head off and Goliath was no more!
   All of Israel's army knew the mighty deed was done
   and in whose name the victory had been won.
      'Not with spear . . .

3 Life is filled with problems which may give us cause to fear.
   But though they seem like giants, just remember God is near.
   He will always help us when we put our trust in Him.
   In the name of Jesus we shall win.
      'Not with spear . . .

476

There is no-one else
(Special)

Words and music: Paul Field

There is no-one else__ like you, there's no-one else like me.__

Each of us is spe-cial to God, that's the way it's meant to be.__ I'm

spe - cial, you're spe - cial, we're spe-cial, don't you see?__

There is no-one else__ like you, there's no-one else like me.__

There is no-one else like you,
there's no-one else like me.
Each of us is special to God,
that's the way it's meant to be.
I'm special, you're special,
we're special, don't you see?
there is no-one else like you,
there's no-one else like me.

Black or white, short or tall,
good or bad, God loves us all.
Loud or quiet, fat or thin,
each of us is special to Him.

There is no-one . . .

477 There once was a man
(Good old Daniel)

Words and music: Anon

Strongly ♩ = 104

Capo 3(D)

There once was a man called Dan - iel (*good old Dan-iel*). And
Dan - iel prayed three times a day (*good old Dan-iel*). But the
King's de-cree said, 'Wor-ship me!' (*poor old Dan-iel*). But Dan-iel would not
bend the knee! (*good old Dan-iel*). So the gates went 'crash' (*crash*), and the

There once was a man called Daniel
(*good old Daniel*).
And Daniel prayed three times a day
(*good old Daniel*).
But the King's decree said, 'Worship me!'
(*poor old Daniel*).
But Daniel would not bend the knee!
(*good old Daniel*).
So the gates went 'crash' (*crash*),
and the locks went 'click' (*click*),
and the lions began to roar,
and the lions began to roar.
But they couldn't eat Daniel if they tried
(*good old Daniel*),
because the Lord was on his side
(*good old Daniel*).

478 There's a song for all the children

IN MEMORIAM   86 76 76 76

Words: Albert Midlane (1825–1909)
in this version Jubilate Hymns
Music: John Stainer (1840–1901)

There's a song for all the children that makes the hea-vens ring, a song that ev-en an-gels can ne-ver, ne-ver sing; they praise Him as their mak-er and see Him glo-ri-fied, but

we can call Him Sav - iour be - cause for us He died.

1 There's a song for all the children
that makes the heavens ring,
a song that even angels
can never, never sing;
they praise Him as their maker
and see Him glorified,
but we can call Him Saviour
because for us He died.

2 There's a place for all the children
where Jesus reigns in love,
a place of joy and freedom
that nothing can remove;
a home that is more friendly
than any home we know,
where Jesus makes us welcome
because He loves us so.

3 There's a friend for all the children
to guide us every day,
whose care is always faithful
and never fades away;
there's no-one else so loyal –
His friendship stays the same;
He knows us and He loves us,
and Jesus is His name.

479   Think big: an elephant

Words and music: Susan Sayers
Music arranged Frances M Kelly

Think big: an e-le-phant. Think big-ger:__ a

sub-ma-rine.__ Think big-ger:__ the high-est moun-tain that

a-ny-one has ev-er seen. Yet big, big, big-ger is

God!__ And He loves us all.__

Accompaniment:

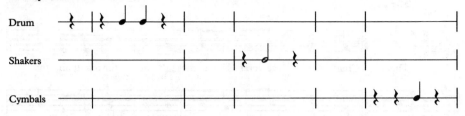

1 Think big: an elephant.
   Think bigger: a submarine.
   Think bigger: the highest mountain that anyone has ever seen.
   Yet big, big, bigger is God!
   And He loves us all.

2 Think old: a vintage car.
   Think older: a full-grown tree.
   Think older: a million grains of the sand beside the surging sea.
   Yet old, old, older is God!
   And He loves us all.

3 Think strong: a tiger's jaw.
   Think stronger: a castle wall.
   Think stronger: a hurricane that leaves little standing there at all.
   Yet strong, strong, stronger is God!
   And He loves us all.

480   This Child

Words and music: Graham Kendrick
Music arranged Christopher Norton

This Child se-cret-ly comes in the night; oh, this Child, hid-ing a hea-ven-ly light; oh, this Child, com-ing to us like a stran-ger; this hea-ven-ly Child. *This* Child, *hea-ven come down now to be with us here; hea-ven-ly love*

1 This Child secretly comes in the night;
  oh, this Child, hiding a heavenly light;
  oh, this Child, coming to us like a stranger;
  this heavenly Child.
  This Child, heaven come down now to be with us here;
  heavenly love and mercy appear;
  softly in awe and wonder come near
  to this heavenly Child.

2 This Child, rising on us like the sun;
  oh, this Child, given to light everyone;
  oh, this Child, guiding our feet on the pathway
  to peace on earth.
  This Child, heaven come down . . .

3 This Child, raising the humble and poor;
  oh, this Child, making the proud ones to fall;
  this Child, filling the hungry with good things;
  this heavenly Child.
  This Child, heaven come down . . .
  This Child, heaven come down . . .

481

This is a catchy songa
(The Christian Conga)

Words: Alan J Price
Music: Anon

Fast ♩ = 132

This is a cat-chy song - a,___ we sing it to the Cong - a,___ we dance and sing to Christ the King. Why don't you sing a - long - a,___ while we dance the Cong - a?___ Praise God a - bove for all His love!

Words: © 1990 Daybreak Music Ltd

This is a catchy songa,
we sing it to the Conga,
we dance and sing
to Christ the King.
Why don't you sing alonga,
while we dance the Conga?
Praise God above for all His love!

1 King David danced before the Lord,
worship filled his heart;
we can dance before Him, too,
this is how we start.
   This is a catchy songa . . .

2 Jesus is the greatest friend,
alive for us today,
He said, 'I'm with you till the end,
I'm with you all the way.'
   This is a catchy songa . . .

Verses spoken, not sung

482 Wandering like lost sheep

Words and music: Andy Silver

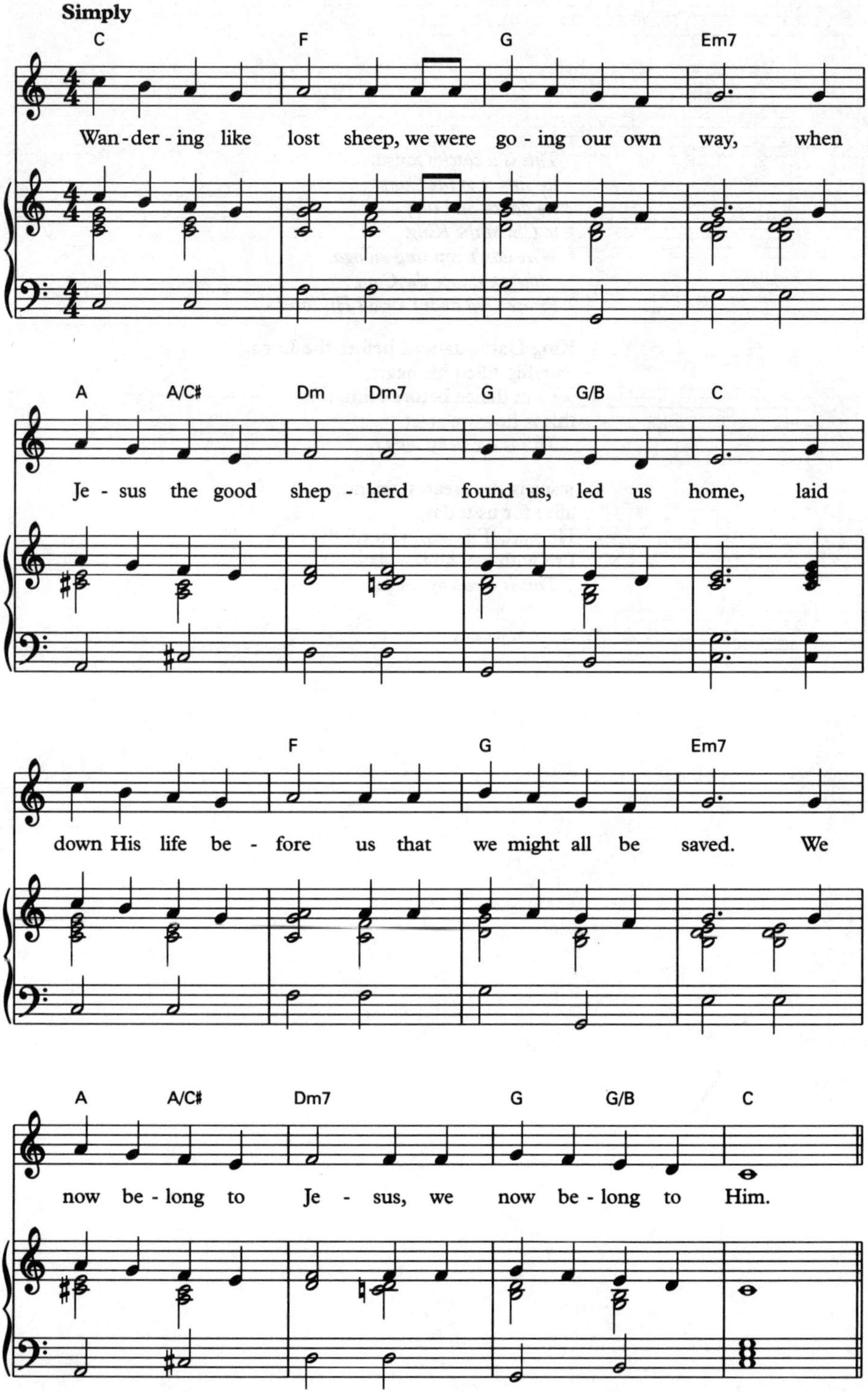

Simply
C F G Em7
Wan-der-ing like lost sheep, we were go-ing our own way, when
A A/C# Dm Dm7 G G/B C
Je-sus the good shep-herd found us, led us home, laid
F G Em7
down His life be-fore us that we might all be saved. We
A A/C# Dm7 G G/B C
now be-long to Je-sus, we now be-long to Him.

Wandering like lost sheep, we were going our own way,
when Jesus the good shepherd found us, led us home,
laid down His life before us that we might all be saved.
We now belong to Jesus, we now belong to Him.
We are His sheep, we are His sheep,
we hear His voice, and follow Him.
We are His sheep, we are His sheep,
we hear His voice, and follow Him.

483 We are soldiers of the King

Words and music: Greg Leavers
Music arranged Phil Burt

March

We are sol-diers of the King, of His vic-tory we will sing; liv - ing ev - ery hour by the Spi - rit's power, march - ing in the name of Je - sus. E - ne-mies are all a -

We are soldiers of the King,
of His victory we will sing;
living every hour by the Spirit's power,
marching in the name of Jesus.
Enemies are all around,
as we praise they're losing ground;
trusting in God's word – it's a mighty sword –
forever friendly, faithful followers fighting for the King.

484   We need to grow

Words and music: Alan J Price

spend some time each day. We'll grow as we wor-ship Him, give Him our love and praise! We need to

B7   E   A   E   F#   B   D.S.

We need to grow, grow, grow, grow,
grow in the grace of the Saviour.
We need to grow, grow, grow, grow,
grow in the knowledge of Jesus our Lord.
We need to grow, grow, grow, grow,
grow in the grace of the Saviour.
We need to grow, grow, grow, grow,
grow in the knowledge of Jesus our Lord.

1 We'll grow as we pray to Him,
   spend some time each day.
   We'll grow as we worship Him,
   give Him our love and praise!
       We need to grow, grow, grow, grow,
       grow in the grace of the Saviour.
       We need to grow, grow, grow, grow,
       grow in the knowledge of Jesus our Lord.

2 We grow as we read of Him
   and the way for us to live;
   we'll grow as we work for Him,
   as our lives to Him we give.
       We need to grow . . .

3 We grow as we learn and share
   with others that we know;
   these are the things to do
   if we really want to grow.
       We need to grow . . .
       grow in the knowledge of,
       grow in the knowledge of Jesus our Lord.

485   We will praise

Words and music: Ian Smale
Music arranged Phil Burt and Christopher Hayward

We will praise, we will praise, we will praise the Lord; we will
praise the Lord be-cause He is good. We will praise, we will praise, we will
praise the Lord, be - cause His love is ev - er - last-ing. We will
ev - er - last-ing. Bring on the trum-pets and harps,

We will praise, we will praise, we will praise the Lord;
we will praise the Lord because He is good.
We will praise, we will praise, we will praise the Lord,
because His love is everlasting.
We will praise, we will praise, we will praise the Lord;
we will praise the Lord because He is good.
We will praise, we will praise, we will praise the Lord,
because His love is everlasting.

Bring on the trumpets and harps,
let's hear the cymbals ring;
then in harmony
lift our voices and sing, sing.

We will praise, we will praise, we will praise the Lord;
we will praise the Lord because He is good.
We will praise, we will praise, we will praise the Lord,
because His love is everlasting.

486   We'll praise Him on the trumpet

Words and music: Ian Smale
Music arranged Phil Burt

Hebrew style

We'll praise Him on the trum-pet and we'll praise Him on gui-tar, we'll

praise Him with a drum and with a harp and a lyre. We'll

praise Him with our voi-ces 'cause we want to lift Him higher; and

all God's peo-ple shout, 'Hal-le-lu-jah!' Hal - le - lu - jah,

hal-le-lu-jah, hal - le-lu-jah, hal-le-lu-jah. Hal - le-lu-jah, hal - le-lu - jah, and all God's peo-ple shout, 'Hal-le - lu - jah!'

1 We'll praise Him on the trumpet and we'll praise Him on guitar,
   we'll praise Him with a drum and with a harp and a lyre.
   We'll praise Him with our voices 'cause we want to lift Him higher;
   and all God's people shout, 'Hallelujah!'
   Hallelujah, hallelujah, hallelujah, hallelujah.
   Hallelujah, hallelujah, and all God's people shout, 'Hallelujah!'

2 We'll praise Him for His favour and we'll praise Him for His deeds;
   we'll praise Him – though the road is rough, He's still the one who leads.
   We'll praise Him for provision as He cares for all our needs,
   and all God's people shout, 'Hallelujah!'
   Hallelujah, hallelujah . . .

3 We'll praise Him that upon a cross the Lamb of God was slain;
   we'll praise Him that He conquered death and now He lives again.
   We'll praise Him – He's the King of kings who will forever reign,
   and all God's people shout, 'Hallelujah!'
   Hallelujah, hallelujah . . .

4 We'll praise Him that He's making us the people we should be;
   we'll praise Him that our chains are gone, we're now completely free.
   We'll praise Him – we don't know defeat, we live in victory,
   and all God's people shout, 'Hallelujah!'
   Hallelujah, hallelujah . . .

487 We're following Jesus

Words and music: Robert C Evans

Lively

We're fol-low-ing Je - sus,____ just like Mat-thew, Pe - ter and John. ____ We're fol-low-ing Je - sus,____ just like Thad-de-us, Phi-lip and Tom. ____ We're fol-low-ing Je - sus,____ just like Si-mon, James and An-drew. Like them, the Lord is call-ing me and you.____

Fine

We're following Jesus,
just like Matthew, Peter and John.
We're following Jesus,
just like Thaddeus, Philip and Tom.
We're following Jesus,
just like Simon, James and Andrew.
Like them, the Lord is calling me and you.

1 They all loved Him (*I want to love Him*),
   they all served Him (*I want to serve Him*).
   They all knew Him (*I want to know Him*),
   they all followed. (*I want to follow*).
      We're following . . .

2 Jesus taught them (*Teach me, Lord*),
   Jesus led them (*Lead me, Lord*),
   Jesus fed them (*Feed me, Lord*),
   Jesus used them (*Use me, Lord*).
      We're following . . .

488   What colours God has made

Words: Timothy Dudley-Smith
Music: Michael Paget

Slowly and simply

What col-ours God has made in flower and field and tree! From spring-ing green of leaf and blade I learn His love for me,

1 What colours God has made
  in flower and field and tree!
  From springing green of leaf and blade
  I learn His love for me.

2 The summer's yellow sand,
  the blue of sky and sea,
  they tell of God their maker's hand,
  and all His love for me.

3 The turning autumn leaves,
  the fruit so full and free,
  the golden glow of harvest sheaves,
  declare His love for me.

4 He frames the winter's skies,
  His silver stars I see;
  He makes the sun in splendour rise,
  the God who cares for me.

5 So sing my Father's praise,
  the living God is He,
  whose colours brighten all our days,
  who loves and cares for me.

489 What do you give

Words and music: Nancy Harrison

Light Latin pulse

What do you give_ a God who has ev-ery-thing?

What do you give_ a God who has it all?

1.
He is the One who flung the shin-ing ga-lax-ies in space!

He is the One who hung the stars in place!

1 What do you give a God who has everything?
What do you give a God who has it all?
He is the One who flung the shining galaxies in space!
He is the One who hung the stars in place!

2 What do you give a God who has everything?
What do you give the maker of the earth?
Give Him your life and let Him guide you;
trust Him in all your ways!
Give Him your heart; He'll fill it up with praise!
Give Him your heart; He'll fill it up with praise!

490

What drives the stars
(It's a miracle)

Words: William and Gloria Gaither
Music: William Gaither

What drives the stars with-out mak-ing a sound?

Why don't they crash when they're spin-ning a-round?

What holds me up when the world's up-side down? I

know_____ it's a mi-ra-cle!_____

1 What drives the stars without making a sound?
   Why don't they crash when they're spinning around?
   What holds me up when the world's upside down?
   I know it's a miracle!
   Who tells the ocean where to stop on the sand?
   What keeps the water back from drowning the land?
   Who makes the rules I don't understand?
   I know it's a miracle!
     It's a miracle just to know
     God is with me wherever I go.
     It's a miracle as big as can be,
     that He can make a miracle of me!

2 Who shows the birds how to make a good nest?
   How can the geese fly so far without rest?
   Why do the ducks go south and not west?
   I know it's a miracle!
   What makes a brown seed so tiny and dry
   burst into green and grow up so high?
   And shoot out blossoms of red by and by?
   I know it's a miracle!
     It's a miracle . . .

3 When a spring makes a brook and a brook makes a stream,
   the stream makes the river water fresh as can be.
   Who puts the salt in when it gets to the sea?
   I know it's a miracle!
   There are thousands of people in cities I see,
   the world must be crowded as crowded can be;
   but God knows my name and He cares about me.
   I know it's a miracle!

491 What a mighty God we serve

Words: Anon
Music: Zulu working song
Music arranged Phil Burt

1 What a mighty God we serve . . .
(*4 times*)

2 He created you and me . . .

3 He has all the power to save . . .

4 Let us praise the living God . . .

5 What a mighty God we serve . . .

492 What made a difference

Words and music: Gillian E Hutchinson
Music arranged Christopher Hayward

With a swing

What made a dif-ference in the life of Saul, to change him from a sin-ner to A-pos-tle Paul? He met Je-sus and sud-den-ly knew that all he'd ha-ted turned out to be true. In-

-stead of per-se-cut-ing those who fol-lowed His name,____ he started in the sy-na-gogue His love to pro-claim. Yes, who'd have thought that Saul could be__ trans-formed __ in-to the great-est mis-sion-ary.__

8va

1 What made a difference in the life of Saul,
  to change him from a sinner to Apostle Paul?
  He met Jesus and suddenly knew
  that all he'd hated turned out to be true.
  Instead of persecuting those who followed His name,
  he started in the synagogue His love to proclaim.
  Yes, who'd have thought that Saul could be
  transformed into the greatest missionary.

2 On several journeys the apostle was sent,
  and suffered many difficulties as he went.
  Beaten, shipwrecked, imprisoned was he
  but learnt to glory in adversity.
  The churches grew and flourished and the Gospel was spread,
  and many found salvation through the things that he said.
  Yes, who'd have thought that Saul could be
  transformed into the greatest missionary.

3 He wrote some letters to the churches he knew,
  to Ephesus, Colossi and Galatia too.
  To Philippi and Corinth he wrote,
  to Rome and Thessalonica, epistles of note.
  Timothy and Titus and Philemon all heard
  and what he wrote has now become a part of God's Word.
  Yes, who'd have thought that Saul could be
  transformed into the greatest missionary.

4 If you've decided that your life must change,
  then give it to the Lord for Him to rearrange.
  He will be your Saviour and friend,
  and on His presence you can depend.
  You may not be a missionary or travel around,
  but all of us can witness to the joy that we've found.
  Yes, what the Lord could do for Saul,
  He's ready now to do for one and all!

493 When I'm feeling lonely

Words and music: Greg Leavers
Music arranged Christopher Hayward

When I'm feel-ing lone-ly,_____ when I'm feel-ing blue,
when I'm feel-ing so fed up, I can al-ways talk to You.
Lord,_____ You hear me when I pray; Lord,_____ You're
near me ev-ery day. Thank You, Lord,_____ You

al - ways see me through;_ I'll ne - ver, ev - er, find a friend as

good as_ You._ I'll ne - ver, ev - er, find a friend as good as_ You.

When I'm feeling lonely, when I'm feeling blue,
when I'm feeling so fed up, I can always talk to You.
Lord, You hear me when I pray;
Lord, You're near me every day.
Thank You, Lord, You always see me through;
I'll never, ever, find a friend as good as You.
I'll never, ever, find a friend as good as You.

494

When the dark clouds
(Talk to the Saviour)

Words: Paul Field and Ralph Chambers
Music: Paul Field

With feeling

When the dark clouds are a - bove you, there's no sun - shine a - ny -
- where; when you feel that no-one loves you, when you feel that no-one
cares; talk to the Sav-iour, He knows how you
feel. His love lasts for - ev - er, His love for you is

When the dark clouds are above you,
there's no sunshine anywhere;
when you feel that no-one loves you,
when you feel that no-one cares;
talk to the Saviour,
He knows how you feel.
His love lasts forever,
His love for you is real.
Talk to the Saviour,
no matter what you do.
You've got a friend in Jesus,
He always loves you.

When the dark . . .

495

When we look up

Words and music: Andy Silver

When we look up to the sky
and we see the sparrows fly,
let's remember that Jesus knows them all.
When we see the lovely trees
and the flowers and the leaves,
let's remember that Jesus made them all.
J.E.S.U.S. C.A.R.E.S.
Jesus cares for all the things He made:
that means you and me,
our friends and family.
Thank You, Jesus, for caring for me.

496 When you're feeling good
(Thumbs up)

Words: Paul Field and Ralph Chambers
Music: Paul Field

With a swing

When you're feel - ing good put your thumbs up.

When you're feel - ing bad put them down.

When you're feel - ing hap - py you can smile all day.

When you're feel - ing low wear a frown. But

When you're feeling good put your thumbs up.
When you're feeling bad put them down.
When you're feeling happy you can smile all day.
When you're feeling low wear a frown.
But don't just follow your feelings.
Trust in God and His word.
No matter what you feel put your thumbs up,
put your faith in the Lord.

497 When God breathes

Words and music: Joan Robinson
Music arranged Christopher Hayward

When God breathes His Spi-rit in my life; when God breathes His Spi-rit in my life; when God breathes His Spi-rit in my life,_____ then I will shine, shine for Him.

When God breathes His Spirit in my life;
when God breathes His Spirit in my life;
when God breathes His Spirit in my life,
then I will shine, shine for Him.

498

Would you walk by
(Cross over the road)

Words and music: P M Verrall

Would you walk by on the oth - er side when some - one called for aid?___ Would you walk by on the oth - er side, and would you be a - fraid?

1 Would you walk by on the other side
when someone called for aid?
Would you walk by on the other side,
and would you be afraid?
   Cross over the road, my friend;
   ask the Lord His strength to lend;
   His compassion has no end.
   Cross over the road.

2 Would you walk by on the other side
when you saw a loved one stray?
Would you walk by on the other side,
or would you watch and pray?
   Cross over the road . . .

3 Would you walk by on the other side
when starving children cried?
Would you walk by on the other side,
and would you not provide?
   Cross over the road, my friend,
   ask the Lord His strength to lend,
   His compassion has no end.
   Cross over the road.
   Cross over the road,
   cross over the road.

499 Yet to all who received Him

Words and music: Ian Smale
Music arranged Christopher Hayward

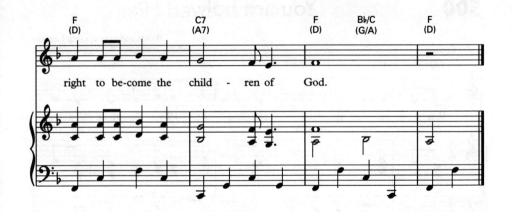

right to be-come the child - ren of God.

Yet to all who received Him,
to those who believed in His name,
He gave the right to become the children of God.
Yet to all who received Him,
to those who believed in His name,
He gave the right to become the children of God.

500 You are holy

Words and music: Greg Leavers
Music arranged Christopher Hayward

You are ho - ly, so You hate all we do wrong. You are lov - ing, for our sin You gave Your Son. You are Fa - ther,___ the great pro - tec - tor; You are migh - ty,___ the great Cre - a - tor; You are

You are holy, so You hate all we do wrong.
You are loving, for our sin You gave Your Son.
You are Father, the great protector;
You are mighty, the great Creator;
You are faithful, You are wonderful,
You are King and You are God.

501 You can weigh an elephant's auntie

Words and music: Chris Brown
Music arranged Noël Tredinnick

You can weigh an e-le-phant's aun-tie, you can weigh a pe-di-gree flea; but_ you can't weigh up all the love that Je-sus has for me, me, me, that Je-sus has_ for me.

Je - sus has — for — me.

1 You can weigh an elephant's auntie,
   you can weigh a pedigree flea;
   but you can't weigh up all the love
   that Jesus has for me, me, me,
   that Jesus has for me.

2 You can measure the length of a wiggly worm,
   or the height of a nanny goat's knee;
   but you can't measure all the love
   that Jesus has for me, me, me,
   that Jesus has for me.

3 You can add up two and two, make four,
   it's as easy as A, B, C;
   but you can't add up all the love
   that Jesus has for me, me, me,
   that Jesus has for me.

4 You can amaze me by subtraction,
   you can even take three from three;
   but you can't take away the love
   that Jesus has for me, me, me,
   that Jesus has for me.

502

You can't catch a plane
(Only Jesus)

Words: Ralph Chambers
Music: Paul Field

You can't catch a plane to take you to hea - ven. Not ev - en a space-ship can get that_ far. You can't take a ho-ver-craft or he - li - cop - ter jour - ney or drive in the fast - est rac - ing car. On - ly Je - sus, on - ly Je - sus, on - ly

You can't catch a plane to take you to heaven.
Not even a spaceship can get that far.
You can't take a hovercraft or helicopter journey
or drive in the fastest racing car.
Only Jesus, only Jesus, only Jesus is the way.
Only Jesus, only Jesus, only Jesus is the way.

503 You're my maker

Words and music: Joan Robinson
Music arranged Phil Burt

You're my ma - ker, You're my mu - sic, You're the Mas - ter of my life. You're my ma - ker, You're my mu - sic, You're the Mas - ter of my life. You're my ma - ker, You're my mu - sic, You're the Mas - ter of my life, and I

love You, Je - sus my_ Lord._

You're my maker, You're my music,
You're the Master of my life.
You're my maker, You're my music,
You're the Master of my life.
You're my maker, You're my music,
You're the Master of my life,
and I love You, Jesus my Lord.

Copyright Addresses

Alexander (Charles M)'s Copyright Trust, c/o S W Grant, 12 Lawrie Park Crescent, Sydenham, London SE26 6HD

Allen, F R, Barton Cottage, Station Road, Blockley, Glos GL56 9DT

Arlott, B M, c/o W S V Kennard, J Kay-Mouat, The Old Presbytery, Alderney, Channel Islands GY9 3TF

Barham Gould, A, c/o D R Gould, 34 Pollards Drive, Horsham, West Sussex RH13 5HH

Barrows, Cliff, 5000 Old Buncombe Road, Suite N, Greenville, South Carolina 29609, USA

A & C Black (Publishers Ltd), Howard Road, Eaton Socon, Huntingdon, Cambs PE19 3EZ

Boosey & Hawkes Music Publishers Ltd, The Hyde, Edgware Road, London NW9 6JN

Booth, J A P, c/o Paul Booth, 2 Old Coastguard Cottages, Waterside, Bradwell-on-Sea, Essex CM0 7QY

Bosworth & Co Ltd, 14-18 Heddon Street, London W1R 8DP

Breitkopf & Härtel, Buch und Musikverlag, Walkmuhlstrasse 52, D-6200, Weisbaden, Germany

Brown, Alan, 11 The Quadrant, Wimbledon, London SW20 8SW

Burt, Phil, 5 Gardner Road, Warton, Carnforth, Lancs LA5 9NY

Bush, Annie c/o Mrs A Spiers, 40 Northumberland Terrace, Everton, Liverpool L5 3QG

Cansdale, M J, The Rib, St Andrew Street, Wells BA5 2UR

Child Evangelism Fellowship, c/o 64 Osborne Road, Levenshulme, Manchester M19 2DY

Christian Music Ministries, 325 Bromfield Road, Hodge Hill, Birmingham B36 8ET

Cliff College, Calver, Sheffield S30 1XD

Cooke, N A M, PO Box 201, West Malling, Kent ME19 5RS

CopyCare Ltd, PO Box 77, Hailsham, East Sussex BN27 3EF

Crabtree, Roy, 7 Ascot Court, Carmen Sylva Road, Craig-y-don, Llandudno, Gwynedd LL30 1LZ

Daybreak Music Ltd, Silverdale Road, Eastbourne, East Sussex BN20 7AB

Dudley-Smith, Timothy, 9 Ashlands, Ford, Salisbury, Wilts SP4 6DY

William Elkin Music Services Ltd, Station Road Industrial Estate, Salhouse, Norwich, Norfolk NR13 6NY

Franciscan Communications, 1229 South Santee Street, Los Angeles, California 90015, USA

Fudge, Roland, High Grain, Eldroth, Austwick, Lancaster LA2 8AN

Gill, D M, Kerry Hill, Hawling, Andoversford, Glos GL54 5SZ

Hall, Archie, Lochinver, 69 King George V Avenue, Kings Lynn, Norfolk PE30 2QE

Harper, Jeanne, Stanfords, 27 Muster Green, Haywards Heath, West Sussex RH16 8JB

HarperCollins*Religious*, c/o CopyCare Ltd, PO Box 77, Hailsham, East Sussex BN27 3EF

Herald Music Service, 28 Church Circle, Farnborough, Hants

David Higham Associates, 5-8 Lower John Street, Golden Square, London W1R 4HA

High-Fye Music, Campbell Connelly & Co Ltd, 8-9 Frith Street, London W1V 5TZ

Hooke, Ruth, 10 Bridgeway, Lostock Hall, Preston, Lancs PR5 5YJ

Horrobin, P J, Ellel Grange, Ellel, Carnforth, Lancs LA2 0HN

Hughes, Andy, c/o Holmleigh, 8 Church Road, Upton, Wirral, Merseyside L49 6JZ

Hutchinson, G E, 158 Lansdowne Road, Worcester WR3 8JA

Jones, Ron, 2 Dean Avenue, Wallasey Village, Cheshire

Jubilate Hymns, c/o Mrs Bunty Grundy, 13 Stoddart Avenue, Southampton SO19 4ED

Keats, Carolyn, 12 Salisbury Road, Swanage, Dorset DH19 2DY

Kerr, B K M, Wayside Cottage, East Dean, Eastbourne, East Sussex BN20 0BP

Kersys, Steve, 136 Main Road, Danbury, Essex CM3 4DT

Kingsway's Thankyou Music, P O Box 75, Eastbourne, East Sussex BN23 6NW

Leavers, Greg, 1 Haws Hill, Carnforth, Lancs LA5 9DD

Leosong Copyright Service Ltd, Greenland Place, 115-123 Bayham Street, Camden, London NW1 0AG

Lewis, Peter, 22 Marlborough Rise, Aston, Sheffield S31 0ET

Lindsay Music, 23 Hitchin Street, Biggleswade, Beds SG18 8AX

Little Misty Music, P O Box 8, Perth, Scotland PH2 7EX

Make Way Music Ltd, P O Box 263, Croydon, Surrey CR9 5AP

Kevin Mayhew Ltd, The Paddock, Rattlesden, Bury St Edmunds, Suffolk IP30 0SZ

McCrimmon Publishing Company, 10-12 High Street, Great Wakering, Essex SS3 0EQ

Meredith, Rev Roland, 1 Deanery Court, Broad Street, Bampton, Oxon OX18 2LY

Methodist Church Publishing House, 20 Ivatt Way, Peterborough, Cambs PE3 7PG

National Christian Education Council, 1020 Bristol Road, Selly Oak, Birmingham B29 6LB

Oaksprings Impressions, P O Box 394, Fairfax, California 94930, USA

Oxford University Press, Hymn Copyright Department, 70 Baker Street, London W1M 1DJ

Oxford University Press, Music Department, Walton Street, Oxford OX2 6DP

Paget, B, Chansons, 23 Ellesmere Road, Uphill Village, Weston-super-Mare BS23 4UT

Public Trust Office, Stewart House, 24 Kingsway, London WC2B 6JX

Reith, Angela, 47 Mayton Street, London N7 6QP

Robinson, Joan, 47 Woodlands Road, Beaumont, Lancaster LA1 2EH

Rusbridge, R, 9 Springfield House, Cotham, Bristol BS6 6DQ

Sanchez Jr, Pete, 4723 Hickory Downs, Houston, Texas 77084, USA

Scarr, S Lesley, 15 Church Park, Overton, Morecambe LA3 3RA

Scott, Lestria, 5 Church Street, Pershore, Worcs WR10 1D7

Scripture Gift Mission, Radstock House, 3 Eccleston Street, London SW1W 9LZ

Scripture Press Publications, 1825 College Avenue, Wheaton, Illinois 60187, USA

Scripture Union, 207-9 Queensway, Bletchley, Bucks MK2 2EB

Sea Dream Music, 236 Sabert Road, Forest Gate, London E7 0NP

Silver, Andy, Bell House Farm, Dalton, Burton-in-Kendal, Lancs LA6 1NN

Simmonds, C, School House, 81 Clapham Road, Bedford MK41 7RB

Stainer & Bell Ltd, PO Box 110, 23 Gruneisen Road, London N3 1DZ

Taylor, P A, 1 The Baulk, Worksop, Notts S81 0HU

Waif Productions, 1 North Worple Way, Mortlake, London SW14 8QG

Josef Weinberger Ltd, 12-14 Mortimer Street, London W1N 7RD

Westworth, M, 3 Greengate Lane, Crag Bank, Carnforth, Lancs LA5 9JJ

Notes for Guitarists

An important part of the concept for this book is the addition of guitar chords to the music for all the hymns and songs. For, in a growing number of church and school situations, the guitar is an important instrument for leading singing and worship.

We appreciate that the experience and ability of guitarists varies considerably and we have, therefore, attempted to make the arrangements as simple as possible without destroying the richness of the music. We suggest that if your chord knowledge is currently very limited it would be well worth while learning a few more chords (e.g. F#m, C#m, Bm, Gm B♭ and diminished chords), for you would then be able to play nearly all the hymns and songs we have included.

To enable relatively simple chords to be regularly used we have often included two sets of chords, so that with the use of a capo, as directed at the top of the music, the guitarist can follow the set of easier bracketed chords e.g. E♭ (Dm).

We want guitarists to enjoy their playing, but we also want to encourage those with limited ability to learn new chords and techniques. Here are a few practical tips:

1. Practice strumming so that you learn what types of rhythm suit particular sorts of hymn. If you have a steel strung guitar, get used to using a plectrum.
2. Be confident when you lead. Practice does make an enormous difference! You will find that people will sing confidently if you play confidently.
3. Learn the chords well so that you don't have to stop half way through a song to look one up in the chord chart.
4. Make sure your guitar is in tune, (i) with itself, and (ii) with any other instrument you're playing along with.
5. Make sure you and any other instrument player know what key you are going to play a particular song in.
6. Lastly, but most importantly, pray about your music. Don't just treat it as a hobby but see it as a privilege to lead others in worship and singing.

Greg Leavers

Chord Chart

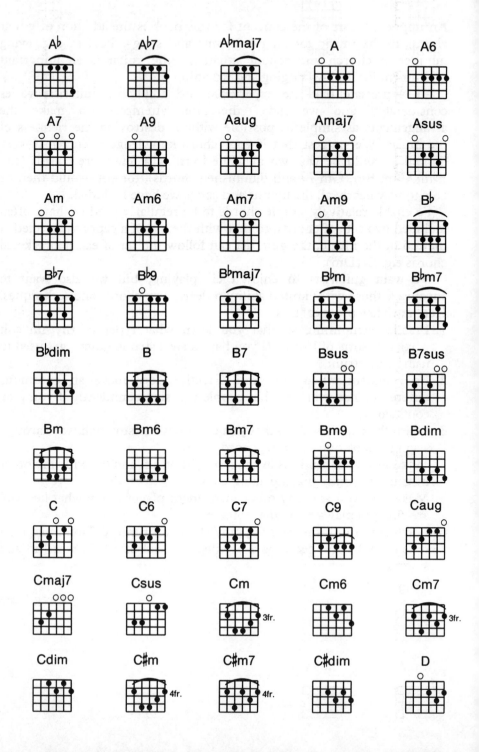

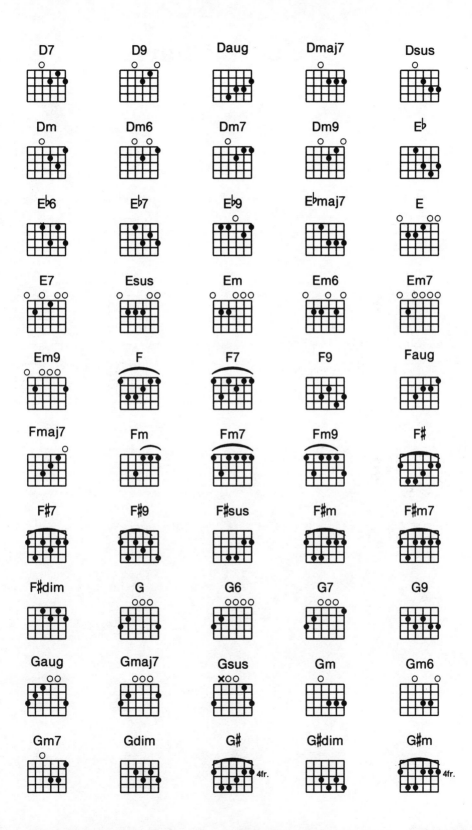

Subject Index

A: Seasonal

1 Advent

2 Ascension

3 Christmas

4 Easter and Holy Week

B: The Godhead

C: Subject Headings

17 The Church

18 Commitment (dedication)

Index of First Lines

Titles which differ from first lines appear in italics